UNITED STATES DEPARTMENT OF JUSTICE

FEDERAL BUREAU OF INVESTIGATION

WASHINGTON 25, D. C.

November 13, 1959

Mr. Joseph R. Conlon
Federal Bureau of Investigation
Los Angeles, California

Dear Mr. Conlon:

I have just been informed of the arrival of your daughter, Maura Ann, and I want to extend my hearty congratulations to Mrs. Conlon and you on this occasion.

My wish is that your little girl's future will be blessed with an abundance of joy and happiness.

Sincerely,

J. Edgar Hoover

FBI girl

how I learned to crack my father's code

MAURA CONLON-MCIVOR

WARNER BOOKS

NEW YORK   BOSTON

This story is based on historical events and is told through the memory and imagination of the child, who sees always by way of the heart. Certain names, locations, and descriptive details are changed to protect the identities of individuals, their families, and environments.

Excerpt from "The Dry Salvages" in *Four Quartets* copyright 1941 by T. S. Eliot and renewed 1969 by Estne Valerie Eliot, reprinted by permission of Harcourt, Inc.

Excerpt from *Twelve Angry Men* used by permission of Ellen Rose for the estate of Reginald Rose.

Warner Books

Time Warner Book Group
1271 Avenue of the Americas, New York, NY 10020
Visit our Web site at www.twbookmark.com.

Printed in the United States of America

First Printing: August 2004
10   9   8   7   6   5   4   3   2   1

Library of Congress Cataloging-in-Publication Data
Conlon-McIvor, Maura.
   FBI girl : how I learned to crack my father's code / Maura Conlon-McIvor.
     p. cm.
   ISBN 0-446-53310-6
   1. Conlon-McIvor, Maura—Childhood and youth. 2. Fathers and daughters—California. 3. Daughters—California—Biography. 4. U.S. Federal Bureau of Investigation—Officials and employees—Family relationships. 5. California—Biography. I. Title.
   CT275.C7628A3 2004
   306.874'2'092—dc22
                                        2003024317

For Joe, Jr.

. . . These are only hints and guesses,
Hints followed by guesses . . .
The hint half guessed, the gift half understood . . .
—T. S. Eliot, *Four Quartets*

FBI girl

My father is bee-utiful when
he swings the bat.

chapter 1

Bang. Bang. Bang.
Strike three.
You're dead.

I practice these lines because the world is a dangerous place.
I lie in bed at night with my yellow-daisy sheets up to my nose,
and Dad comes in my bedroom to snap shut my window. He is
like one of those monks from *Robin Hood,* moving slow, his toes
cracking as he walks from one room to the next. He does not explain why he locks everything up, but I have figured it out: the
world is packed full of criminals, and it is the job of my father,
Special Agent Joe Conlon, to keep them out of our house.

I pull my sheets closer, fall asleep thinking about the smell of criminals in the trunk of my father's car.

• • •

On Saturday morning, Dad stands just outside the doorway, with his hands in his pockets, waiting for me to look up from my book and notice him.

"It's *The Clue in the Crumbling Wall*," I say. "Nancy Drew is just about to crack the case." I can barely read all the words, but Dad must be proud that I am holding such a book, so advanced for my age.

"Uh-huh," he says, rocking back and forth. "I am asking you and the others if you'd like to go up to the St. Bede field in fifteen minutes and play ball." Dad never asks us ahead of time. It is always a surprise, one that doesn't happen all that often. It's like it has to boil up inside him, and then his invitation comes like a dandelion that I wish upon, its feathers blowing through the air, whooshing farther away in the wind.

Before we play baseball, we kids—Michael and me and Julie and John—rush to complete our weekend chores. Julie and I make our beds, then we grab Windex and swipe the dining room, living room, and family room windows. I'm older—seven years old—so I reach for the high spots. We compete to see who can squeak the loudest. Mom dusts the furniture after she's finished typing up all the news for the St. Bede Catholic Church bulletin. Michael mows the lawn because he's the oldest. Dad vacuums the new pool in our backyard and then inspects the lawn-mowing effort. His hands make fists in his pockets. He shakes his head no to Michael's job.

"Can I be in charge of collecting the baseball mitts?" I ask Dad before anyone else gets the chance. I ask this every time. He pulls his head back as if an idea has landed in the thin air between us.

"Come with me."

I follow him into the house, down the hallway lined with framed pictures of our New York relations. We are the only ones who live far away in California, just us four kids, Dad, and Mom. I follow as Dad turns into his bedroom and walks straight over to his ash-blond dresser, which is a foot taller than the curls on my head.

In the top left drawer, Dad stores his white, folded handkerchief, ChapStick, brown comb, and the little black pens that say *U.S. Government.* In the middle drawer, he stashes car keys and the blue-and-black–covered booklets that say *Savings.* In the top right drawer, Dad stores his badge and FBI gun. I have never seen him stash the gun there, but I can tell it's in that drawer. When I walk past his dresser, slow, with crouched fingers like Nancy Drew, I feel that haunting gun stare at me. I keep the perfect distance, three feet away. I know if I get too close, the gun will go *bang* and Dad will discover that I spy on him.

He takes his keys from the dresser and thumbs through them as if they are dollar bills, then hands me the specific one for the trunk of the FBI car. The special key is as silver as the fish Mom cooks Friday nights. He looks at his watch like I have exactly two minutes to complete the mission. "Go ahead and get the mitts in the trunk—and come right back."

"Can I wear your mitt?"

"Just get the mitts."

I hold the key up to my chest, skip out into the hot and dusty sun, past the red-rose bushes that Mom says always bloom too late in summer. I climb through thick, tangling, ankle-high ivy until I reach the trunk of Dad's black FBI car. The silver key fits, twists perfectly, just like the last time. It makes a popping noise as I turn it, like the loud snap of bubble gum. The trunk lifts higher than my arms can reach, so I let it sail up like a kite into the air.

Heat rises from inside the trunk, spreading the smell all around me. I look down and see the mitts: Dad's black and oily one stitched with white shoelaces, Michael's with his handwriting that says *Mickey Mantle* in its meat, mine with its fresh leather, and two shrimpy junior mitts for Julie and John. The mitts are scattered among the golden bullet shells, hundreds of them, everywhere in the trunk, swimming in the creases of the leather gloves. I close my eyes and breathe deeper. The bullet shells smell like the clothes gangsters wear. Mitts and golden bullet shells and gangster smells lying in Dad's trunk, on their bellies, their sides, on their backs.

Bang. Bang. Bang.

The shiniest bullet shell stares at me. I pick it up and blow on it like it could be a whistle, making a whirring sound, then I hold it right up to my nostrils and breathe deep. Its smell is serious—a blue smell, like the cannons exploding in the Pirates of the Caribbean ride at Disneyland, where Father Jack takes us when he visits from New York. Father Jack isn't like Dad at all, even though they're brothers, and I remember how my uncle put his hands over my ears when the Pirates' gunfire scared me so bad. His hands landed like butterflies, and the cannon pounding got softer, but the smell of blue smoke kept coming.

I reach up for the trunk, high on my tiptoes, muscles twitching in my legs, and slam it shut. I take Dad's mitt, throw it as high as I can, and catch it right at my belly. I love the smell of Dad's mitt the best. Inside my throat, I yell *yahoo,* then run back to the house and find Dad where I left him, standing next to the ash-blond dresser, his palm open, waiting for the safe return of the silver key.

•   •   •

We play ball at the St. Bede field, which is on the same block as our parish church. Michael is the first to push out of the car. His cleats dig into my white sneakers and I thwap his leg with my mitt.

"Slow down, will ya." Dad hates it when we get so excited. I settle down, pull myself out, and after me come John and Julie, jumping up and down next to Mom's belly that's large as a watermelon. Mom is about to have our new brother or sister. Mom loves babies. She and Dad tried for seven whole years after Michael to have me. She says she will take as many babies as God will give her.

When Mom is not having a baby, she throws the baseball left-handed. She calls herself a southpaw. I am proud to have a mother like that. She loves the Brooklyn Dodgers even though they are not in Brooklyn anymore. "Isn't it funny how the Dodgers followed us from New York to Los Angeles!" That is what Mom said to Dad once, like she had something to do with it. Dad hates the Dodgers. Mom says he is a Yankees man, even though he's just switched to root for the California Angels. They play not so far from our house, and very close to Disneyland.

"I get center field." Michael swings his arms around. He thinks he can take any position he wants since he is the oldest.

"Maura, why don't you stand in the outfield this time?" Dad pulls two fingers out of his green pants pocket, motions for me to go position myself. I scratch my head because I usually just hang around shortstop and pick up slow-moving grounders and try hard to get them back into Dad's mitt, even though I still can't throw that far.

Dad trudges to home plate and I follow. The closer I get to him, the farther away the outfield seems, so far away a covered wagon would have to pull me there. I walk on the dirt, which is red, like brick dust, and follow Dad's shadow, so quiet behind him he has no idea I am there until he turns around and almost hits my head with the bat.

"What are you doing?"

"I don't know."

"Come on, we don't have all day, get out in the outfield."

"Can you just tell me something?"

Dad lights up a cigarette. He stands behind home plate and signals Michael to scurry deeper in the field. He tosses the base-ball, speaking through his cigarette smoke that I should back away so I don't get hurt. He tosses the ball again and swings, and the ball sounds like a greasy cheeseburger as it flies away. Michael screams *weeeee-hah* as the ball swerves into center field, where I am supposed to be standing.

"Okay, make it quick." Dad keeps his stare to the outfield, sending out puffs of smoke that look like small balloons.

"Those gold things in the car?"

"What are you talking about?"

Dad lifts his arm as Michael throws from center field, snatch-ing the baseball flat in his naked palm. Dad backs away, pelts the next ball, this one sounding like a firecracker. A shriek, then it's gone, the ball whirling way out, past Michael's head, all the way to the boundary fence, where the St. Bede baseball field runs right into the Jacaranda Navy Base.

"The golden bullet shells, Dad. The trunk is filled with them."

Dad drops his bat, ignoring Michael's return ball, which goes sailing by, banging against the wooden backstop behind us. He bends to pick up the bat, gripping it in the middle.

"Who said you should be paying attention to those?"

"They're all over—they smell like gangsters." I watch gray cigarette smoke snaking all around him.

Dad wipes sweat off his thick arm, then lifts his cigarette so that it's staring down straight into my eyes. Its red lava glows as he sucks on it.

"You ignore the bullet shells, you hear. Otherwise"—he

shifts his jaw—"otherwise, I'll have Michael be in charge of the equipment." He tosses the ball, once, twice, three times, snapping it up louder each time as I wonder how Dad can smoke and snap at the same time. "Now, are we here to field balls or talk about something we should not be talking about?"

Mom, in her green-and-white-striped shirt, stands up in the dugout like she is my coach, and claps her hands like maybe it's more important to catch balls than pester Dad. "Maura, aren't you going to play today?"

Michael yells from center field, "What's the holdup?" as Dad leans on his bat, folding his tight arms. I tie both my sneaker laces, then run past shortstop. It seems like it takes me forever before I leap into center field, stepping on boatloads of dandelions. Even though Dad doesn't say a word, I can tell by his posture he is pleased I am standing out in the field. I wonder if the next ball will come my way, but before Dad swings, I inhale deep into my mitt. It has the blue smell. Dad hits a high fly ball. I wobble, trying to spot it, my arms outstretched to the sun.

• • •

On Sunday night at eight o'clock, our whole family watches *The F.B.I.* It is our tradition. After we eat mashed potatoes, green peas that taste like mushy Wonder bread, slices of beef that float in red meat juice, and ice cream with Bosco chocolate syrup, we pile into the family room. This is after Dad has washed the dishes and dried them—it's never good enough just to wash them without drying them—and Mom has asked us to put our brown-checked St. Bede school uniforms and clean socks out for the next day.

During the first commercial break, I roll over on the spindly green carpet and look at Dad. He sits in the corner of the blue tweed couch, wedged in like apple pie.

"Dad, I think Inspector Erskine—I mean Efrem Zimbalist, Jr.—is the tannest movie star I have ever seen."

"Is that right?" His eyes zoom like a fastball from the TV to the *Los Angeles Times* open on his lap as the commercial continues.

"Dad, do you have to go on car chases and jump over buildings and handcuff those smelly gangsters, just like Inspector Erskine?" I ask, nice and slow.

Dad does not say anything. He stretches the newspaper past his face, like it is a curtain. I wait for it to drop. Instead, he keeps turning pages. I wait for him to speak. Dad turns another page, the newspaper crinkling in his fingers. Maybe he would be put on detention at work if he told how they catch criminals. Maybe that information is top secret, to keep the gangsters from finding out.

Billy Romero, the first kid on our block to get a ten-speed bike, tells me they are out to get us. Every time I pass his house on my way home from St. Bede Elementary School, he zooms out of his driveway, sits on his seat, and crosses his arms, right in the path of my stingray bike.

"Hey, Maura, your father could be killed by criminals anytime—did you know that!" That is what he yells.

"No. Never," I say, veering past, like I am the mermaid captain of my own ship, although I say it so soft Billy Romero must not hear, because he already blurts his next warning.

"And *you—you* could get kidnapped on your way home from school. FBI kids get nabbed all the time."

I keep riding my bike, faster, in my heart of hearts saying, *Bad things will never happen to my family, because Dad is tougher than the worst criminal out there.* No gangster would dare come close. They could never outmaneuver Dad. He is the smartest special agent in the whole FBI.

Dad clears his throat when the second commercial comes on, finally dropping the newspaper.

"What is your baseball mitt still doing in here?"

The mitt, which I have worn all day, sticks to my left hand. I shrug my shoulders.

"Why didn't you give it to Michael to put back where it belongs?"

Before I can answer, the Crest toothpaste commercial ends, and that special-agent music starts up again to tell us we are back to *The F.B.I.*

It is time for the epilogue. Inspector Erskine and his agents capture the bad guys each week and sentence them to prison. After we know they are locked up for sure, spicy FBI music begins.

I stare straight ahead to the picture of J. Edgar Hoover, my dad's boss, that hangs on the wall above the television. Mr. Hoover must wear that stiff Brylcreem, like Michael does since he started St. James High School, to keep his hair straight and narrow. Mr. Hoover's looks are serious, like he has not had a dessert for twenty years. I switch my eyes back and forth, from Mr. Hoover to the television screen. I imagine it is really Dad's boss talking to me as Inspector Erskine points to the poster behind him with the black-and-white photographs of the Ten Most Wanted. Inspector Erskine's voice sounds like gravel. He tells us to be on the alert. The gangsters are armed and dangerous. They could be in our neighborhood.

I roll over on the carpet and look at Dad and wonder if he thinks a gangster would ever sneak around Thrifty's Ice Cream or the Fox Movie House or the St. Bede ball field. I wait for Dad to notice me, but he is busy inspecting the faces of the Ten Most Wanted.

"Dad, does that mean armed and dangerous with golden bullet shells?"

Dad's eyes clamp onto the television screen in such a way I know I should stay quiet. He folds his legs, the newspaper dropping to the floor, and he barely opens his mouth. "The inspector means you should play it smart. Otherwise, you'll get hurt."

"How do you play it smart?" I crawl just a bit closer toward his dark shoes.

He lights a cigarette, cups it, curls of smoke escaping the cracks between his fingers. Mom stares at Dad like she would prefer for him to talk about pleasant things, to switch the topic away from how we have to worry about all the danger. Dad looks back at Mom with that face that says he has nothing pleasant to say. Then he slants his head and squints his eyes.

"Avoiding dangerous areas is one way to play it smart."

I gulp. I watch him turn up his sleeves and stare straight ahead like one of the Ten Most Wanted has just jumped through the television screen into our family room. I turn back to watch the set. The camera zeros in on one criminal, the gangster's face hogging the entire screen. I lower my face and let it rest in my mitt.

"Maybe you shouldn't watch this part, Maura. This may be what's giving you those nightmares." Sometimes Mom rubs my back when I have my nightmares of houses catching on fire, but lately, she just sleeps when I tug at her at night. I stand in the dark room and watch her pregnant belly go up and down like the ocean, and listen to Dad snore until I am so sleepy I am forced to go to bed alone.

"No, I like this part—it's my favorite."

I dare myself to stare the guy in the face. I drop my mitt and watch from under my eyelids. This criminal looks like a grizzly bear, like he is so hungry that if he found you on the playground, he would kill you for your hot dog or Cream-a-ling apple pie. He's got scars and bruises and a crooked nose. His eyes look watery and silver, like our steak knives when they soak in the sink.

I grab my mitt again and lift it up and smell it and wait for

Inspector Erskine to end this Ten Most Wanted part. I sniff closer. I smell the stitches in the leather, the meat of the mitt where Dad says you should catch the ball. I bury my face in it, breathe in and out like the doctor says to do when you sit on his cold table. I breathe so much that soon I can't smell or even see anything else.

"What in God's name are you doing with that mitt?" Dad says as he gets up to turn off the television. He steps my way and grabs the mitt stuck on my hand. "I've never seen a house like this in all my—"

"Dad, I don't want us to ever get hurt. Can't you teach me—"

"Maura, come on, now. Don't let your imagination get the best of you." Mom stands up with her hand on her belly. "No one is going to get hurt. Now—bedtime!"

It looks like her belly is smiling, which makes me think my imagination is getting the best of me. Still, I study Dad to see if he agrees with Mom. He waves at the air, then walks out of the room without saying a word, just like he does every Sunday night after we watch *The F.B.I.*

· · ·

From Monday to Friday nights, I sit in my corner bedroom, by the window, and wait for Dad to come home. I look up and down our street, Margaret Rae Drive, and think of all those pictures that come on the news every night, all the guns and soldiers and hippies in torn clothes who yell and shake their long hair.

Finally, Dad's FBI car rounds the corner, slow, and pulls into our driveway. The headlights stream through the holes of my yellow lace curtains. I duck so Dad can't tell I watch him take off his black hat, which is called a fedora, as he gets out of the car. I get ready to run and greet him at the front door as he goes slower than a snail up the walkway. The fedora rests in his hand, soft next to his important black trousers. I tell Dad he is the smartest father in the whole world, and then I lean into his cheek and smell the blue smell.

Posing like I am Julie Andrews.

chapter 2

t is Friday night and all I do is drum my fingers as I sit at the kitchen table, staring at the pink telephone and counting from one to ten, hoping for an invitation from our neighbors the Flanigans to see *The Sound of Music*. Mom is busy with the new baby, who's three months old today, busy talking to doctors. She tells me she needs privacy when the doctors call. She asks me to go outside and play with Julie and John for a while. I always do, dreaming that the Flanigans will let me watch *The Sound of Music* three times in a row and then take me out for a banana split. When the Flanigans took me to see *Mary Poppins,* Mrs. Flanigan handed me a Mary Poppins coloring book. I wonder what she will give me this time.

Mom and Dad sit at the kitchen table at night after we all go to bed. Their voices hide in whispers. I hear them from my bedroom, hear spoons clank inside cups, then small slurps. Dad's voice is low like the heater. What they say is top secret. They don't want us kids to hear. I wonder if Dad caught one of the Ten Most Wanted at work. I creep out in my purple pajamas, sneak up to the shut dining room door, but Mom must sense I am near, because right away she pops up and escorts me back to bed.

"You and Dad. What are you talking about?"

"Adult things. Everything is fine. Now it's time for sleep." Mom does not have her orange lipstick on. Her lips are faded, like roses thirsty for water.

"If it's time for sleep, then how come you and Dad aren't sleeping?" I get into bed with her hand on my back, but I refuse to lie down. Mom does not say anything at first, and I can hear the kettle whistle in the kitchen and Dad's chair scraping against the floor.

"Daddy and I have some things to talk about—"

"There's no gangsters on the loose, right?!"

Mom fluffs my pillow. "Gangsters?" She chuckles, catches herself by surprise, and then swallows like there's words tangled in her throat. "No, no. Just things parents talk about. Everything will be fine."

"Dad says you have to play it smart for things to be fine."

Mom looks at me and pulls back the covers. I swing my legs in.

"You can play it smart by getting some rest. Good night."

The heater clicks on, and soon its roar travels through our house on Margaret Rae Drive like a choir of ghosts. I lie in bed and touch my warm cheeks and think of our new baby brother. I love the new baby's feel, his skin so soft, like Jell-O. His hair is red, and Mom says wouldn't you know, the fifth baby to arrive is the most Irish-looking of the bunch.

He came home from the hospital wrapped in the official Conlon baby blanket, the one our Gramma Molly made for the rest of us. Dad did not say much when the baby came home. He thanked the Flanigans for baby-sitting, then put his FBI badge in his gun drawer. I saw him do this. I don't know why agents need badges at the hospital. Someday I will ask. Dad is lucky. The new baby is named after him—Joe, Jr. We will call him Joey. His skin is light, like Dad's, and so far, his eyes are just as blue, like the eggs robins lay.

• • •

I finish my Friday night dinner of tomato soup, fancy fish sticks, and french fries and then go back to staring at the phone. Finally, it rings in a special way, and I can just tell it will be for me. I leap for the phone, skirting past Michael, who is getting ready for sports night up at his school. It is Mr. Flanigan on the other end.

"*Ho ho ho.*" He says this each time he calls. "Guess who this is!" Another *ho ho ho* and a snort.

"Mr. Flanigan!"

"How'd you guess?"

I bite my nail and worry he will not ask me to come along to the movie, and instead will ask for Dad, who always lights up a cigarette when you tell him Mr. Flanigan is on the phone.

"Do you want to talk to my dad?"

"No, honey, we'll leave that ole Irishman alone. Listen, how would ya like to see that new movie up at the navy base tonight? We've got room in the car."

"*The Sound of Music?*"

"And, honey, I got a free pass just for you." He snorts again.

Mr. Flanigan always says he has a free pass. He was in one of those big wars, just like Dad, but Dad was in the army and had to go to faraway places. Mr. Flanigan gets tickets for half price when a new movie comes to the Jacaranda Navy Base theater, but he calls it a free pass because free pass sounds more exciting than half price.

I put the phone down and run from one room to the next, asking Julie and John where Mom is and they shrug their shoulders, playing Mother Goose. I find Mom in the back bedroom. She wears her pink sweater and scoops down to Joey. She holds his hands together, rubs something off her cheek with her shoulder, as she sings low. She says the lyrics, line by line, from "The Farmer in the Dell." Joey's eyes smile back even though his mouth falls open and saliva covers his chin. Mom wipes it up.

"Hi, Mom."

She looks up, startled, and I see tears shining on her cheeks. Her eyes are red with veins. Before she says anything, I become a tornado and run out of the room back to the kitchen. Dad walks in with his tin bucket full of sudsy water, sets it down, and leans over to start mopping the floor, just like he does every Friday night. First he flicks on the radio to listen to a California Angels game, then turns it off when he spots the phone off the hook.

"What's going on here?" Dad says this like any moment a call could be coming in from J. Edgar Hoover and we should remember to keep the phone free.

"Ooops. I'll get it." I pick up the receiver, pull the phone cord as far away as I can, and whisper, "Mr. Flanigan, my parents say it is okay for me to go." He tells me to get ready right away because the Flanigan family will honk their horn in five minutes.

I hang up the phone, so quiet. Dad sets the mop down, stretching his neck like a turtle.

"What do you think you're doing?"

"Nothing."

"Who was that on the phone?"

"I'm going to see *The Sound of Music* with the Flanigans." I say it so fast I nearly choke.

"Did you ask your mother?"

"No, she's with the baby . . . She's cryin'—"

"Did you ask me?" He leans forward, crosses his arms again to inspect how I will answer his question.

Dad doesn't have any scars on his face, just a tight grin. He has that look that says I should be careful if I want to get away with going to the theater with the Flanigans.

"Can I . . . see the movie?"

He shakes his head, then turns to the heating vent in the wall as if ghosts live there. "I've never seen a house like this in all my life," he says. The ghosts must listen, because he says this all the time, even if none of us ever mutter a word.

"Please, Dad?" My tongue tightens.

Mom comes out with Joey in her arms. She looks at my scrambled eyebrows, then looks at Dad.

"This one here." He points to me.

"Mom, Mr. Flanigan invited me to see *The Sound of Music*. They're going to pick me up right now."

"How wonderful! That sounds like a terrific invitation." Her eyes roll back over to Dad.

Dad mumbles under his breath. "How is Joey feeling?"

Mom clears her throat, nods her head so Dad will remember me.

"Oh, sure, okay." He reaches into his pocket. I hear the tinkling of metal whirling about. Sparkling coins come out from his trousers, as if they could be wishes tossed into a fountain. He turns quarters in his wet palm, looking for the right one.

"What do you think, little Joey? Do you think we should give her twenty-five cents?" Dad talks to him like he is his partner, like talking to Joey will keep the FBI protection over him. Dad walks in twice to lock our windows at night ever since Joey was born.

Dad drops a quarter in my palm. I stash it deep in my pocket.

"Don't forget to bring back the change."

"Okay."

I always do. Even though I buy Milk Duds, Good & Plenty, or sometimes Chocolate Flicks, I surprise Dad with a nickel back.

Honk, honk. The Flanigans are here! I kiss Mom good-bye. Dad goes back to his pail of water, looks up at me, then at the floor. I think maybe he is waving good-bye with his eyes. FBI agents always communicate in code.

•　•　•

Mr. Flanigan jumps out of the car and opens the door for me, just like they do in the movies. "Nice to see you, honey!"

I climb into the Flanigans' backseat, sitting next to Fergus, who sits next to Donal, who sits next to Fintan, who sticks his tongue out to Jimmy in the front seat. The boys scoot away from me immediately because I am a girl, they say, and there's no way they want girl germs. Mrs. Flanigan leans over the seat just as Mr. Flanigan snorts, but all I see is Mrs. Flanigan's white helpless face.

"You boys straighten up. You hear?"

It must be terrible for the Flanigans to have all boys, four pesky sons who act as tough as cowboys. Last summer they cycled over to my corner lemonade stand, where I was selling Michael's old model airplanes for twenty-five cents apiece. The Flanigan boys grabbed half the planes and escaped back down the street while I sat there frozen, afraid to tell a soul for fear they'd come back to beat me up. Tonight I try hard to give them my calm Nancy Drew look.

Wind blows my light brown curls as we head for the theater, driving past the St. Bede ball field. I think of all the times I have climbed to the top of the bleachers to see the Jacaranda Navy Base theater and the green tanks and the huge gray airplanes that shake our classroom windows when they fly overhead. Mr. Flanigan says they store something called nuclear weapons there, but I forget about all that when the man in the white cap salutes Mr. Flanigan, and we enter the base.

Mrs. Flanigan, with her night-black hair, turns around in her seat. "Did you bring a sweater, Maura?" she says, smiling at me before she asks, and then smiling afterward. It's like she dreams up a question just so she can have a reason to look at me. I smile back. I know if the Flanigans could, they'd give anything to have me as their daughter.

Sometimes I lie in bed and think of Mrs. Flanigan's look when she tells Mom how lucky she is to have a daughter, and I think how if our house ever caught on fire and I was the only one left alive, I would go live with the Flanigans because they'd spoil me rotten, making me my favorite dinner every night, which is meat pie with a Bisquick crust. They would give me an extra-large bedroom with white fancy furniture and a playhouse even taller than the one Dad built for me, a playhouse with its very own electricity so I could plug in my Suzy Homemaker oven.

I look around the navy base theater. It is not like the other movie theater where my parents took us once, the one with red curtains and dark velvet cushions and little lights like fireflies.

In the navy base theater, we sit on cold chairs and there are no curtains ahead, just bluish green walls. All around the theater are men wearing strict-looking uniforms. But all that disappears when the lights go off for one second, then two seconds, then three seconds, then the movie projector flicks on.

I can hear the voice of a woman, and there she is, on top of a mountain packed with purple and yellow flowers. She swirls and she swirls, and her arms are out to the world. I lean forward in my cold seat, and the hills *do* come alive when she sings—I can hear the crickets and the wind and the brook and practically even the flowers start to sing with her. During the show, Mrs. Flanigan smiles at me some more. I wonder if she will sew me a new wardrobe, using fabric from the Flanigans' bedroom curtains, just like in the movie.

• • •

After I see *The Sound of Music,* Mom takes me to Mildred Perry, who smells like hair spray as she snips, and who gives me a butterscotch candy when the cut is over. When I come home, I walk into my parents' bedroom and look in the mirror. I have no more curls. Instead, I just have eyes, which seem even bigger, and now I can see my entire neck and my ears and all of my forehead too.

Mrs. Flanigan comes over to help Mom with the new baby, and when I answer the door, she gives me that look of appreciation.

"Why, Maura . . . you have a Julie Andrews haircut!"

I gulp. "I do?"

I run back to Mom, who holds a warm bottle up to Joey's mouth. Mom is quiet when she feeds the new baby, and she gives him a long look each time he tries to gulp. His saliva gets bad, and his gulps are slow. His tongue is thicker than most babies'.

That is what the doctor told Mom, but I think when he gets older, that condition will just go away.

"Mom, do I have a Julie Andrews haircut, do I?"

She wipes off the baby's face and pulls him up in his bassinet because he's constantly slipping down, she says, this one, constantly slipping.

"Yes, Maura. You have an *official* Julie Andrews haircut."

I go running back to the mirror in my parents' bedroom to look at myself. My hair is just like Fräulein Maria's. I spin around three times. I run out to Mom, jumping up and down, but I can see Mom is busy talking, munching on words like roast beef. Mrs. Flanigan doesn't notice me either when I walk into the kitchen. Instead, she digs her fingernails into one cheek and stares at baby Joey.

"Oh, my. But does the doctor—"

Mom turns around and sees me and hushes Mrs. Flanigan. "Oh, hello."

Mrs. Flanigan snaps up and tries to give me that look of appreciation. I smile in a gray way. I stand with my new haircut, like Fräulein Maria when she arrives at Captain Von Trapp's house for the first time and her mouth drops open and she stares all around her, like she is on a new planet and she barely knows what to say. I try to give Mom and Mrs. Flanigan my own look of appreciation.

Later that night, I sneak into the living room when no one is looking, and start swirling around, singing to myself so soft that no one will hear my voice, "The hills are alive with the sound of music." As I twirl, I think how in one week, I will start second grade and no one will recognize me. They will think it is Julie Andrews who has come to attend St. Bede school. I spin so hard my father steps into the living room in his white shirt and black tie and tells me to stop making myself dizzy.

•   •   •

The winds blow in September, kicking up hot, sizzling air. You have to be sure to hold on to your skirt when you walk outside. Mom says the warm winds are called the Santa Anas because they come in from the desert. They blow in brown tumbleweeds that go skipping along the school pavement, across the St. Bede ball field, whirling in circles. Tumbleweeds scare me. They are like Gypsies, like wild ghosts who have no place to go.

I put on my St. Bede uniform of brown plaid and a brown sweater, complete with a sewn badge that says some motto in Latin. I arrive at the classroom of Sister Norah, wondering if any of the other kids will notice my haircut, but no one, not even Sister, says a word.

Our first month of school we begin to learn how to write in cursive. The letters from big *A* and little *a* to big *Z* and little *z* are spread above the brown chalkboard. Sister Norah is plump. Her habit hangs in heavy pleats as she grabs her pointer stick and follows the outline of each and every letter, telling us that this, *this* is how we will be writing in no time at all.

Each letter comes easily to me. I stare down at my notepaper and watch them slip out of my hands. A beautiful *A*. A fine *B*. A nice *C* and a dandy *D*.

"Those are beautiful letters," Sister Norah says to me, her mole above her lip moving up and down as she speaks. The cloth from her habit swipes my pencil when she turns around, marching to the front of the classroom.

"Next week we begin our *E*s. Is everybody clear on that?"

"Yes, Sister Norah." We speak all together at once. I am not worried, since all of my other letters have been perfect

The following week is when the troubles begin. I try and try but cannot write the *E* like the *E* on the official chart. My hand is in a dream, for I add an extra curlicue on my capital *E* because I think *E* is sad and plain just as it is, and in my opinion it screeches out to be dressed up. Sister Norah starts pacing past my desk all week, telling me I am not making the capital *E* in the proper way. She will not let me move on to the other letters—as the rest of my class does—until my *E* is just perfect. One day she slaps my hand with a ruler, telling me I must once and for all get my *E* right.

After school, I jump into my shorts and T-shirt and run out to my playhouse. I try on the dresses Mom gives me, the ones that are wide like spinning tops with colors of Life Savers. I put on her old pointed shoes. I sit and watch my yellow windows fill with shadows of tree branches. I nestle close to the window, pretending the shadows are dancers who touch my skin. I think of Mom inside the house and wonder if I should tell her about the problem with my *E*s.

I sneak back into the house to find her. She sits alone in the living room, where I used to swirl around. She is crying again and listening to music on the console, but then she sees me and smiles a little bit and turns the music down.

"Are you having fun in your playhouse?" I nod my head yes to her. "How would you like to bake me a little chocolate cake on your Suzy Homemaker?" she asks.

"Okay, I would like to do that," I say.

I go and pluck two eggs from the refrigerator and run back out to my playhouse filled with sun and the odor of old rug squares Mom bought for me at the carpet store. I stand over my box crate, crack the egg. It spills into the flour. I add a snatch of water, swirl it around with my pink spatula until I have a mixture smooth as silk. I spoon the wet mixture into my magic baking pans, dash to my bedroom where Suzy Homemaker sits, and pop the pans in the oven and watch the two lightbulbs bake my

The world feels different in second grade.

cake for almost two hours. When the cake is ready, I bring it out to Mom. I hope my cake makes her happy.

• • •

The next day in school, Sister Norah moves me up to the front of the class, seats me just behind Peter Norden. She is now more determined than ever for me to write my *E* correctly. I am afraid she has told the principal, Mother Perennial, about my weakness, for now I see Mother Perennial scowling in the school corridor, and I think Sister Norah has also told Reverend Father McKinley, who comes now to our classroom more often. When he enters the room, right away we must stand up and all together recite, "Good morning, Father McKinley," as he looks through his thick glasses right at me.

During recess, when Adele Romero and Jane Fitzgerald and pretty Elizabeth DuPoint and the other girls play foursquare, I decide to go to the nurse's office. Mrs. Canopie is the school nurse, and every time I walk in, she looks at her desk and lines her pens up perfectly.

"Can I help you, sweetheart?" she says.

"My stomach feels awkward."

Then she tells me to sit down on the cold folding chair and open my mouth for the thermometer.

"You are Mary Conlon's daughter, aren't you?" She doesn't look at me the special way, like Mrs. Flanigan, which I guess means she has a daughter of her own. "You look fine, dear. If you want, go ahead and rest on the bunk bed for twenty minutes." She reads my temperature, telling me it's normal.

Once a week, sometimes twice a week, during recess, I go visit Mrs. Canopie and tell her I am not feeling so well. My stomach is twisted up, I tell her. She takes my temperature each time and tells me again I am normal. I ask her if I can lie down on the bunk bed with the smooth, plaid bedspread, and she says that is okay. I lie down on the bed and it is peaceful. I breathe deep, smell rubbing alcohol, and watch cotton balls sit in the glass jar like sleeping fish. The breeze outside picks up, the hanging blinds blow in and out, clanking against the wall.

After recess one day when I have been lying on the bed for twenty minutes, Mrs. Canopie comes over and scrunches down.

"You are fine and healthy as can be, young lady. You've been here an awful lot. If you keep coming in, I think I ought to call your mother."

I look at Mrs. Canopie with wide eyes and think of Mom and how she is busy helping the new baby, how Mom puts her head into Joey's tummy and cries sometimes, and how Dad is so quiet at night, walking around the house holding Joey close as we watch from our bedrooms. I think the nurse should not call my mother. I will stop coming to the clinic when knots go wrapping around my stomach.

On the one day I force myself to play it smart and stay away from the school clinic, I throw up all over Peter Norden, the boy who sits in front of me and writes his letters more perfectly than anyone.

Sister Norah with the mole on her face and the ruler in her hand comes flying at me. My face is full of my lunch of ham sandwich and Ding-Dongs, and Peter Norden is crying because he's not used to having warm vomit ooze down his little neck. Sister Norah looks at me, a little devil who should be red with embarrassment.

"Oh, Maura. Why didn't you tell me!" She gathers me, pulling me up from my waist. "Why didn't you tell me you were feeling so ill!"

"I—I didn't know."

She takes me away, out of the classroom, and as I turn around, I can see the face of Peter Norden, who looks like he has been hit with lightning. Sister Norah pulls me alongside her, whisking me down the corridor, which smells like chalk and fluorescent lights. There I am once again before Mrs. Canopie, who looks at me now with her hands to her face.

"Oh, poor thing!" She cleans me up and pulls down the cover on the lower bunk bed, then reaches for the phone as I crawl in.

I wait. Maybe she is calling the janitor for that white powder they throw on barf, but right away I can tell I am wrong.

"Yes, yes, Mary. She's fine, but, you know, she's been in here an awful lot." Mrs. Canopie listens and shakes her head, then hangs up.

"Your mother will be here shortly. You stay right there."

My body stiffens in the cold sheets as I count the metal springs on the bunk bed above mine. Twenty-nine springs later, Mom arrives in our brown Chevy station wagon. She signs me out and I grin because I realize I will not have to go back to

Sister Norah's class that afternoon to work on my *E*s. Instead, I will go home and rest and wake up in my bedroom with the Suzy Homemaker oven, as green and blue as the walls at the Jacaranda Navy Base theater.

By three o'clock, the official time when school is over, I get tired of lying in bed. I decide I will make hot chocolate for me and Mom so that we can feel better right away. I heat up milk, pour hot chocolate into a teacup with roses. I bring the teacup to Mom. She is in her bedroom, where it is quiet and she has fallen asleep. That is, until Joey begins to awaken.

"Shoosh . . . shoosh. It's okay," I say to Joey, and think maybe I could make him a hot chocolate, but remember he is still too young.

I rub Mom's shoulder.

"Mom, Mom . . . the new baby is starting to cry."

I run around the foot of her bed and touch her soft shoulder from the other side.

"Mom?"

Again I nudge her. Joey watches me, it seems, with bright but confused eyes.

Mom. The new baby is starting to cry. That's what I want to tell her, but I don't. Because even though Mom opens her eyes and looks up and smiles, I see her cheeks are still wet.

"Thank you very much." She gives me a small kiss. She sees my hot chocolate, takes a sip, then puts it down on the night-stand. She picks up Joey and takes the crying baby away into the living room to put on some soothing music. I sit down on her bed and watch the steam slowly disappear from the teacup filled with hot chocolate.

• • •

That is the night the phone rings and I pick it up and freeze because I hear Sister Norah's voice on the other end. I did not know nuns were allowed to speak on telephones, or even if they could have one. No human being, besides the nuns, has ever stepped inside the big white convent with its stucco roof, and so who could ever guess they held the power to call your home?

"Hello . . . Is this Maura?"

I think I should say, *Yes, Sister,* but instead, I just hold on to the phone as if it is a piece of china that will break into a thousand pieces if I move the incorrect way.

"Excuse me. This is Sister Norah. Would this be Maura?"

"Yes."

I barely push the word out of my mouth. I am afraid to think of why Sister Norah is calling. I want to tell her I am sorry for throwing up all over Peter Norden, tell her I am so sorry I cannot write my *E*s properly, but instead, I just heave a quiet sigh.

"I would like to speak with Mrs. Conlon, Maura."

Sister Norah says my name with the same accent my Gramma Molly has, the one that comes from Ireland. She says my name as if there is a huge waterfall underneath her voice. As she speaks, I feel the whole world could be blown away by the strong voice of Sister Norah.

"Yes, Sister." I hold on to the phone and wait.

"Thank you, my child. You have become so, so sad."

I don't know what to say because I do not know what Sister is talking about, and so I run and find Mom, who is rubbing Vicks VapoRub on baby Joey's chest.

"Excuse me," I say. "Sister Norah is calling on the phone."

Mom looks up.

"Oh . . . whatever for?"

She asks me to sit next to Joey as she goes off to the pink telephone in the kitchen. I look at Joey, who smiles up at me. I stare at him and try to smile back. He looks into my eyes, his lips thick like they are ready for kissing.

"I'm not just a nice Irish girl anymore, Joey," I tell him. "That's my teacher on the phone and she says I am a sad girl."

Joey's eyes twinkle, like he wants to tell me that Sister Norah doesn't know what she is talking about.

• • •

Mom takes us all into the living room that night. Michael, who is always playing Dave Clark Five albums, and me and Julie and John, who sucks his thumb, we all sit together like birds on a telephone wire. Dad comes too, but he is at the edge of the room, standing in the hallway. He looks like Special Agent Captain Von Trapp, so still, motionless, like barely any oxygen goes in and out of his mouth.

Joey is in the middle of the room, in his bassinet, and Mom is on the floor next to him. We are like the wise men gathering around Joey, who looks like Jesus, wriggling, with soft stars in his eyes. He's got on blue pajamas with white plastic feet, and he keeps reaching for his zipper. I don't think Jesus would do that. Jesus would lie in the manger, staring straight up to heaven, waiting for us wise men to shower him with gifts.

"Joe, will you come into the room?" Mom looks to the hallway where Dad leans against the wall filled with more photographs of our New York relations. His elbow rests against the picture of our Uncle Father Jack, who I think would be Dad's favorite brother even if he weren't his only one.

"I'm fine here . . ."

Mom looks at him with straight eyebrows. She doesn't say a word, just looks back at us.

I keep my eyes glued on Dad's. His eyes get misty. I don't know why. Maybe he looks at Mom and thinks how beautiful she is, just like Captain Von Trapp looks at Fräulein Maria like she is so pretty he could just get up and dance. I don't think that is it, though. Maybe Dad is concerned that the phone might ring any second and that J. Edgar Hoover might need him.

Mom smiles a little at us like she is about to give a big speech. The speech must be about Joey because she keeps looking down at him, then takes his chubby little hand and swings it, just like when Dad takes us to the park and pushes us back and forth on the swings. I watch Mom's and Joey's fingers dance together and wonder if this is why we are gathered in the living room.

After it's quiet for a while, she starts to talk. "This is a special night," she says.

It is special because this is the night she tells us Joey is a special baby, that he has some condition that will make him develop slowly. His condition is named Down's syndrome. Then she says that God sent Joey to us as a gift. That is when I look back at the hallway and see Dad. He stands out there like some guy in the rain. His hands are tucked snug in his pockets and his head tilts backward and tears get locked up under his eyes. If God has given Joey as a special gift, I wonder if now would be a good time to start singing "Do-Re-Mi." I close my eyes and imagine myself swirling about. Maybe if we sing, Dad would come in and sit with the rest of us.

I look over to Dad. He is gone, even though the phone did not ring. We kids file out of the living room. I look up and see the photo of Father Jack hanging crooked on the wall. Mom straightens it just perfect, and I ask her when Father Jack will come and visit us again. She's not sure, but she bets it will be sometime soon.

• • •

After Sister Norah talks to Mom on the telephone, Sister stops slapping my hands in class. She allows me to add the extra curlicue to my *Es*.

One day just before recess, she excuses the rest of the class and asks me to stay behind. I sit at my desk and wait for her. She bends down, takes my hands, and looks at me. She must know something I do not, why I am a sad girl.

"Your mother has informed me about your new brother."

She releases my hands, then puts hers together as if to start a prayer.

"This is a difficult time, my child. But indeed"—she whispers over my face like a low cloud—"God will bless your family . . . and your Mongoloid brother."

My cheeks broil. I have never heard anyone call Joey Mongoloid, a Mongoloid brother. Mongoloid sounds bad, like when you flub up in kickball and no one wants you on their team again, or like you are a monster with three eyes who is too weird and ugly to love. I want to scream at her that he is not Mongoloid at all, but I don't. I just sit like how we are taught, with hands curled in laps.

Sister excuses me. I walk out of the classroom slow, then start running past the other kids playing and laughing and yelling. I run for the baseball field at the edge of the playground and climb the bleachers, high, so I can see the navy base theater, its copper trim hanging over dark helicopters. I open my mouth and wish I could sing, but all I do is stand there, feeling hot winds whip dirt up from the field, blowing it all over me.

Dad's brother, my Uncle Father Jack.

chapter 3

Dad dresses in a regulation uniform. He wears a freshly ironed shirt, its collar stiff as cardboard, black trousers, a black jacket, a black fedora, and black tie. Dad's boss must be even stricter than Mother Perennial. Mr. Hoover demands that agents keep a full tank of gas in their FBI cars—half a tank is like a mortal sin. He also must require agents to keep their refrigerators stocked with milk, because every time we are low, Dad shakes his head and goes out for more, as if it is an emergency procedure.

Dad walks through the front door each night at six o'clock sharp, a brown shopping bag tucked under his arm. He investigates who is in the vicinity, then heads for his bedroom. He stashes his badge and gun, lights up a cigarette, and with his bag goes in search of Joey.

I follow him, then return to the kitchen when I've confirmed there's nothing for me in that brown bag. It's always for Joey, every time, a new rattle or a new bib or bouncing ball. I tell Dad that Joey is too young to appreciate gifts, and he gives me that look that says I ought to wash my mouth out with soap. So I stay quiet and breathe in Dad's smoke as I imagine Joey spreading his hands flat over Dad's cheeks like a magician, like he does every night, making Dad chuckle as he kisses Joey twice. I don't know how Joey does this trick. Chuckling and kissing are not normal FBI activities, just like I think it's not so normal for our mother to cry.

Mom stands over the pink sink and peels a carrot fast, her shoulders slumped a little. I stand next to her and start on the yellow potatoes, but she is much more skilled than I am. When I cut my finger, I just stand there and stare at it. You have to be tough to look at blood—the way it oozes out, so red and slow. I bet Mr. Hoover demands that from FBI agents, but before I can ask, Mom hands me a paper towel.

"Maura, please be more careful."

"Sorry."

"Are you concentrating on what you're doing?"

"Maybe I'm just reckless."

"Reckless?"

"We learned that word in school today."

Mom smiles. "I see."

Sometimes after we eat, she brings to the dinner table vocabulary quizzes stored next to our *World Book Encyclopedia*. She tests us several grades higher than we are, because our family is good with word definitions. I tell her we learned "r" words in school today, and she smiles an even bigger smile. A radiant smile.

Dad wanders through, locking all the windows and shutting the drapes before we even eat dinner. Sometimes he does this while holding Joey. Dad says retarded people are innocent lambs who need our protection. I wonder why a Ten Most Wanted criminal would be interested in Joey, and then I remember the kidnapping warnings from chilling Billy Romero.

"Dad, how come you go and check all the windows *twice?*"

He scowls, loosens his firm white collar. "Don't you have anything better to do? Are these your shoes here? Why don't you put them back where they belong?" He blows out smoke and doesn't move until I do.

I throw my sneakers into my closet, where I keep my stash of Nancy Drew stories. My latest episodes include *The Whispering Statue, The Clue in the Jewel Box,* and *The Bungalow Mystery.* I trade books with Adele Romero when I can sneak past Billy, who says only boys can become detectives, who says Nancy Drew is a made-up fake because who would wear high heels and perfume on crime investigations? I want to tell him that's not true, but Billy Romero with his thick neck makes my knees shake.

I'm still staring in the closet when Julie peeks around the corner. She speaks in a husky tone because her asthma is acting up. Mom keeps a vaporizer that looks like a gurgling gumball machine in our room at night to help Julie breathe. It makes our room moist as a jungle.

"I've got something to tell you," she says.

"Yeah, what?" I shut the closet door with a bang.

"First you have to guess."

"No, I don't wanna guess, just tell me."

"Mom and Dad are talking about it right now. It's a surprise."

"You *know* what they're talking about?"

"Yes." She folds her arms, as if she's such a charm.

"Well, then, it's not a surprise. So what is it?"

"It's about Father Jack—he's coming here in three weeks."

"Here! Three weeks! Here?!"

I look in the mirror, see the reflection of myself jumping up and down, and run to the kitchen. I smile to Mom, even though it's just the back of her red apron I see. I look at Joey. He smiles too, but that's nothing new for him. Dad crouches down low in front of the refrigerator, pulling out one bottle after another. This is the time of night when he searches for the juice from the cherry jar. He pours this into a drink called a Manhattan, which is another name for New York, the place where Father Jack lives.

"Dad, is it true? Is Father Jack coming to see us?" I ask, standing behind a kitchen chair, biting my nail.

Dad keeps shuffling things around in the refrigerator. Mom steps back from the frying pork chops to look at me and then Dad. The air is full of greasy fat.

"Where is that jar of cherries?" Dad asks. He has stacked ten bottles—pickle relish, ketchup, mustard, mayonnaise, salad dressing, tartar sauce—on the countertop. His cigarette sits like a cannon on the edge of the refrigerator door. I think maybe Dad will notice me if I use my new impressive vocabulary.

"Is Father Jack coming to see us radiantly?" I ask.

"I've never seen a house like this in all my—"

"Here. You must be looking for this." Mom reaches up to the cupboard above the stove and takes out a huge glass jug filled with red cherry juice, the container that arrived by special delivery today. It is the response Mom received after she suggested to the head of the maraschino cherry company that they put more juice in their cherry jars.

"And where did this come from?" Dad's hands fall on his hips.

"Remember that letter I wrote a few weeks ago?" Mom gives Dad the container of cherry juice as if it's a trophy, the kitchen light bouncing from the red jar, casting a glow on her cheeks.

•   •   •

Dad never answers me about Father Jack, but one Saturday when I spy on him washing the brown Chevy station wagon, I know that soon we'll be off to the Los Angeles International Airport. He bends over the hose nozzle, which is just under my corner-window sill. Through my lace curtains, I watch him soap up the car as if he might shave it. He places three rags in special positions on the driveway. After the car is soaped and rinsed, he picks up the rags, drying the car with a specific FBI method. I run out of the house to the driveway and put my hands on my trim hips, red elastic polyester shorts snug around my waist.

"Father Jack's gonna be here any day, huh?!"

Sure enough, the next day Dad and Mom pile us kids into the brown Chevy station wagon and we go to pick up our uncle. I watch Dad's eyes check the rearview mirror as we race down the freeway, then I look at all the other license plate numbers. We pass 123 ATS. *123 Apple Tart Sauce* or *Alligator Turtle Sausage.* I wonder if Father Jack will remember me. I hope he will tell us more stories this time around. When I listen to Father Jack, I feel like I am dancing over the rainbow and that its pot of gold has my name inscribed on every coin.

Mom sits with us after Dad pulls up to the curb at American Airlines and climbs out. Cars whiz past us, and each time one of them blows its horn, Julie and John bang on the window, as if to stop the noise. It seems like it takes hours, but finally, I see two figures in the crowd walking slow, step by step, out to our car. Dad grips a black suitcase, his other arm close to the arm of Father Jack. My uncle holds a black hat, one like Dad's, and a white priest collar glides all the way around his neck. Father Jack gives Dad a pat on his shoulder before he looks our way. I almost duck when he spots us. He unbuttons his black jacket, stoops down, his hands resting on his knees before he points and waves. I think he is looking right at me, like one of those floodlights in the night sky whose job it is to grab stars. I gulp and try to smile.

"Wave back! Wave back!" Mom says, wearing her tangerine-orange lipstick and tangerine-orange blouse. She jumps out of the car, dashes ahead, shakes Father Jack's hand, then points to the passenger seat. When the door finally opens, my lips freeze. Father Jack pops his head inside. He has lots of hair, sandy blond, like the beach, and his eyebrows reach the sky.

"Well, well, who might we have here? It looks like the talented Julie Andrews!" Father Jack climbs in, reaches back, whisks me on the head, and looks around. "And Julie and John—growing up so fast. And Michael? Hmmm. I bet he's out playing baseball." Father Jack looks at Dad, saying "baseball" with that New York relations accent, his words bouncing after they fly out. He shifts his weight, looks around again. "And where is my brand-new nephew?"

Dad lights up a cigarette. "We all in?"

"Aw, come on, Joe, don't tell me you're keeping the best for last!" He turns around, winks at us, rubs his hands together with respect.

"Jack, we are so looking forward to you meeting Joey. The Flanigans were kind enough to come over and baby-sit during his nap time." Mom leans forward, her white purse falling into my lap.

"How is the little one doing?" Father Jack looks at Mom and then the rest of us. "How are all of you doing?"

"Oh, doing just . . . fine." Mom opens her mouth, her cheeks a little pale compared to the bright shine of her lipstick. She reaches over, rolls down our back window a bit. "Now, Jack, you're not going to need that jacket—this is California!"

I like the way Mom says "California." She says it like "peaches," like it's a magical place, filled with orange groves and strawberry fields and palm trees, and miles of the Pacific Ocean, the bluest sea in the entire world.

"It'll take me all of ten minutes to get used to this California sunshine." Father Jack lets out a big chuckle, loud, shaking his head as if he thinks something is funny. "You know, I still get a kick over the way Muth speaks of Cally-fornia."

I tug on Mom's bare arm and lean in closer. "Who is Muth?"

"Muth is Gramma Molly," she whispers.

"What does Gramma Molly say about California?" I whisper back.

Father Jack turns around when he hears me. "Was that a whisper or a question I heard back there, from Miss Andrews?"

I have never been called Miss Andrews before by a New York relation. I sit taller in my seat and clear my throat like my voice might swirl deep in there. If I am Miss Andrews, maybe I can ask my question louder.

"Father Jack, what does Gramma Molly say about California?"

Father Jack swerves all the way around so he can face us, his arm draped over the seat, nearly touching Dad.

"*She says*"—Dad interrupts, keeping his stare straight ahead, one hand on the wheel, the other clutching a cigarette—"she says it's a damn desert out here."

We all stay quiet for a second, except for Father Jack, who manages to chuckle a third time, and Mom joins in. As for me, I am not used to hearing Dad say the "damn" word.

"Aw, well . . ." Father Jack looks out the front window again, then turns back to us. "But, you see, your Gramma Molly proclaims that 'Cally-fornia is a desert' with a thick Irish accent!" Father Jack rolls his words out in a sweet brogue and we all giggle—except for Dad, who is busy keeping us safe on the road.

• • •

Mom always used to hold big dinners or even throw a party when the New York relations would come to visit us. She loves parties just like she loves the Brooklyn Dodgers. She says watching the Dodgers was like being at a party, because in Ebbets Field you sat so close you could practically touch the players. I think Dad feels the same about parties as he does about Mom's favorite team.

After Grandpa Conlon died, Mom had the neighbors over on St. Patrick's Day. The Flanigans and the Romeros and the Lukovichs ate corned beef and cabbage and told stories and laughed, but Dad sat in the back bedroom playing Chutes and Ladders with us, talking to fat Dorothy, our baby-sitter. Mom kept coming back, saying, "Joe, will you please come to the dining room and join the party?" Dorothy turned red, and Dad's eyes shot out like marbles. "Can't you see I'm having my own party back here?" That was the last St. Patrick's Day celebration we had, and since Joey's been born, Mom's too busy to give any parties at all.

But now she decides she will ask the neighbors over because they whisper to her that Father Jack is their favorite priest. "So approachable," they say, "and what a lovely sense of humor." Mr. Flanigan sometimes calls him St. Jocko.

Mom must be thinking of these things tonight, because her cheeks shine as she props up the velvet pillows in the living room. She wears a red satin dress with thick straps. It shows off her hourglass figure. Mom says hourglass figures are a good thing, they make you feel like a woman—but I'm not sure that's so good, if being a woman prevents you from doing crime investigations.

I sit on the couch with our Conlon family album resting open on my lap. Sometimes I just like to pull it out, look at photos of Mom and Dad when they were young, and study all the pictures of our New York relations.

"Mom, do we have to come out and say hi to the company tonight?"

"That would be very nice, good manners—don't you think?"

"Ugh. No. I don't think so."

Father Jack walks in and looks up to what Mom calls the cathedral ceilings.

"Getting ready there, are you, for the evening festivities?" His glance then falls right to me, just as mine returns to the family photo album. Father Jack comes over and stands behind me, stroking his chin. I can tell because I can hear the sound of whiskers.

He bends low and points to a picture of Mom. In the photograph, she stands with a bunch of other ladies in a long line. She wears a tan bathing suit, and there's a white rose in her hair.

"Well, look at that, Mare. Joe never let on you were in a beauty contest down at the Point."

Mom turns from the soft, gray couch, grasping the last pillow she is about ready to fluff. Her hair is in small curls, slightly stiff from the Final Net hair spray, and her cheeks run deep red.

"Oh, my. I forgot about that picture. Geez, that's so long ago—I probably was all of eighteen . . ."

"Were you married to Dad then?" I pipe up, proud to hear my voice.

"No, no. That was before I met Daddy."

I look back down at the photograph. It's hard to imagine Mom before she ever met Dad. She smiles big in the picture, bigger than she has in a long while, since before baby Joey was born, for sure. I feel Father Jack's warm breathing behind me, and I think—I hope—that maybe now that our uncle is here, Mom can smile, maybe even laugh some more.

"Mom, were you the queen in all the beauty pageants?"

Father Jack sits down and gives me a smile, like that is a good question to ask.

"All the pageants? Oh, goodness, I barely made it to that one!" Mom walks to the desk by the stereo console and takes Dad's ashtray, empties it into a small brown bag, careful to not let the ashes touch her red dress. "My father, your Grandpa Hogan, was strict, you see. He came right out and forbade me to enter that contest."

"He did?" I gulp, trying to remember what "forbade" means.

"Oh, and my brother Ed, he didn't take to the idea either. This was just after Ed was ordained."

Father Jack leans back, his hands holding his head as he looks around the walls filled with framed pictures of forests and oceans. He looks at me, winks, and nods to Mom, who crumples up the paper bag and sighs a little.

"So, what happened then, Mare?" he asks.

Mom's cheeks get as red as the maraschino cherry juice when Father Jack calls her Mare. I think she likes being called that name. She looks around the room for the next chore, but since they are all done, she sits down in the love seat across from us, her knees pulled tight together. I watch how her tongue pokes the inside of her cheek before she finally tells the rest of the story.

"Ever since I was a young girl, you see, I dreamed about entering the Jetty Point beauty contest. I was so silly then, really." Mom adjusts a curl draping down her neck, then glances at her fingernails. "You sure you want to hear all this?"

"We have all evening." Father Jack smiles. I nod hard.

"Well . . . it was right after I graduated from high school in 1945. I sent in my application, signed it *Mary Hogan,* bought a new swimsuit at Lord & Taylor in New York, then all summer long splashed ocean water on my face, so I could get the nicest tan. Geez, the things that were important . . ."

"Then you had to sneak past strict Grandpa Hogan? Did ya, Mom?"

"Maura, now, remember, you should never do anything like this!" Mom straightens up, then leans forward, and I can smell her perfume, which she wears only on special occasions. "Before anyone was awake, I put on my swimsuit, pulled on a trench coat, slipped out of our bungalow, and headed for the contest at the Admiral Inn. Well, first, your nana, my mother, was waiting for me by the back door. She handed me the white rose, for my hair. She had plucked it from the wild bushes outside."

I look down to the photograph. I see little stars in Mom's brown eyes, like she is on a roller coaster, like her eyes are cups that hold the thrill of wind and laughter. Her smile is like a movie star's, one that glows more than anybody else's in the whole world. With my pinkie finger, I trace the shape of her eyes, which are wide like almonds.

Father Jack clears his throat and sighs like he could sit forever and listen to Mom tell her story. "That's great. Those were some summers at Jetty Point, huh? You must have had the time of your life down there." Father Jack looks back up to the cathedral ceiling, rose pink, in the light of the room. "I always enjoyed coming down to visit when you and Joe were courting. Seems like just yesterday, doesn't it?"

Mom blinks a few times like she hasn't thought about Jetty Point in a million years, and she doesn't say anything else except that she better get Joey into his pajamas and check the pot roast because the company will be here anytime.

I stay seated. So does Father Jack. Mom begins to scoot to the edge of the couch.

"Ah, please." Father Jack puts his hand up. "You just relax, Mare. I'll go ahead and take care of little Joey."

Mom fidgets a little, gathers her dress, then lets her shoulders drop as Father Jack smiles at her and leaves the room. I stand up too, lug the photo album and rest it on Mom's lap.

"You are the prettiest lady in the whole world," I say, looking at her warm cheeks. "I better go. Father Jack may need my help."

I run down the hallway, toward the back bedrooms. Father Jack stands next to the changing table in Joey's room, but he's not alone. Dad lifts Joey and starts to put on the new diaper. A

Mom and her hourglass figure.

soft orange lamp lights up the walls where shadows of Father Jack and Dad move. No one says a word. It's like they are busy concentrating on getting the diaper just perfect, Dad turning Joey side to side as Father Jack waits close by, like Dad's assistant. Usually if you get too close, Dad nudges away, but this time he doesn't.

"Jackie, can you hand me those safety pins?"

Father Jack says sure, reaches over to the dresser where Dad's cigarette rests, and hands Dad the diaper pins. Father Jack is not as tall as Dad, not as muscly either, maybe because he is younger. His shoulders are soft, whereas Dad's are broad, and even the way Father Jack stands, it's like he's telling you a story. I hear Joey, who is nearly asleep, yawn as my uncle leans down and kisses his cheek.

Dad holds baby Joey.

chapter 4

M om sits in front of her bathroom mirror, the beige one lit by four bright bulbs. She straightens her eyebrows with a finger and applies her lipstick. The doorbell rings. Before she has a chance to jump up, I tear out of the bathroom, go pounding on everyone's door. "They're here!" I shriek. "The company is here—hide, hide!" Michael turns up the volume on his new album to drown out my knock. John, with his little buzz cut, bolts out of his bedroom and starts jumping up and down. I bang on the remaining doors while Dad appears out of nowhere.

"What's all the commotion?"

I turn around, my mouth open, a hand still fisted from the pounding.

"I expect it to be quiet."

"Okay." I stand alone, with John hiding behind my legs.

"I'm gonna play Little Piggy with baby Joey," John says, his voice as sweet as strawberries. John always plays this game, mostly at night, just before he and Joey fall asleep, holding hands across their beds.

Dad walks away, shaking his head with each step.

I count up to ten seconds, turn off the light when Dad shuts the hallway door behind him, and then crawl on the carpet from one end of the hallway to the other. I crane my neck to the door that is made of wooden slats—perfect for spying. I take small breaths as I lie in the dark, the small chandelier from the dining room streaming light through the cracks. I squint my eyes, seeing perfectly into the kitchen. Even the copper bottoms of the hanging pots shine, reflecting all the excitement in the air.

Mom, already gleaming, opens the front door. "Welcome, welcome. So nice to see you." She takes everybody's umbrellas as the adults—the Flanigans, Romeros, and Lukovichs—fan like peacocks, shaking rain off their backs.

"Who would have suspected a rainstorm this time of year!" Mrs. Flanigan wears the pinkest lipstick and a silver necklace that flashes in the light.

"Just for old times' sake, I took out my rubber booties from New York. I'd almost forgotten that I'd kept them!" Mom says, opening the dining room closet to hang up the coats.

"My God—we wore galoshes in Seattle for three months straight. Of course, our boys can't stand the rain."

I duck when Mrs. Flanigan says "our boys," her eyes traveling to the slats in my door.

"Call me a romantic, but I love the rain. It sounds like music," Mom says, dancing a few steps. Mrs. Romero nods her head yes.

"Mary, I'm sure the rain thinks you're music to its ears, honey." Mr. Flanigan speaks so loud, almost like he wears a secret microphone. All eyes fall on him as the ladies start smoothing their hair and adjusting their dresses. They drop off fruit salad with miniature marshmallows, string beans with almonds, chocolate cake, and dinner rolls before heading for the living room. Mr. Flanigan meanwhile looks all around. "Now, where's the good father?"

Dad walks out from the living room, where he has turned down the Mitch Miller music coming from the console, and nods to the ladies.

"You talking about me, Lou?"

"Funny, you ole secretive Irishman. Now, where's the genuine article—that priest brother of yours—out from the old country?"

Father Jack grins, shakes Mr. Flanigan's hand. "Hi ya, Lou. Good to know New York ranks right up there with the old country!"

"Great to see you, Father Jack. Welcome back." Mr. Flanigan almost looks like the guard at the navy base saluting when we drive in.

"It's always a pleasure."

Mr. Flanigan talks in a little Irish brogue, maybe because he knows Father Jack is the son of Gramma Molly, whose brogue is as thick as pancake mix. "Father, Norma and I received your Christmas card, thank you very much. You're at some new church, St. Ignatius parish, Father—is that right?"

Father Jack nods, his hand gesturing. "I'm flattered, Lou. You have a terrific memory. Now, I hope you don't have that kind of memory for how the Yankees did this year."

Mr. Flanigan snorts. "Not a chance, Father. This Joe character here keeps us tuned to the Angels now, so don't be talking about any other high-class teams. And well, you know, that O'Malley character, with the Dodgers, I hear what a cheapskate he can be."

"You don't say?"

"Well, that's what Joe would tell ya, right, Joe?" Mr. Flanigan slaps Dad on the shoulder. "Joe keeps us sharp, on our toes if you know what I mean." Mr. Flanigan lets out a *ho ho ho* and Father Jack chuckles too. Mr. Romero and Mr. Lukovich smile as all the ladies glide out of the living room to say hello to Father Jack, shaking his hand like petals. They look like girls lining up for their First Communion, so honored to meet my uncle.

"We're not used to having dinner with an actual priest—in someone's home. It is so wonderful to have you here. Or so wonderful to be here with you." Mrs. Flanigan almost curtsies, giving Father Jack a holy look of appreciation.

"Well, I hope you don't do anything differently on my account!"

The ladies all titter and grab one another's arms and walk back into the living room with Mom. Dad walks over to the secret cabinet above the phone alcove where he keeps the adult drinks. The men set down bottles of gin and whiskey. Dad pulls out tumblers, four of them with a special letter *C* for "Conlon." The men dodge from one foot to the other. I wonder if Mr. Flanigan will ask, "What do you have when the doctor removes part of your colon?" (The answer is a semicolon.) Or if he will tell one of those jokes I don't understand and Mom will look at me in horror when I ask about it, warning me to never repeat those words again.

"Manhattan, anyone?" Dad pulls ice out of the freezer. "Jackie?" All the men veer their heads to Father Jack to see what he will say.

"With two cherries, Joe, if you don't mind. Thanks."

The men relax, still swishing coins around in their pockets like they want to see who has the most change, or they can't figure out what to say except to tell a joke, but Mr. Flanigan still doesn't do even that. Maybe because Father Jack is here and they want to comb the conversation, like hair, into a new style.

"So, looks as if those Angels had a pretty rocky season this year," Father Jack says.

"And what else is new, Father? But that won't stop Joe here from listening to their games morning, noon, and night."

Father Jack looks at Dad, then goes around to all the men, his eyes catching light. "Well, how about baseball on all other fronts? What's the latest with the field up at St. Bede, Joe?"

"It's going gangbusters—four years in a row now!" Mr. Flanigan roars, grabbing a few olives from the table, chomping on one until the bulge in his cheek disappears. "I guess Joe's told you nearly a hundred boys played this season—more on the waiting list for next year!" Mr. Flanigan swallows, reaches for more olives. "These kids woulda been on the streets if it weren't for ole Joe."

Father Jack says thank you as he takes the drink from Dad and leans to the table for an olive. "Kids need a place to go, especially these days. But one hundred boys? Joe, that's a bona fide league you got going—uniforms, umpires, the whole nine yards?" Father Jack pauses. "You still have that nice sod?"

"The softest sod on earth, right, Joe?" Mr. Flanigan says, nudging Dad's arm again.

Dad stares at the vegetable tray, almost as if his eyes are penetrating the table it rests on. He opens his mouth, reaches in to pick something out of his teeth as Father Jack takes another quick sip, then clears his throat. "Well, we sure had our days, Joe and I, playing ball. Of course, back then, it was all that hard pavement . . ."

Dad takes a step back, leans against the refrigerator, standing just outside the circle of men, who say they remember those good old days too.

"Yeah." Mr. Flanigan takes a few slurps from his drink. "Go ahead, Father Jack, fill us in on the mystery of Joe Conlon and his obsession with baseball. I never met a man who follows the game the way this fellow does!"

Father Jack looks at Dad and smiles, then gazes up to the ceiling as if he is waiting for a story to fall from the wood beams. He wipes his mouth with a napkin, then chuckles. "How could I forget this one? Joe, you remember that afternoon on Good Friday Muth caught you sneaking out with your mitt?" Father Jack folds his arms and rubs his chin. "She took a look at the likes of you, and out came her fist from her pocket: *What are you thinking, running out to play baseball on a Holy Day of Obligation! You ought to be ashamed! You had better be heading for the confessional!*" Father Jack says this using Gramma Molly's Irish brogue, and the men's laughter tumbles out of their throats like screws, because that Irish brogue has a way of breaking the ice. "Well, that was some kind of game, wasn't it?"

"Jackie, I don't seem to recall that particular day." Dad folds his arms, his hands flat against his chest.

"Aw, you're pulling my leg, Joe." Father Jack lights up a cigar, blows out a few puffs, his voice a deep purr. "Well, anyhow, try to keep my big brother away from baseball!" More puffs from his cigar. "Of course, you could always blame the neighborhood kids—they were always coming around, pestering Joe to come bat for their team. Anyhow, I followed Joe out. Sure enough, he walloped quite a homer that Good Friday."

Mr. Flanigan booms with his imitation brogue. "Is that right, Joe, defying your good mother like that? You ought to be ashamed."

Dad does not return his huge poke, so Mr. Flanigan grabs the vegetable tray, passes it around, then bites down on a couple of radishes, waiting for Father Jack's story to continue. Meanwhile Dad reaches into the refrigerator for the maraschino cherry jar. He pours in more juice, then lobs another ice cube into his tumbler, the men keeping their glasses close to their chests.

"Let's see. Joe, you slid hard into home after running the bases. And, of course, given that it was Good Friday—" Father Jack watches Dad at the refrigerator, then looks into his drink and swirls the ice around. His eyes look soft. "Well, I forget exactly how to tell it best."

Dad caps the cherry juice, sips his drink, then lights up a cigarette, inhaling twice before speaking. "It's safe to say, Jackie, the story had an unhappy ending, if I recall correctly." He takes a longer sip and pulls his head back.

"Yes, well. I guess the worst of it was that Muth found out." Father Jack grins at Dad, his chin pointed forward, and Dad sneaks a look in return.

"Hey, ole Joe, and what the hell was your punishment for that transgression? Were you out hoeing potato fields for the next fifty years?" Mr. Flanigan snorts through his drink. "Or did you commit the worst mortal sin and ask ole Hoover to ship you to L.A.?"

Mr. Romero and Mr. Lukovich turn to Dad, chuckling and scratching their necks. Dad looks out the window as rain taps harder. He studies his cigarette, then sucks in its red fire. Nobody moves. The rain is now banging upon the roof like hammers.

"Well, as I said, that was some afternoon." Father Jack rests his cigar and glances up to the ceiling.

"Jackie, enough stories for now," Dad says.

Father Jack in his light blue shirt with a soft collar takes the cigar up to his mouth again and looks at Dad. "Sure, Joe."

Just then I feel someone's foot crushing my leg. I put my hand over my mouth so I don't let out a shriek. I turn on my flashlight, point it up. It is Michael, on his way to the bathroom.

"What're you doing down there?" His whisper is loud.

"Hey, guess what! Dad knocked out home runs when he was a kid. All the neighborhood boys worshiped him."

"What are you talking about?"

"I just heard it from Father Jack. Dad sneaked past Gramma Molly to play on a Holy Day of Obligation. He hit a homer, maybe even a grand slam." I flick off the flashlight, not wanting to call attention to my position.

Michael kicks his sneaker against my leg. "Does Father Jack say if Dad's ever gonna hit us balls again?"

Dad never asks us to go to the field anymore since Joey's been born. He never goes himself. It's almost like he has forgotten it is up there. Even though we do our chores, there is hardly an invitation and we're forced to play on the street, always stopping for the drivers who don't care to watch us toss balls or field grounders. Sometimes we'll play on the grass, but Dad shakes his head because he hates how our skids mess it up and encourage all the weeds to grow.

"Father Jack hasn't asked Dad that, but I bet he will."

"Maybe Dad'll listen to him. We ought to play on the field Dad built."

"Huh?" I sit up, careful not to push open the door. "Dad built *our* field?"

"Yep. Of course."

"From scratch?"

"Yep. It used to be ugly, just full of weeds. Dad and his crew got bulldozers from the navy base. They ripped out the weeds, then set the whole thing on fire. The sky was black and smoky for hours. You're too young to remember." Michael walks on toward the bathroom, then turns around. "And if Dad catches you spying, the weeds won't be the only things burning."

I listen to his warning, then slide back down, peering through the slats anyhow.

Father Jack undoes the buttons on the cuffs of his long sleeves and turns them up a bit. "Well, anyhow, Joe, those boys at St. Bede must love that thick sod."

"That's right," Mr. Flanigan says. "And speaking of the ole sod, has Joe told you about this ambitious Irishman we've got as our new pastor?" His voice circles the room like a boomerang.

"What's that, now?" Father Jack asks.

"Well, he's a big change from the last one we had."

Father Jack glances at Dad, then raises his glass, barely touching his lips. "And what was the issue with the old pastor— Father Wheeler, wasn't it—or should I ask—"

"That's right, Father Wheeler. Well, you know, a terrific priest, but he sure as hell liked his Scotch, and after piping in the booze he was up to some crazy shenanigans." Mr. Flanigan punches Dad on the shoulder and Dad ignores him, like what is with this Flanigan character always slapping him in the shoulder as if that will make Dad tell the stories. "Come on, Joe, it's all yours."

"Ah, Lou, not this one again." Dad grabs an olive, then pulls out another cigarette from his shirt pocket.

"Yeah, all right, then." Mr. Flanigan loosens his belt buckle as if this story is about to take all his breath. "So, Father Wheeler gets on the phone after he's had a few and calls England—Buckingham Palace—and asks for the queen! Can you for crissakes believe it—the queen of England, he asks for the damn queen. God only knows what he planned on saying to *her*."

Mr. Flanigan roars so loud the ice cubes in his glass wiggle and chink. He hits his pant leg, starts chuckling again, so much he can barely continue his story. "Father Wheeler hangs up with Buckingham Palace. I don't know what they say to get him off the phone, the queen's in the bathtub or something. Then he goes, makes another call." Mr. Flanigan snorts again. "This time he's calling the Soviet Union—the damn communists—and he's trying to get through to Khrushchev!" His nostrils flare wide, and his laugh comes out sounding like a hyena.

"I think I see where this is headed." Father Jack raises his eyebrows, sets his cigar in the ashtray, and looks at Dad. "Joe, you never mentioned doing intelligence work on behalf of the parish!" I think Father Jack likes to hear about Dad's job with the FBI. I wonder if Dad tells him everything when he phones every couple of Sundays, calling right after we talk to Gramma Molly, who lives in Queens, just like Father Jack. Dad always uses the bedroom phone to talk to Father Jack. I can hear his low voice trading a story, a few laughs coming from under his closed door. I wonder if they have some secret pact.

Dad nods. "The suspicious calls appeared on our records. I had a conversation with Father Wheeler. We took care of things." He crunches on his ice.

My flashlight hits the door by mistake and Dad turns his head. I hold my breath, hoping I am not discovered. Then Mr. Flanigan jumps in. "Yeah, and it was ole Father Wheeler who gave Joe the green light to build the baseball field. Makes you wonder if we have the queen of England and Nikita Khrushchev to thank. Odd bedfellows, right, Joe?"

"Well, and what about those Dodgers!" Father Jack raises his hand. "I still admire what you did, Joe, calling on the Dodgers like that, during that Chavez Ravine remodel, asking them if they'd donate their old sprinklers to your field."

"Yeah, well. That's years ago." Dad turns red, just as Mr. Flanigan jumps in again.

"Hell, Father. Joe tell you he got Pee Wee Reese to show for a St. Bede's sports benefit? Proceeds paid for the uniforms first year around. Yep, the FBI's got them cream-of-the-crop connections, everybody wanting to stay on Hoover's good side, eh?"

Father Jack smiles. Dad lifts his head, looks out the window. Father Jack lights his cigar, takes a few puffs, and watches Dad. "Yes, the FBI does all right." His next puff lands right in front of Dad's face. "Well, anyhow, Joe, the children must be overjoyed to play on a field built by their own father."

Dad glances at Father Jack and doesn't say a word. Instead, he steps to the hot oven, peers in the window, holding his black tie close to his shirt, his shoulders slumped.

The men say nothing, just stand with hands in trousers, dodging from foot to foot. You can tell they are trying to figure out the direction of the conversation, to think of some manly thing to say next. The smell of cigars and cigarettes fills the house, as does the chatter of the ladies, who sound like a chorus of angels in the living room. Meanwhile the men stay firm, like they know they've got more serious topics to discuss. Still, no one says a thing as Dad finally turns away from the oven.

"Speaking of the FBI," Mr. Flanigan shoots out, barely a beat between his words, "what in God's name's happening at the Jacaranda base? Rumors of nuclear weapons are flying like hot potatoes. Joe—you ever gonna tell us what the bejesus is going on?"

Dad keeps a blank stare.

Mr. Flanigan checks out the eyes on the other men, then pulls up his sagging belt, and his trousers follow. "So close to that ball field you built. Sure would hate to see the commies blow up the whole damn thing." He turns to Father Jack, who lets his gaze fall. "I know you are a man of the cloth, Father Jack, but—"

"Why don't you call me Jackie?"

"Okay, Father—Jackie." Mr. Flanigan swallows, lowers his voice into a nasal whisper. "You and Joe must talk about these things—the commies infiltrating the country, Martin Luther King riling up all the Negroes, the whole goddamn nation going to pieces."

Father Jack's face softens. "Lou, anyone say you have a way with words?"

Mr. Flanigan snorts. "Coming from you, Father, I'll take that as a compliment."

"You certainly know how to stir up conversation." He nods and clears his throat. "Sure, Joe and I might hold different opinions, as you would expect. We're both on the streets every day—just privy to different conversations. Wouldn't you say so, Joe?"

Dad sucks on his cigarette, leans over the table, flicking ashes into Father Jack's cigar tray.

Father Jack continues. "My support of King—well, maybe the FBI might find that somehow related to the troubles you speak of, Lou. But then again, maybe not. Who knows? All I can say is that I'm seeing people's lives transformed, people who've never had much, you know, respect and opportunity. You can't argue with that."

Dad sends out pillars of smoke, sending them high, spiraling like slow twisters into the air. He glances toward the slat dining room door and I crouch low to the carpet, hearing him clear his throat. But Mr. Flanigan jumps in.

"Father Jack, don't you think this whole Black Power thing is some sort of conspiracy drummed up by the—"

I inch higher to the slats above. Father Jack's cigar has gone out, but he lights it up again, taking one, two, and then he speaks through the third puff. "Fellows, if I may say—the FBI may have access to specific information. But really"—he pushes out a long exhalation, just as Dad's lips fall into a long O, breathing in Father Jack's words—"information coming from the Bureau, or what have you, is of little relevance to the people I see day in and day out in my parish. I'm seeing real signs of hope, and if there isn't anything as compelling as—"

"You saying, Father Jack, your parish is mostly Negro?" Mr. Flanigan folds his arms over his wide belly.

"I'm saying, Lou, that my parish consists mostly of poor folk who've been as downtrodden as our own people were in Ireland."

"Jack, another drink?" Dad reaches for his glass, but Father Jack waves the idea away.

"I'm okay, Joe. That first one did the job of two." Father Jack scans all the faces in front of him, ending with Dad, as each man lights up another cigarette. All the blue smoke gathers together, turning gray as it drifts toward the ceiling.

Mom arrives from the living room and the men take a step back. She pops a meat thermometer into the roast, then pulls it out. "We're about ready for dinner. You all enjoying yourself out here?" She eyes all their drinks.

Mr. Flanigan does not do a fat wink this time, just stays quiet. Dad walks to the living room. It's time for Mitch Miller and his band to end for the night. Mr. Flanigan takes another sip, whispers loud to Father Jack. "Given these nutty times, we're doing all right with Hoover at the helm. Father, you're in good hands if you got Joe on your side."

"Well, in the end we all meet in the same place, don't we?" Father Jack sets down his cigar and puts his hand out to Mr. Flanigan.

"I think we're ready for a good Irish joke. Lou, do you have a clean one on hand?" Mom smiles, slips an apron over her hourglass figure.

• • •

The next afternoon me and Father Jack take baby Joey out for a walk. This is the fourth afternoon in a row that my uncle waits while I get into my play clothes. Mom says Father Jack is not like some priests who look the other way when they see someone like Joey come along. Father Jack pushes the carriage and I walk by his side, making sure Gramma Molly's crocheted blanket stays tucked over Joey's white legs.

We walk past Janella Reid's house. Her entire front yard is full of roses and you can smell them a mile away. On Saturday mornings, I get up before everyone in the neighborhood and ride my bike to the Reids' even though it's only four doors down. I sneak up to the roses, look both ways, then fill my paper bag as fast as I can with petals. Sometimes I pick a few flowers, sometimes a dozen. I take them home and drop the petals into a bowl of water from on high. They dive down like ballerinas, spinning in midair before they land on the water to sweeten it with their rose juice. As Father Jack and I walk past, I stare at the roses still left and wonder if I am committing a sin by stealing them.

"Those are some roses, huh?" Father Jack points to the yard.

"Yes." I gulp and pick up my pace. "I can push Joey now . . ."

"How about in a little while? Meanwhile why don't you tell me something?"

"Me?"

"Hmm. What could it be?" Father Jack begins to whistle for a few seconds, then stops as if he's just found the great idea. "Why don't you tell me what you would like to be when you grow up?"

"I don't think I want to grow up."

"Oh, and why is that?"

"I don't know. I think baby Joey needs me . . ."

"I see. Well, he loves you very much."

"I love him too. He's lucky—he's named after Dad, you know."

"Yes, I know." Father Jack steps away to let me push Joey now, leaning over to make sure he is okay. "They are some pair, huh, Big Joe and Little Joe."

A kid from Rushmore public school wearing a black-and-white-striped shirt heads our way. He looks down and stares at Joey, a nonstop stare. You can tell his severe look says there is something wrong with my brother. Father Jack opens his mouth and says, "Hello, young lad, what is your name?" But the kid just runs on.

"Well, he's only a young boy, huh? He still needs to learn." Father Jack smiles and looks down to me and waits for me to smile back, as we continue our walk. "You know, I was thinking. I've seen your handwriting and it is very nice. Maybe sometime you can write a letter and send it to me in New York. You can write anything, even what you'd like to be when you grow up!"

"Dad writes a letter to Gramma Molly every week. Just before dinner on Sundays."

"I think she counts the days until the next letter."

"Dad says she never reads his letters, because he always has to repeat the information on the phone. We talk to Gramma some Sundays. . . . She's not so glad about Joey."

"Why do you say that, Maura?" Father Jack puts his hand on my shoulder, for just a second.

"I can tell—by Dad's face. He just stares at the wall when she's on the phone. Sometimes I think our walls have ghosts." I look up to Father Jack. He takes my hand, swings it, then lets it go.

"Not to worry, okay? Everything works itself out. Joey is

special. And so are you. Do you know that?" I think for a minute, but I am not so sure.

"And when you get older, you will come to New York and I will take you to the Statue of Liberty, and I bet you may even like it better than Disneyland. And then we'll have a big dinner and you'll meet all your New York relations. You've got one of the most Irish names of the whole bunch, you know."

"I do?"

"Yes."

" 'Maura' is Irish for 'Mary,' you know."

"See what I mean—you *are* special." Father Jack stops short when he says this, and I look at his lips, which I can tell want me to believe them, so I nod my head.

We arrive home, after going around the block, and Mom asks Father Jack if he would like a cup of coffee, which is the most popular question adults ask.

Father Jack lifts Joey out of the carriage, places him back in the bassinet, strokes his red cheeks.

"Does he need to be fed?"

Mom is not so used to other people helping out with Joey, I guess, because she can't figure what to say next.

"Oh, well, yes, that would be . . . just terrific, Jack. Are you sure?" He says of course, and Mom finds some creamed food for baby Joey.

"And I will take that coffee later. Thanks, Mare." Mom's cheeks and forehead turn red, but I think they're getting used to it.

I watch Father Jack spoon-feed Joey. Joey can't say *ummm, ummm,* but I can tell he would if he could. Father Jack then gets up to make his coffee. I have never seen a real live priest fill up a kettle with water and set it on the stove and turn it up to high in such a holy way.

"I think I'll sit outside for a bit. Get some more of that fresh California sunshine. Maura, would you like to join me?"

"No, I will stay here." I know I don't have anything to say.

When the kettle starts to whistle, Father Jack gets up, but Mom comes back, waves him to sit down, and after she pours the hot water, she asks if I would like to serve Father Jack his coffee.

I look out to the patio. Father Jack folds his hands together and looks out to the pool. The wind has picked up and scales ripple on the water's surface. Huge maple leaves float down, landing half on the pavement, half in the pool. I put on a red and white apron and tiptoe with the coffee cup to the patio filled with seashells Mom has collected from Delphina Beach, which is only six stoplights away.

"Here's your coffee . . . Father Jack."

I look up into his eyes. I have never looked at them up close. They are just like Dad's eyes but with green, like frogs, mixed into the blue. His eyes bend slightly in the corner, like they want to reach down to his mouth, which says nice and gentle words.

"Thank you . . . and could you be so kind as to bring out the cream?" His eyes are like Christmas tree lights, twinkling on and off.

I could be a ballerina, with a rose in my hair, I think to myself. Maybe that's what I will be when I grow up, but then I remember that I would be too shy to dance or curtsy, and I wonder how I could be a ballerina if I was always wanting to run behind the curtain.

"I'll be right back."

I sneak back into the house and look out the window while Father Jack peers down to his hands and rubs them. I open the refrigerator, and I think what a wonderful thing it is that my Uncle Father Jack likes cream in his coffee.

Fitting in with all the dreaming flowers.

chapter 5

I love the smell of May. It is the month of flowers. Even though I am in fourth grade and I know it's a sin, I still ride over to the Reids' house early in the morning. I lay my gold stingray down on the sidewalk and creep up to the rosebushes so I don't wake them up. They are moist with clear teardrops and too sleepy to know what's happening. Some are the kind of pink you want to wrap yourself up in. Some are orange with red in the center—they call your attention like the singers on *The Ed Sullivan Show* with their wild clothes and high boots who sing so loud Mom says this indeed must be a new generation.

In May, though, I don't make the rosewater perfume. I steal

the rose petals for Mary. May is the month of Mary. That is what we learn at school.

Our teacher for fourth grade is Sister Rita. She speaks in the same brogue as Sister Norah and Gramma Molly. She says that in May we will not be saying Our Father like we normally do. We say Hail Mary instead because Mary is the queen of angels and, she repeats, May is her month.

The statue of Mary is situated at the head of the classroom, facing us. She wears blue garments; her arms are outstretched, and she stands on top of two snakes. Snakes are evil creatures. Mary stomps them out, doing it with a smile like it's a piece of cake.

"Okay, boys and girls, shall we talk about the importance of May? Who would like to go first?" The sun charges into our classroom and lands on the fuzz of Sister Rita's cheeks.

I want to raise my hand and say sweetly it is May, it is the month of Mary, but it's not my custom to pipe up like that at school. I look around the room and see the more popular and talkative kids raise their hands, their eyebrows going up in excitement because it is obvious they have the answer and can't wait to say it and whoever Sister calls upon will be the new class star.

Miriam Daniels, with skin so clear you can see right through to her veins, gets to answer.

"This is when we honor the Blessed Virgin, Mother Mary."

"Very good, Miriam. And in what ways do we honor Mary?"

I feel Sister Rita's eyes veer over to me. She always looks and wonders—just like the other teachers I've had—waiting for me to raise my hand, but I never do. I am in my own quiet space. I sit and think and watch and feel like the ocean that just goes in and out and back and forth, saying very little but always capturing someone's attention.

Once I was sent to remedial reading because I could not find my voice when asked to read out loud, but I was sent back to normal reading class the next day. Still, I hope Sister Rita will call on someone else. I straighten my posture and lean to the right, where the angels await. The devils lurk to the left. I always fall asleep on the right side of my bed and hope the devil does not steal my soul if I roll over to the left, by mistake.

"Again, how do we commemorate—" A few hands shoot up, including those of Elizabeth DuPoint, who remains the prettiest girl in our class, and Adele Romero, who beats me in basketball, and Peter Norden, who still has not forgiven me for throwing up on him after I was nervous when Joey was born.

I glance to Sister Rita as she peers through her round gold glasses. I think she must hear my heart beat louder than the basketballs the boys sneak into the hallway and dribble during recess. I know the answer, but I just can't push the words out of my dry throat with loads of lumps and frogs and maybe even souls from purgatory who are stuck and can't find their way out.

I feel a moan inside, like the sound of Dad's FBI car motor warming up in cold fog, and I feel ice on my tongue and try to heat it up. I think of how it could sound to hear my voice say, *May is the month when Mary rules. We praise her by singing songs, having May processions, and making special crowns.* I imagine saying this in front of everybody, and how all the talkative pupils might look at me and think, *That girl has a majestic voice.*

I sit at my desk and stare down at the wood grain and the little indentation that holds my yellow number 2 pencil, which I always sharpen at home because I am too afraid to get up in front of class and use the one on the counter.

"Maura?"

I bow my head low and feel the entire class, every face, turning to mine, waiting, waiting for the sister of the mentally retarded boy to speak. I press my thumb down and my pencil goes flying and rolls on the floor. I let it sit there by my sneakers as my face steams up.

"Okay, then." Sister Rita finally gives up on me, unfolds her arms, and turns to the other side of the room. "Elizabeth Du-Point, why don't you go ahead?"

I don't hear a word Elizabeth says. I keep my head low and draw a picture of a jeweled crown for Mary, one with sharp points to keep all evil away. I draw this in the new spiral note-book I asked Dad to buy me. I didn't tell him what I wanted it for. On the outside, my new FBI log looks just like an ordinary notebook, black cover and all, but inside, it's full of important facts from my investigations. Almost every day, I scribble down the makes, models, and license plate numbers of vehicles on our street that I don't recognize. Sketches of Mary's crown also de-serve to be in the log that gives me secret power—Mary is the queen who runs surveillance on the snakes of the world.

• • •

During May, we don't work on our Catholic dictionaries, learn-ing all the rules and regulations about religion, but I can still re-cite the seven evils and all the sins like mortal, venal, and a few other types. I still know that unbaptized babies go to limbo and the people not good enough to go to heaven get parked in pur-gatory, and we have to pray for their souls, keep praying for them so that God will open the heavenly gates and allow just a few of them in, hunchbacked and wearing old, holey coats, one at a time, with a hundred of our prayers on their backs.

After school one day, I tell Janella Reid with all the rose-bushes that I am a Catholic, which means I belong to one holy and apostolic church started by Jesus Christ that got handed down to Peter while he stood on a rock, and then he passed it on to the popes, who have Xs and Vs, code numbers, after their names.

Janella stuffs her mouth with Ritz crackers. I don't blame her. I like them too, much better than our usual saltines, which is what Dad buys when he goes to Hydro's Supermarket.

"Are you a Catholic, Janella?"

She reaches for the peanut butter, slaps it on her crackers. "Nah—I am American."

"I'm American too." I swallow my peanut butter, my mouth still sticky. "But if you are *just* an American, how can the souls ever get out of purgatory?"

"I don't know. I'll go find out." She goes to ask her parents and she returns and says they are not sure. Her parents do other things than think about purgatory. Mr. Reid likes to look at photos of nude ladies with boobs as big as the blimps that float by in the summer. I found his stash of magazines in the bathroom when he was out fertilizing the roses, but I didn't tell anyone. Now Janella says her family is moving, which keeps me from worrying that I can't be her friend anymore because I might end up in purgatory for looking at those pictures and she might never bail me out.

• • •

Soon after Janella moves away, a blue and white moving truck, license plate 240 KQT, slides up our street. I take my FBI log, hide behind tree trunks, sneak around cars, and then crawl through rows of juniper bushes. I crouch low, uncap my pen. A lady with beehive hair marches out of the pink house, waving her arms like she is going to stop the truck herself.

"Whoa, boys, whoa there."

The movers lower the drawbridge. Out of the truck parades the furniture, including a birdcage without a bird, a fish tank without fish, gold-trimmed tables, and a dark piano she orders them to roll into her garage.

"Over there, over there. It's gotta go over there!" The new neighbor whirls her hands about like she is directing traffic. The movers plunk down the piano in one spot and wipe sweat off their sideburns. "Oh, wait, oh heck—the piano can't stay there. Nope, nope, nope." I never knew you could just move a piano like that. Ours has sat in the same corner of the living room for centuries. "Over in the other corner, pleeeeez." She winds her arms up in the other direction and the movers follow. "Oh, yes—that's much better. You boys, now, you're perfectly wonderful, you know. Can I get you some lemonade or something?"

The movers say no and take off. The lady sits down in her garage and plays a song on the piano. It sounds like thunder clapping, with seagulls churning above. I have never heard music just roll down the street like that, making the shrubs stand at attention. After the song, the lady runs back into the pink house. I check her garage the next five days and never once does she close her garage door. I scribble these notes down in my FBI log, then ask Mom if she is aware of the strange new neighbor living on our street.

"A new neighbor on the street? And they've already moved in?"

That afternoon we are there, Mom and me, walking over a Betty Crocker's devil's food cake with homemade chocolate frosting. I keep my eyes on the dark frosting while Mom bends to look at a calla lily.

"Look at this—the flowers are blooming so nicely this year. A good sign."

"Good sign for what?"

"That we will have lots of flowers all summer."

"Mom, can I lick that frosting falling off the side?"

"Come on, you should know better."

Just then Mom peers into the garage as we head up to the doorstep. "Look at that—a piano in the new neighbor's garage!"

"The garage has been open for five days and five nights." I squeeze my FBI log, which hides underneath my shirt. "Smell that cooking meat coming out the kitchen window. The lady must be home." My skills at collecting evidence are becoming quite excellent.

Mom reaches for the doorbell. The porch light flicks on, fast, as if our new neighbor has been waiting five days for the door-bell to ring. The lady with hair so tall it's like the Matterhorn towers over me. Mom's orange lipstick glistens.

"Hello. I am Mary Conlon, your neighbor down the street. I just wanted to say welcome!" Mom smiles and the lady looks at Mom and looks at me and eyes the cake, then starts oohing and aahing all over it. It's the nicest one Mom and I have ever made. I wish our new neighbor would tell us chocolate gives her an upset stomach and that we should really bring it back to feed our starving family.

"Lovely. Oh and chocolate is my absolute favorite. How nice of you, neighbor . . ."

"And this is my daughter Maura."

Mom touches my shoulder, as if I belong to that crop of flow-ers, preparing to bloom all summer.

"Could that be *M-a-u-r-a?*"

I nod.

"Well, of course it is! And look at those darn purty green eyes. If those aren't the greenest eyes I've ever seen, then Mrs. O'Leary's cow never started that ole Chicago fire."

Mom laughs and I gulp down a wad of saliva.

"Well, I am Abigail, Abigail Eveready, and it's a pleasure to meet you both. You'll be meeting my husband soon enough—

he's still closing things down in Texas." Her hand shoots out as if it has been hiding in a holster.

"Maura said she saw you move in last week. I'm sorry it took a while to get over here . . ."

Mrs. Eveready bends down. "You the one spying on me from the junipers when I was ordering those darn moving men around?"

My face drops into my green collar, eyes shut for longer than a blink.

"Well, that was awfully nice of you to be so curious about someone new on the block. I think I'll just call you my little spy!"

I look up at her and smile, even though I feel bad about my horrible technique, getting caught in the act and all. Then Mom tells Abigail she noticed that piano in the garage and asks does she by chance take students and would she consider taking me on? By the time we say good-bye, it is arranged.

• • •

Mom calls Sister Rita and tells her about my lessons, and I stop speaking to Mom for a whole day when I find out, because now Sister asks me to play the song that signals it is time to place the new crown on Mary. Each of us in the class is assigned one day in May for Mary to wear the crown we've made from scratch.

"Maura, Maura? It is that time—would you please come up to the front?" Sister folds her hands promptly.

I walk up to the front of the room, keeping my eyes on the small organ keyboard, and play with shaking fingers four lines from "O Mary, We Crown Thee with Blossoms Today." The whole class sings along and their voices distract me and I start to mess up the notes. Before I'm even done hitting the last one,

I run back to my desk, as if fifteen seconds is more than enough time to be standing in front of the class.

Even though I am safe in my seat, I know I've got to quickly gather enough courage to return to the top of the class because this is my day to place the crown on Mary. I look behind Sister Rita and study Mary's eyes, trying to figure out if she is happy or sad or somewhere in the middle. I wonder if Mary is shy like myself and think she might be because she always lets Jesus do the talking, and even when the angel Gabriel came, she didn't say too much, not even when the angel announced that she would have a baby born on Christmas Day when all the trunks of the palm and oak and jacaranda trees on our street are wrapped in foil.

"All right, let us see here." Sister bends down over her beige notebook where she keeps the list of our names in alphabetical order. "Let us see here," she says, pushing up her bifocals.

I look up at Mary. Her flowing garments drape over the world. I can almost see her tapping her fingers, like she's getting impatient as she waits for my special crown. I try not to make it too obvious how much I stare at her, but already my heart pounds harder.

"Yes, it appears that it is *Maura's* turn today—*Maura's* crown will now be placed on the blessed head of our Virgin Mother." Sister looks up from her notebook. I wonder why she says my name twice. Maybe she thinks shy girls can't hear the first time around.

"Maura?" She steps toward me, saying only my first name, not my last, which she does for the other kids. Maybe it's because I am the only Maura at St. Bede and in all of Jacaranda Highlands and maybe in the entire state of California. I wonder if Mary and me—we don't need last names.

I reach under my desk, pull out my lunch sack, open it up,

and immediately, the smell of egg salad sandwich hits me in the face. I reach in and grab my Baggie with my crown for Mary and hope it won't smell like egg salad, and I put it perfectly in my palm and look up to Mary, who stands waiting at the top of the room for me. I glance around and see all the glum faces watching me and wondering if my crown will look as good as theirs.

I pull myself out of my wooden desk, walk to the top of the room, past Sister Rita, past the wool of her black habit and the smell of holy soap. I try hard not to trip or drop my crown. I bow before Mary and then slide toward the thin silver stepladder, which shakes as I take my first step. I look at Sister and hope she will hold the ladder, but she just stands with folded arms. I take my second step, my knees wobbling as I hold my breath and reach up to Mary's head. The ladder makes a shuddering sound. I tell my knees to hold still, and I pray I won't fall backward in front of everybody, or worse, push Mary over and shatter her into a thousand pieces.

I let go, and my crown of white roses, orange ribbons, and orange beads falls on Mary's head. I try to ignore the snakes underneath her feet who sneer at me, saying who do I think I am giving Mary this mighty crown that will help her drive evil out of the universe? I wonder how Mary likes stomping on snakes without wearing any shoes. That is something Nancy Drew would only dream of doing.

The crown sits on her head the way the little girls in France wear their tiny berets. I adjust it a little so it looks more like how a queen would have it.

"That's lovely, Maura. Well, quite original."

I almost lose my breath because I think it is the Virgin Mary speaking to me, but it's not, it's Sister Rita, who looks at me and nods her head, and I wonder if she has nodded as much to the other crowns as she does now to mine.

"You may be seated."

"*Orange* crown . . . *orange?*" I can hear whispers from the class.

I look at Sister through shy eyes and look at the class and wonder if they like my crown. I want to tell them about Joey and how he helped me make it in the bedroom. I wonder if the Virgin Mary knows Little Joey helped, that he kissed each one of the roses, but I don't say a word. I look at Elizabeth DuPoint. She puts her face to the air like no one could ever make a crown as good as hers, even though hers looked so rigid. Adele Romero's mouth hangs open like she thinks my orange crown is strange, that something is not right, like it could be a retarded crown. Peter Norden fakes like he is going to throw up.

I pull my brown plaid uniform over my knees, feeling the stillness in the room. Sister begins to speak and says it's time to move on to our next subject. I don't hear a word she is saying. Instead, I just look up and stare at Mary's creamy skin under her crown of orange, her lips full of holy love. I wait for her to speak to me, to tell me she likes my creation, that it makes her happy, that no one has ever made a crown like this for her before.

Sister Rita leads us into spelling, then math, and then on to our history lesson, which is about the California Indians, but I still don't hear a word she is saying. I just watch the sun glide across the classroom like a dazzling circus pony, its gold resting right on top of Mary. I stare hard, wait for her to smile or even wink at me, but her face still does not move. I think if I stare even harder, then maybe she will change her mind and swivel her entire head and look me in the eyes. I tighten my eyebrows, look serious like a real FBI agent, not noticing that Sister Rita has stopped at my desk.

"What is the name of the first California mission founded by Father Junípero Serra?"

I look up to the cross around the neck of Sister Rita, who decides not to wait for me to raise my hand.

"Maura, can you please tell us?"

My forehead gets red as a devil's pitchfork because I cannot remember what Sister has just asked, and even if I did, I could not speak, just like that, in front of everybody.

"I know, Sister," Elizabeth DuPoint says.

"Thank you, but please wait until I call on you . . ."

I bite down on my lip and make my eyes very big, so big that they will let Sister know I forgot the question.

"What is it that you are doing, Maura? What are you thinking about all the time, that you can't even pay attention in class?"

I do not tell Sister that I've been staring at the statue of Mary waiting for her to speak.

"Maura, name—the—first—" Sister's voice sounds like thunder booming from Mrs. Eveready's piano.

I look around the room, and this time almost all the hands shoot up. I stare again at the Virgin Mother and see her smile just an inch bigger than the last time. I hear her tell me to imagine the orange crown on *my* head, so I can find my voice and speak as queens do.

I bite my tongue, and it stings, but finally, I feel a rumble inside and I open my mouth and to my surprise words fall out. "The answer"—Mary now smiles as big as those Hollywood movie stars—"is Mission San Diego. Father Serra banished the heathens, just like Mary drives out snakes, and just like the FBI wipes out all evil."

"Well, yes, that's very good," says Sister Rita.

I look back up to see if Mary likes my answer, likes my voice, but now she is back to her same old face, watching us all, our class of thirty boys and girls in brown and white Catholic school uniforms. Her arms are outstretched, inviting us to her, as if we should come her way.

• • •

That afternoon I bring my crown home. The flowers fade a little, but the orange beads glisten. Mom gives me a little statue of Mary she keeps in her stationery drawer. I go to my bedroom and make an altar and rest my crown before Mary's feet. I stick sweet-smelling roses in little vases and put a white candle inside Joey's empty baby food jar. I kneel on the cushions before the altar and fold my hands together and pray my crown will look new forever, that it will stay my good-luck crown.

When Dad pulls into the driveway at six o'clock sharp, I ask him if we can go to Sears on Saturday and get a special jewelry-type box, for my crown.

"We'll see."

Two nights later, he places a small wooden object on my desk.

"What's this?" I am not used to Dad walking into my room and handing me a gift.

"It's a box."

I inspect it up close. It is not a jewelry box. Instead, it is husky and square. I tap my short fingernails on top of it. "Is this for my crown?" I hope it's large enough.

Dad retreats to the doorway, puts his hands in his pockets, and sucks in his cheeks. "It's an old card box I don't need anymore. I assume you'll put it to good use. If not, I'll take it back to the office."

"This box . . . is an *FBI box*?" I gasp, holding it firmer in my hands.

"So, take good care of it." Dad walks away. I insert Mary's crown for protection, grab a white sock, dust off the box and smell it. It has the FBI smell, like Dad, the smell of blue and wood together.

Dad takes Michael's troop to visit FBI headquarters in Los Angeles.

chapter 6

I t is so hot the summer after fourth grade all we do is jump in and out of the pool, then suck on cherry Popsicles. Mom leans over the black Singer sewing machine with straight pins in her mouth, her face dripping with perspiration as she puts in another new hem for Joey's pants.

Down's kids tend to have shorter legs. Dad had to build special wooden blocks for the pedals of Joey's tricycle so his legs could reach, and add special straps so his feet would not keep slipping out.

I sit down on the blue tweed couch, ready to hand Mom the next pair of Joey's pants. "Do you think you'll be taking up hems for the rest of Joey's life?" I ask.

She looks at me. Her shoulders sigh. "We take it one day at a time, don't we?" she says, wiping off sweat with a washcloth.

J. Edgar Hoover stares down at us, surrounded by all his framed letters to Dad. One offers sympathy on the death of Grandpa Patrick Conlon, who Dad never says a word about. The other letters congratulate Mom and Dad every time they have a child, except for Joey. There is no congratulations letter for him, even though he is already three. Maybe Mr. Hoover does not want to draw attention to Joey because Joey's so friendly he'd be easy to kidnap.

• • •

Late in the afternoon, I walk down the block, inspect each parked car, and enter a few more unfamiliar license plate numbers into my log. The clouds start to thicken, turning black in their centers, and the hissing crickets begin to sound like snare drums. I go back to my bedroom and shut the windows, then sit and wait for Dad's FBI car to round the corner. I sit at the edge of the bed for almost two hours, but tonight he doesn't come home right at six o'clock. Dad always walks in on time, and if he does not immediately smell supper, he investigates the scene, uncovers what could be distracting us from preparing the important meal.

At six-fifteen, I go into the kitchen and ask Mom why Dad is late. She stirs the spaghetti sauce, then drains fat from the sizzling ground beef. She says she has not heard anything from Dad. My heart races, but I sit down quietly and stare hard at the pink telephone, which does not ring. At six-thirty, Mom smiles. "I'm sure it's nothing, Maura. Dad will be home any minute."

At seven o'clock, we eat dinner silently. Afterward, Michael takes out the trash and John brings in the plates and Julie helps Mom with the dishes, and at eight o'clock, I help Joey get ready for bed. When I sing to him, I try to make my voice come out even: "Doe, a deer, a female deer." Joey sings with his hands. We lie in the back bedroom in the dark where Joey can't see my frozen face. I listen to the dryer in the garage growling through the wall. It rumbles like a spaceship ready to leave for the moon. The dryer shakes harder, then starts to echo, and in the echo I think I hear Dad's FBI car pulling into the driveway. I finish the song for Joey because he would be disappointed if I quit in the middle. Then he says *please,* because he wants me to sing it again. I hum low and can tell it's Dad's car for sure, and now the front door opens, then closes with a soft shove. I wait for the smell of cigarette smoke, for Dad's footsteps in the hall, while I sing another chorus to Joey, but Dad doesn't come back. Even the ghosts in the vents stay silent. I plant a kiss on Joey's cheek and make my way carefully to the end of the hallway, peering into the kitchen through the slat door shut tight.

Mom bends over Dad. He sits on a kitchen chair, his legs stretched out on the floor. His black fedora has fallen off next to Mom's cup of Sanka. The kitchen smells like it does when we come rushing home all scraped up and Mom applies rubbing alcohol, which makes us howl. It smells like blood. I push open the door and plant myself in front of Dad's black shoes. His eyes are shut, one of them bulky and purple as a grape.

"Who's there?" I see Dad's nostril twitch like he's trying to sniff me out.

"M-me."

Dad says, "Can I help you?"

I wonder what that's code for, and why he's talking in code at all when his head is streaked with blood. "Why—what happened—wha—" I want to throw my arms around Dad, but instead, I touch Mom's arm as she leans over him.

Dad waves, his eyes packed shut. "Had a fight with the butcher, that's all. Sold me chops and I wanted steak."

I look at Dad and watch his chest breathe in and out, slow and deep. I want to tell him I know *Butcher* must be some villain's code name, like Penguin or Riddler on *Batman*. Mom reaches for another hot washcloth, and steam floats up from the bowl. Dad takes the cloth from her and rubs it on himself, not screaming, not even flinching one bit.

"You give Joey a good-night song?" Mom says this like she is calm and wants me to see how calm everybody is, like this is a normal thing for Dad to come home so late at night with cuts across his forehead and cheeks.

"Dad?"

He holds the brown cloth against his wet skin, sweat sneaking from under his ears.

"It's okay. The butcher turned out to be a nice guy."

"But you've never. Did you catch—"

"Off to bed." Dad waves his hands as if my voice is a bumblebee. I want to ask him if he threw the Butcher in the slammer for life, but Dad just shoos me away again. I go back to bed and wait for him to come in and lock the bedroom windows. I prepare my speech, ready to say I will protect him from all the Butchers, but that night his creaking toes never come in. I lie there, hear him snoring all the way from my parents' room. I look over to my FBI box holding the dried-out crown of Mary. She would just get up and lock the windows herself, so that's what I do. I lean all my weight in and shove, then crawl back into bed and wonder how Dad locks them with barely a touch.

Dad does not tell us how he got beat up. I beg Mom to tell me, but she says she does not know. It is confidential, she says. FBI agents are forbidden to talk about these matters. I write down in my log, *Butcher, code word*. When I pass Dad in the hallway, I whisper, "Butcher," under my breath, but he does not stop, just carries his FBI shoes out to the garage, where he keeps his shoeshine bench.

One night when Dad's bruised face is turning from purple to yellow, he stops in the hallway. I think maybe he is going to talk, especially when he says, "Has your mother told you about the summer?" Sometimes he says *has your mother told you* when it's really he who wants to say something. But when he finally speaks, it's nothing about the Butcher. Instead, he announces we will be flying to the East Coast to meet our New York relations. Dad says he must stay behind in California because he's in the middle of a case. My stomach gets all wadded up because I think that must mean the Butcher is still on the loose. I say extra prayers each night from then on, asking God to make sure my father comes home safe each night.

•   •   •

One Saturday in the middle of August, Dad drives our family to Los Angeles International Airport and walks us to the terminal. He stands firm, shakes everybody's hand, then tells me to be careful three times. He folds his arms, his muscles stretching like brown hills across his chest.

"I wish you could come with us and see the New York relations," I say.

"Some other time," he says, leaning down to fetch Joey from the stroller. He lifts him high into the air. "You take care of your mother and your sister and brothers." I don't think Joey can understand Dad, but he gives Dad a slobber kiss anyhow.

A deep voice announces that it's time to board our airplane to New York. I turn around and wave good-bye to Dad and he waves back. I nudge Mom's shoulder. "Dad's waving good-bye," I say. By the time she turns around, the five of us surrounding her on the walkway, Dad's hands have fallen into his pockets, but he gives us one nod, his eyes watching our every move. I tell Mom we will have to call home every night to make sure Dad is okay, and she nods yes.

Michael is the first to step onto the plane, followed by Julie, John, Mom with Joey, and then me. The plane smells like shag carpet and is filled with tall, mustard-colored seats.

"Beautiful children," the stewardess says to Mom, who has Joey already sleeping in the seat next to her. I wonder if the stewardess will notice Joey has Down's syndrome. "Lovely—all of them," she says.

Mom nods yes. I think the stewardess is wonderful, like Glinda the Good Witch. I look at Mom. She gives me the same smile she gave the stewardess, who leans down to talk to me. I have never seen a real live stewardess before. I admire the stiff blue hat she wears.

"What's your name, young lady?"

"Maura."

"Such a pretty name!"

I look to Mom, who smiles as she watches me, and nudges her shoulder up like I should talk some more. "It's Irish. We are going to see our New York relations."

"Oh, how nice! They must be Irish too?" The stewardess looks at Mom and winks.

"My Gramma Molly is the most Irish. She has the brogue."

The stewardess hands me a deck of cards that reads *American Airlines*. She says when I get to New York, I might like to play cards with my grandmother, but I don't think Gramma Molly does that kind of thing.

We fly all day. Every hour I ask my mother what time it is. I ask her if she thinks the New York relations are just as excited to see us as we are them, and she says of course.

I sit back and wait, just like the time I waited all summer for Gramma Molly to come visit us in Cally-fornia, when I was five. I wonder if Gramma's legs are still white as salt and if when she sees my tan, will she wave at me, complaining that a girl like myself shouldn't be getting so much sun on her legs, but then I'll tell Gramma I get tan like my mother, and she'll say, "Oh, yes, I see."

I got so tan the summer I waited for Gramma Molly. I stood outside day after day and watched Mr. McGibbons, the construction man, and Dad build the pool in our backyard. They built it eight feet in the deep end, wet cement on the bottom, a diving board on top, and just up to my shoulders in the shallow end. The night the pool was filled with water, Mom took me outside to look at the reflection of the full moon, and later there was Dad, swimming up and down like a white fish, the muscles in his arms and legs kicking water over the edges.

"Do you think Gramma Molly will wanna swim or go to the beach when she comes out to see us?" I remember how I asked Mom questions about Gramma Molly all summer long.

"Hmm, I don't think so. Gramma Molly has that fair Irish skin, like Daddy."

When Gramma did arrive, it turned out what she liked to do was talk, something that did not happen ordinarily at our house. Her voice flew through the rooms like a bird looking for the sky, talking about one *crissakes* thing or *good God* another, her hands twirling this way and that, while Dad kept shaking his head and saying, "Is that right, Muth?" Dad knew exactly when to say that, because right when he did, Gramma would sigh like she was glad Dad was listening, and return to her story. I watched her hands, which were freckled like Dad's, hoping she might reach into her suitcase and pull out a special present for me, maybe a Pebbles doll dressed in a cave girl outfit, her red pony-tail fastened with a saber-toothed tiger bone.

The first night after she arrived, I lay in bed, hearing Gramma come down the hallway repeating, "Oh, dearie," all the way to my bedroom, where her suitcase waited in the closet. I didn't want her to think I had been waiting desperately for my gift, so I pretended I was sleeping. Even so, Gramma started talking in her brogue.

"Dearie . . . are you awake?"

I turned in my bed, starting to snore until I heard a strange, fidgeting noise—the sound of the closet doors creaking, creaking open. I squinted to see what Gramma Molly was doing.

"Now, dearie, 'tis a shame you're sleeping. I have a little something—especially for you."

Something for me! I wanted to wake up just like that, with a snap of a finger, but first I had to stop snoring, saying *aaaaaaah, aaaaaah.*

"Oh, well, I'll have to save the present for one of your cousins back in New York."

Oh, not one of my cousins—Theresa, Kelly, Colleen, James, Noel, Fitz, and then all the others that belong to Dad's sister, Aunt Veronica. My New York cousins get to see Gramma Molly all the time—Sunday suppers and Easter and Christmas and Thanksgiving and Halloween and First Holy Communion. I felt jealous because our cousins got to have a grandmother and aunts and uncles, like Father Jack, and second and third cousins, and all we had in California was each other.

A zigging and zagging filled the room, the sound of a zipper on a suitcase rolling up for good. The room fell nearly silent, the lace curtains sagging to the ground, the zipper gliding along until it hit a snag and Gramma called out, "Damn thing!"

"You okay, Gramma?" I shot straight up in bed.

"Oh, and whose voice might that be?"

"Mine."

"And who's mine?"

"Maura."

"Oh, so it is. Well, very good, now. I thought you were sleeping . . ." And with that, she fastened tight the zipper and slammed the closet door.

"But, Gramma . . . what about the brown suitcase?"

"It sits in the closet. Good night, dearie."

"But what about . . ." I could barely spit out the words. "Gramma—what about the present in your brown suitcase that you brought especially for me?"

Gramma Molly heaved a long sigh, then flicked on a little table lamp with white daisies at its base.

"Stay right there," she said, trudging back to the closet. She pulled open the door, yanked her suitcase zipper, and turned her head, fast, like a hot potato.

"Close your eyes and don't be opening them until I say."

I closed my eyes like when Michael watched *Dark Shadows* in the afternoon, always refusing to change the channel.

"Okay, then, hold out your palm."

I held out my palm.

"Ah, but your eyes are not closed. Close your eyes."

I shut my eyes, feeling Gramma place something cold and metal in my hand. It felt like a game piece for Monopoly.

"Open your eyes, dearie." Gramma stood with her hands on her hips and gave me three seconds to tell her if I liked it or not.

I looked down.

"What is it?"

"What is it! Oh, holy night, what do you think it is?!"

I watched her stomach stretch out as far as her potato breasts as she sat down. Her mouth clicked together. "It's a thimble. You wear it like this . . ." She fit it right over my middle finger.

It looked odd. "Is it for good luck?"

"It's for sewing, dearie. Soon you will learn how to sew. And that's when you will wear the thimble."

"Maybe I'll be nimble when I wear the thimble?" I smiled at her.

Invisible bees must have been buzzing by, like they do for Dad, because she looked at me and waved at the air. "I don't know what you're talking about." She hobbled back to the closet and reached down again into her suitcase, pulling out a piece of thread and a needle.

"You may as well learn this now." She bit a piece off the spool and showed me how to pull the thread through.

"Here, lick your finger to get the knot right." I let the thread twirl and roll along the side of my dampened finger until it formed a knot.

"I love this—"

"That's good enough . . . Now, off to bed."

I sat up taller. "Did someone teach you how to thread a needle too? Did your gramma teach you?"

"Off to bed."

And with that, she turned off the lights, unzipped her dress and hung it up. Silver streamed in from the streetlight outside as Gramma pulled on a nightgown, the type a fairy-tale gramma wears, so fluffy you can't tell if there's a body in it. Then she rolled into the bed next to mine and started a Hail Mary.

"Gramma?"

Her prayer grew softer, as if it were a personal affair.

"Gramma, are you there?"

No sound at all, not a prayer, not even a breath, and I wondered if Gramma Molly had died.

"Gramma?"

"All right, what is it that you want now?" Her voice vibrated like a brass organ, and I jumped under my sheets.

"Was your gramma from New York?"

Gramma Molly started praying again, saying, "Ah, Jesus, Mary, and Joseph, will this damn child ever leave me to rest!"

"I promise it is my last question."

"No more questions!"

I held my breath, listening to Gramma Molly. In between *Hail Mary* and *full of grace* and *the Lord is with thee*, I heard her whisper, as if she were telling only the pillow and not me, "She came from where your people come from."

I pressed down on my thimble and whispered back, "Thank you," to Gramma, so low that it seemed I was talking to the pillow as well.

Mom loves her old jetty, and now she takes us there.

chapter 7

Our plane lands in New York City, and our uncle, who is Mom's older brother, picks us up. Father Ed looks like tall Mr. Green Jeans from *Captain Kangaroo*. He drives a car called a Checker cab that is painted deep blue. Father Ed says his long legs require a big car. Mom sits in the front with Joey. Michael, Julie, John, and I crawl into the back. We sail away from the airport just as two men pull out their thumbs and yell, "Taxi, taxi!" Father Ed comes to a stop and rolls down his window. He explains to them even though his car looks like a taxicab, he is not a cabdriver, and the men back away when they see the white collar around his neck.

That night we go to the beach bungalow in Jetty Point

where Mom grew up in the summers, and when we arrive, we eat saltines with tuna fish. I can barely hear the ocean in the background because the breeze is so loud it blows up the trees' skirts. The outside umbrella spins around like a bright blue top.

I am up at six o'clock in the morning because the sun shines early in New York, the heat sticking to the air like Scotch tape.

"Where are the palm trees, Mom?" I look out the window of the bungalow and see only wild sea bushes growing out of the sand.

"Palm trees in New York?" She laughs. "Maura, the first time I ever saw a palm tree was after the FBI transferred us to California. Daddy and I drove across the country, and as soon as we got to Los Angeles, Daddy knew the first stop—the Pacific Ocean. Those palm trees looked so exotic."

I think "exotic" means you get possessed by so much joy it forces you to hug or kiss something. I try to imagine Mom hugging a palm tree.

"Okay"—Mom claps her hands—"let's have some breakfast. And then we'll go for a walk and I'll show you around."

Father Ed is sitting in the corner of the front room, his head leaning into his Bible. He says he does this every morning as part of his meditation. When he does not read the Bible, Father Ed travels here and there and teaches people how to talk to one another. That is what he does as a priest.

After breakfast, Michael and John stay behind and listen to Father Ed's stories about love and family communication. Mom puts Joey in the red wagon stuffed with pillows, and we stroll with Julie along small, sandy sidewalks, past rows and rows of little wooden bungalows with flags whipping high in the wind. Some of the flags are American flags, but most of them are green with four-leaf clovers. We arrive at the bay full of bobbing boats and gulls landing on gray buoys. The water is deep blue, small waves lapping in the strong breeze.

"Look, there it is!" Mom bends low and grabs my wrist and points to hundreds of buildings way out across the water. "You've heard about Manhattan—there it is—and if you look right in the middle of all the buildings, you will see the tallest skyscraper in all of New York City."

"The Empire State Building?"

"Yes."

I look through the tumbled vines of buildings stretching out there, miles ahead, and find the one with the pointy top. "Wow. I can't believe it. I can't believe I am actually seeing it. The Empire State!"

"Hey, do you see King Kong?" Julie asks.

Mom takes a deep breath. She closes her eyes and sucks in sea air as if it is made of flowers. She breathes in and out, the breeze tossing back her curls. I look around Jetty Point. It is filled with so many cute bungalows, each painted a different color and each with a front porch and tables and chairs and people sitting and reading the newspaper and eating breakfast and saying hi to everyone who strolls by.

"Is this how Jetty Point looked when you were a girl, Mom?"

She opens her eyes, her lips fresh as cantaloupe. "Oh, yes. Some things don't change—it is as wonderful as ever." She takes my hand, points in another direction. "Now, you see this water right down here?"

"Yes."

"Your Grandpa Hogan and Nana came down here in the mornings and clammed. Nana made clam chowder at night. We'd sit on the front porch with our clam chowder and a hurricane lamp and listen to the waves. Oh, and your great-grandparents would come down from Brooklyn. The ocean was much closer to the bungalow back in the old days. And all day long, all we wore was our bathing suits. That's all you ever needed."

"Wow." I try to imagine having a great-grandmother and living in my bathing suit and eating only Nana's clam chowder at night by the light of a hurricane lamp.

"Did you read books? Did you read detective stories?"

"I'm sure I read all sorts of books."

"Did our nana like it here too?"

"She lived for the Point. She loved the light . . ." Mom's face beams like the sun bouncing off the sidewalk. "Those were happy times."

Behind Mom, the skyscrapers stretch like a gargantuan jungle gym as far as my eyes can see. Gray ships sail like floating ribbons in the sea. They look like they're headed straight for the tall buildings.

"Mom, where are those ships going?"

"Into New York Harbor. Now, when I was a girl, I'd be walking along these sands and watching the *Queen Elizabeth* and *Queen Mary* sailing out there."

"Where were they going?"

"New York and England. Back and forth. Two stacks and I knew it was *Queen Elizabeth,* three stacks and it was *Queen*—"

"*Mary?*"

"That's right."

"Wowee kapowie," Julie pipes up.

Mom turns and looks down by the waterside to a white building with wooden slats, a boardwalk leading down to a metal plank not too far away. A fishing boat pulls up, its motor rumbling. Some men hop out and shout, "Flound-uh, flound-uh!"

"What are they saying, Mom?"

"Flounder. That's a fish."

Mom takes the handle of the wagon and we all walk closer to the building. I watch gulls fly in and out of the dark brown beams holding up the boardwalk, and hear the building's shutters go smacking in the wind.

Joey starts to get fidgety in the red wagon. He has just lately started to say "Mom," because Down's kids learn to talk later than normal kids. The way he says it is cute, more like *maamee*, like he says it inhaling and exhaling at the same time. She lifts Joey out of the wagon and he throws his white arms around her neck. We step onto the spongy gray boardwalk and I feel the sway from the water's pull. The white building looks deserted. Mom covers Joe's eyes from the sun, then situates him back in the wagon. She walks almost in slow motion, before leaning into the window. I peek in too and see a hardwood floor and a stage with what looks like red velvet curtains. I hear birds caw, and the clanging of bells from the buoys.

"Look at that." A few cobwebs hang from the chipped ceiling. "Is this where they showed movies in the old days?"

At first, Mom is silent as she cups her eyes to the window. "Oh, no . . ." She looks back to the wagon to make sure Joey is okay, then peeks back in. "Do you remember when I told you about the old beauty pageant?"

"You mean *the* beauty pageant!"

"Yes. This is where it all happened . . . the 1945 Miss Jetty Point Beauty Pageant!"

"Whoa." My nose and hands are plastered against the window as I study the velvet curtains hanging long, their thick hems making a puddle on the hardwood floor etched with black cracks. I imagine Mom up on the stage, showing off in her swimsuit, with the white rose in her hair from my nana, who loved the light here in Jetty Point. I look at the stage, close my eyes, and see Mom walking across with her tall, tan legs, swirling about as the audience goes wild, whistling through their fingers.

"I can't believe it—I can't believe we're here!" I stare into the window until I see a reflection in the glass of a man walking up behind us, his footsteps coming closer. Mom swings around first, and soon we all do. She smiles at the man, then reaches down and puts some lotion on Joey's face to keep it from burning, softly tugs the blue baseball hat that says *Dodgers* on his head.

"Hello. Is that you? Mary—Mary Hogan?!" The man has stiff hair that hangs across his forehead. "It couldn't be, could it!" He talks thick, a thick New York accent.

Mom turns around and smiles. She doesn't say anything. The man begins to pat his stomach.

"Paul Ramsey, Mary! Oh my Gawd, look at you, I don't believe my eyes . . . The Hogan beauty queen has come back home." The man stretches his words out longer than taffy.

"Paul Ramsey?" Mom purses her lips. "Oh, my . . ." She puts out her hand and he shakes it until I think it may fall out of Mom's arm socket.

"Good to see you, Mary, good to see you. Gawd, what a surprise. Geez, how long has it been, Mary? Twenty, twenty-five years, good Gawd, could it be that long?" Paul Ramsey crosses his arms, like he's got something important to say. "Last I heard, you married some G-man who swept you away to the West Coast."

"Oh, yes, we've been in California for quite a while. And I haven't been back to the Point here in, well, ages . . ." With her free hand, Mom tugs her cotton blouse over her hips, and her head bends to us.

"These are my daughters, Maura and Julie."

Mr. Ramsey bends down and shakes our hands like electricity. "Did you know your mother was one of the most gorgeous broads in all of Jetty Point? Well, of course she's still a beauty, eh? All the guys called her the cat's meow. I bet you didn't know that, now, did ya?"

I shake my head no, looking back to the white building, the reflection of the water moving on its underside, and imagine Mom being called a cat's meow instead of "your mother."

"You know, we used to dance together in the old days—remember all the bands they had at the Inn? Nothing like all this rock and roll these here kids listen to—and they call that music." Mr. Ramsey lights a cigarette, inhales, then exhales, for almost two minutes. He has not even looked at Joey yet. "So, where's the mister? And how long you out for?"

"Joe's got a case with the Bureau back in Los Angeles."

"Married to the FBI—those guys with all the secrets, huh, Mary?"

Mom picks up Joey, adjusts his weight around her waist. "Paul, I don't believe you've met our youngest. This is Joey."

Mr. Ramsey's shoulders cringe. He does not lean closer or back away. He takes a minute to think of something to say, looking at Joey, then looking at Mom, then back to Joey, whose eyes are sleepy because of the strong sun.

"Joey's our special fellow." Mom bounces him up and down.

"Yeah, yeah. Uh, I see that." Mr. Ramsey spits out a chuckle, looks down to Julie and me. He places his lobster-red hands on his long black walking shorts like they've got nowhere else to go, then he scratches his head. "Hey ya, Mary—" He leans closer to Mom like he is saying something we are not supposed to hear, but I don't think anybody in New York ever talks that low. "Mary—I am so—sorry."

Mom smiles as if she is back onstage at the beauty pageant

and why would anyone in the world think to say those particular words?

"Paul, you haven't told me a thing about Maggie and your family. How are your children?"

He looks down to his feet. "You know. Hey, uh, you remember Tom and Wilma Johnson? Back in Queens?"

"Tom and Wilma Johnson?" Mom takes a second, looks at us, then turns toward the skyline of New York in the distance, as if we should be watching the jolly skyscrapers too. "Well, of course . . ."

"Yeah, well, they had a daughter like this one here, you know, your youngest one here. She's upstate now, some institution . . ."

"Really." Mom's smile now is held up by toothpicks. Her eyes squint, like the time Dr. Hodges whispered that word "institution" after Joey was born and her face hardened and she thanked the doctor and we never drove home so fast as we did that day, Mom even running through a stop sign. "I am glad the Johnsons are doing well. And, Paul—it's just been a pleasure. You know, we really ought to be getting ba—"

"Ah, really, Mary, the pleasure's all mine." Mr. Ramsey takes Mom's hand, barely shaking it, just holding it, maybe like he used to when they were at the dances at the Admiral Inn. "You stop by anytime, you hear? Maggie and I are at 189 Conch—the bungalow with nine leprechauns out front. Maggie, you know, she's always liked the leprechauns." Mr. Ramsey tugs himself backward, the boardwalk squeaking, and studies our faces. "And I am so—"

"Please say hello to Maggie. Tell her I've never forgotten her scrumptious peach pies . . ." Mom's lips quiver, just a trace.

I turn around and look at the white building, the pole alongside it with its red, white, and blue flag shaking high up in the wind, as sand starts to blow in our faces. I wish we all could sneak in the white building, go run around up onstage and pretend the velvet curtains are our capes, but I don't ask as Mom nestles Joey into the red wagon, her curls wild in the breeze as she takes extra time to sandwich in his pillows.

"Mom?"

She leans up, salt in her eyes. "I think it is time to get back to the bungalow, okay?" She puts on a kerchief, just like the movie stars do when the wind roars and they don't want to mess their hairstyles. She ties it into a neat knot and puts on her sunglasses.

"Are we ready?"

I look out to the bay, its small beach with sand sizzling so hot in the morning. "Hey, Mom, look at this." I leap out into the sand, dodge sharp shells, pick up a twig, and trace a huge heart. When I am done, I wait for Mom to give me her reaction.

"What's that?" she asks, her voice split in two, a high wind and a darker, low one.

"It's a heartprint, that's all. It's my heartprint on the sand."

She smiles and then turns, pulling Joey behind her. I put on my baseball hat and follow the red wagon. We pass by other people pulling their red wagons. They stroll from the grocery store, wagons loaded with bags of food. No cars are allowed in Jetty Point—just red wagons and the tiny bungalows and the sidewalks and the people and the front porches and the sand and the water and the skyscrapers of New York City winking like jewels in the far sky.

I can't believe I'm standing so close to the Lady!

chapter 8

Father Jack comes down to the bungalow the next morning after we finish our Lucky Charms. He claps his hands and asks if we are ready for the Big Day, which is supposed to be a surprise, but I am pretty sure about where we're going. Father Jack strokes Joey's back, gives him a peck on the cheek, and then tells Mom to relax and enjoy the sea while he takes us kids on an adventure today. Mom says indeed she will as we follow our uncle out the door and down the sandy sidewalks to the parking lot.

I keep the window rolled down as we drive along the water, wind rushing in my face, messing up my hair, but I don't care. Michael hits my shoulder and points out to the distance, and I can see her just like in my history book, the Statue of Liberty, who is so tall her torch nearly touches the white clouds. Her crown is different than Mary's—it has more spikes, like she is serious about the words "liberty and freedom for all." I wonder if she feels all alone standing by herself in the middle of the harbor, waiting for us to come see her.

"I knew all along Father Jack would take us here."

Michael rolls his eyes. "I'll beat you to the top."

•   •   •

We all stand in a huddle as Father Jack buys tickets for our trip, then comes back, puts his arms around us all, pointing out to sea. "The Statue of Liberty is what your Gramma Molly saw when she came to America from Ireland."

"How many years ago?" I ask, squinting, my hands trying to block out sun.

"Many. You'll have to ask her."

I stare at the statue and blink my eyes to make sure she is real. Maybe that is what Gramma Molly did too. Today the air is hot and filmy. Father Jack grabs Julie's and John's hands and suggests we have a hot dog first. There are so many people around us. They speak so fast and walk faster than they speak and radios blare and the hot dog man wants to know if I want sauerkraut on my hot dog and I've no idea what he is talking about.

"Mustard should be fine. You like mustard, if I remember, right, Maura?" Father Jack hands me a steaming hot dog wrapped in white paper, and off we go for the boat. The Statue of Liberty holds her torch up with a strong arm and clasps a book to her chest. I can't wait to see what she likes to read.

Father Jack squints into the sun. He wears a brown-checked top with no collar so no one can tell he is a priest. I like how priests can change identities just like that. He looks down to me as I peer up to him, one eye open.

"What do you think so far, Maura?"

"I like it. I like being here." I close my eyes, the roar of the motor tingling under my feet. I think of how I will tell Dad about our time with Father Jack, and then I think about what Dad is doing and how his face looked when he came home late that night. I tug on Father Jack's shirt. "Did Dad tell you he got beaten up by a criminal?"

"No, he didn't tell me about that."

"The criminal's code name is *Butcher*. There were cuts all over Dad's forehead."

Father Jack pulls the hair out of my face and says, "There's no need to worry. No one can outsmart your dad, okay? Just relax, enjoy where you are, on a boat sailing out to see the Statue of Liberty, okay?" Father Jack smiles and I nod my head, letting the salty wind and sun take turns licking my cheeks.

The rest of the afternoon is a hum of endless spiraling stairs, a view from the crown with boats below rocking like sea horses, cotton candy on the ride back, and Father Jack telling us not to tell Gramma Molly about our pink snack. Gramma Molly, after all, will be having us for dinner.

But first, Father Jack takes us to his neighborhood parish. He says it will be fun for us to see our father's ole stomping grounds, which is some place called Knighton, Queens. We drive up to a brick church, with a basketball court and a rectory next to it, as the bells ring six times.

Father Jack opens up the door and in we walk to his rectory. I've never been to a rectory before, only watched Father McKinley and the St. Bede priests sweep in and out of theirs. Inside, a sweet lady with butterscotch hair is cooking what smells like Saturday supper. She comes out and introduces herself as Helen, the housekeeper, and asks if Father Jack will be joining the other priests for the meal. "No," he says, "we are only here for a short while."

"Why don't you kids make yourself comfortable here? I've just got some papers to sign and then we'll be on our way." Father Jack leans down and clicks on the television as Helen brings out lemonade for us and turns on the fan.

"Oooh, far out—the Yankees are on." Michael grabs Julie and John, who scoot close to him on the couch.

"I love the Yankees!" John jumps up and lands on the floor.

"Not as much as me." Julie crouches low.

"What about those Angels?" Father Jack folds his arms.

"That's Dad's team," Mike says, leaning toward the television.

Father Jack laughs. "But of course."

I look around the rectory walls. They are full of shelves loaded with books with red covers and some with gold-trimmed pages, and already it smells like an altar with several holy candles burning. I ask Father Jack if I may walk around and look at the rectory and he says that is fine.

One wall features several beautiful photos. In one picture, Father Jack shakes the hand of a young man who has black skin. Then I realize everybody in the photograph has black skin except for Father Jack. I remember the first black hand I ever shook, the hand of Paula Jones. We don't have many people who are black living in Jacaranda Highlands except for Paula Jones and her family. Mom invited them to come swimming one afternoon, and Paula and I took turns holding each other, floating in the pool.

In the other photographs, Father Jack stands with old people, so old they look like they could fall over at any second. A few men lean on canes, and one of the ladies has missing teeth.

Father Jack's face beams. A penciled scribble alongside the picture reads *Low Income Rental for the Elderly Approved.* In another photo, he stands with four black children, one of them in his arms. Those children are so lucky to have my uncle close by all the time, cheering them on and lifting the hair out of their eyes when it's windy.

I keep moving down the hallway, looking at everything on the walls, until I end up at the front door with the small stained-glass window. I push the door open and follow the cement path outside and start wandering down the sidewalks.

The houses look different in Knighton, Queens, than they do in Jacaranda Highlands. There are no big lawns here or fences like we have. One tiny yard the size of a hopscotch square creeps into the next. Each house is tall and skinny, with a tiny porch, one creaking with old furniture. One house has a hole in the window. I wonder why the people don't just go up to Haley Hardware and fix it instead of nailing across a piece of wood.

"Hey there, young lady—you lost?" A man with huge hair and black and oily skin steps out of his house. He sets down a paint can in the hot sun, comes walking toward me like a character from *The Munsters.* He wears big pants, and in his pockets I hear no change, just see the shape of his cigarette box, which he reaches for. I want to turn around and run in the other direction, but instead, I stand there, next to an old fire hydrant where I imagine a million dogs must pee. I see other kids with big hair coming up the block, moving so fast I feel blades coming out of their shoes.

I feel so alone as I turn around and don't see a soul I recognize. Then I hear someone calling my name. I look at the tall, oily man and wonder if he calls my name but he just watches me. I turn in a circle wondering if it is Inspector Erskine looking for me, because no one else knows I am here, in Knighton,

Queens, New York. I turn around again. The voice sounds like Dad's, but then I see it belongs to Father Jack. He strolls down the street, checks his watch, and I wish he would please walk faster.

The oily man stands in a see-through T-shirt with no sleeves and watches my uncle come my way and I hope the oily man will leave us alone, me and my uncle, so we can get back into the car and head over to Gramma Molly's, who has been cooking all day in the kitchen.

"Father Jack!" I turn, go running to him, and he grabs my hand.

"Oh, you're out here having a discussion with Lawrence? Larry's got some good stories, how you doing, Lar?" Father Jack tips his hat even though he doesn't wear one, and the oily man drops his hands and points to me.

"Father Jack, this one belong to you? She was walking around like she didn't know which way was up and what was down. I was about to give her a brush and put her to work." The man talks like music, like taps on a xylophone, and I don't know what to say, so I look up at Father Jack.

"This is my niece Maura, from California."

"California! Where all those rich movie stars live?" The oily man, Lawrence, looks at me like he's never met anyone from California in his entire life. I have never met anyone like him either. I nod my head yes as the screen door pushes open and out walks a lady who looks like she could be related to Lawrence.

"Father Jack! A little late for your morning walk? You wanna come in? Fresh-baked muffins . . ." The lady picks up a teddy bear lying on the porch and scoops it under her breasts.

"Lois, thanks so much, but"—he points to me—"I've got nieces and nephews out from California. We're on our way to their grandmother's for dinner."

"All the way from the West Coast! Well, humpf, okay, then." She smiles, takes hold of Father Jack's hand, and looks at me. "You know, you're a lucky girl, having an uncle like this one here." She squeezes his hand and lets go.

I bite my lip, look down at Father Jack's black shoes.

"He's the only priest that's walked this neighborhood in years. He is practically one of our own. You understand how lucky you are? You understand that now?"

I nod yes, twice, since she asked me two times, and look up to Father Jack, who's got his arm out to Lawrence and Lois.

"So, we'll be seeing you Wednesday night at the parish office?"

"Don't worry—we'll be there, Father. And I'll be coming along to that housing meeting next week."

"Very fine. It'll be good to have your support at City Hall."

Father Jack shakes their hands, says good-bye, and escorts me back toward the rectory. Some kids come skipping up, grab my uncle's shirt from behind, and yell, "Hello, Father Jack!" and run along, laughing. Other neighbors look up from their front porch when we pass by. Each one of them says, "How ya doin', Father?" and he says fine and asks them how they are, then before long, we are off to see Gramma Molly.

My stomach growls and feels slightly nervous. I think of Lawrence and the lady, Lois, and I wonder what their muffins taste like. I think of all the other neighbors who live on Father Jack's street and how old and rickety the houses look and those stiff bars that guard some of the windows and the huge cars that hit all the holes in the road. My stomach growls again so loud that everybody in the car can hear it, and Michael turns around to make a face.

"Hold on to that stomach, because we have one more stop to make." Father Jack drives a little while longer, then pulls into a parking lot surrounded by trees taller than any I've ever seen. "We'll make this quick, guys. Come on."

He starts to run and we chase him through a grove of trees filled with wide green leaves. This is like Sherwood Forest, an easy place for Robin Hood to hide and shoot arrows, and still all around people ride bicycles and another man yells out, "Soders, get your soders here." Soon we come out onto a clearing, a small paved area with a little fence and weeds popping in and out of the cracks in the pavement. It takes a few minutes for me to realize that before us is an old baseball field. I see chipped cement, a faded yellow line connecting first, second, and third bases.

"You all love baseball, right?"

We all nod our heads as Father Jack points to the field. "This is where your dad and I played when we were kids, like you."

I look at Father Jack, then stare at the pavement, trying to imagine Dad playing ball here, on this tough cement. I keep trying to imagine Dad as a kid, but it's difficult. I blink my eyes and still can't see him being anything but my father the FBI agent, wearing his black hat, stashing his gun, and protecting us from the danger in the world.

"Your dad was something else. The best center fielder around."

"Did you two play on the same team, Father Jack?" Michael asks.

"Well, we had nothing like the league your dad's set up in California. We played pickup games." He smiles, motions for us to follow him.

I kick small pebbles along the way and scratch my new mosquito bite. It seems like the day is getting hotter and my face feels like a butterscotch candy sticking to its wrapper. I take a huge yawn and sigh. "Are we almost to the place you are taking us, Father Jack?"

He walks a bit more, then stops. "Yes—this is it. We are

here!" He points to the ground and we all stare at the pavement, Julie and John holding fingers, Michael with his hands on his hips, and me still scratching my neck. Father Jack crouches low. "Did your dad ever tell you about the stupendous catch he made in center field?"

"Nope, our dad's never mentioned anything like that." Michael's quick to respond.

"Well, I'll tell you all about it. Even better, I'll show you." Father Jack stands up and starts moving about. "So the ball flew out, way out, like it was destined to be a home run, but your dad, out here in center field, he started to run quick as lightning." Father Jack's feet skip backward, fast, like a deck of shuffling cards. "Your dad ran with such speed, then faster, and then, shwoosh, with arms outstretched, he leaped up, and oof, snagged the home run ball." Father Jack jumps high, grabs a chunk of air, then falls back to his feet, faking like he holds a baseball. "And what's more, your Grandpa Patrick saw him make that great catch."

I tie the bow on my polka-dot top and look around to a rolling hill in the distance filled with more Robin Hood trees. They have huge winding limbs, gray barks, and leaves wide as rulers. A train rattles from someplace close by as the wind shoves hot air down my back. I try to imagine Grandpa Patrick being alive and watching Dad, even though I have read thirty times the framed letter from J. Edgar Hoover sharing his sadness that Grandpa had to die.

"Dad never tells us about Grandpa Patrick. He just walks away when we ask him."

"He does, huh? Well, that's unfortunate."

"Did Grandpa Patrick hit balls to you and Dad?" Michael asks.

Father Jack puts his hand to his jaw and looks at the four of us, our thumbs hanging out of our pockets and hair all messed up from the boat ride on New York Harbor. "Hmmm. I think I hear the voice of Gramma rumbling through the trees. We better move along."

"Father Jack, can *you* tell us a story about Grandpa Patrick?"

He takes a big breath and looks into all our eyes as we huddle around him. Michael pulls out Bazooka bubble gum and passes out some for everyone. I stick a piece in my mouth and suck in all the sugar while I wait for Father Jack, who barely chews his gum.

"Why don't we head for the car? We can talk while we walk." He takes Julie's and John's hands and I follow a few paces behind, chewing the hard gum. Father Jack bows his head for a while, like he's praying real hard, then he finally turns to look at all of us. "A long time ago, when your dad and I were, say, nine, ten, eleven, something like that, there was something called the Great Depression. Michael, maybe you've already studied about this in school?"

"Sure, well, a little."

"Well, remember, during the Great Depression, many fathers lost their jobs. Grandpa Patrick was one of them. There wasn't a job to be found for years, and this was hard on him, hard on everybody. So, you see, some men didn't always feel like going to a field and tossing balls. Some felt broken down. Money and jobs were scarce."

"But our dad has a good job with the FBI and he never asks us to play anymore," Michael says.

"That's right!" John chimes in.

"He's always busy with Joey." I gulp. "Maybe he's forgotten how to catch."

"Oh, I'm sure not. One day you'll be getting a hit yourself and it'll sail right out to your dad. Mark my word."

Father Jack looks at me and winks, starts chewing on his gum like he's one of those big-time ballplayers on television. He blows and pops a huge bubble and taps Michael and starts running in winding loops, and Michael's face brightens and he starts chasing after Father Jack almost like he's playing tag football, then John darts after both of them, his hands twirling like sprinklers, and Julie grabs my arm and yells, "Let's go get 'em!" They go running around the painted bases, over and again, Father Jack zooming like a rocket, forward, backward, all around, and everyone else does the same, touching home, then circling around again.

I look down to the hard pavement. The heat bounces up and my head starts to ache like pounding nails. I try to picture Dad making some great catch and sad Grandpa Patrick hiding by the trees and watching. But I can't see them, only rings of circles inside my head spinning like a kaleidoscope. The sticky wind kicks up again and the circles zoom faster, purple and yellow, and I close my eyes, then imagine sounds, like the crack of a bat, and I imagine some kid running the bases, but I can't tell who it is, and I hear excited breath, then a sliding, smacking sound. But when I open my eyes, no one is there.

"Maura, Maura—are you coming along?" My uncle comes running back for me. "We better be off."

"Father Jack?" I look up and see sweat covering his face. "Is this the place where Dad played on the Holy Day of Obligation?"

"Ah, so your dad has told that baseball story?"

"No, um, I never heard a baseball story," I say, turning red.

Father Jack scratches his head, looks down to his watch, then rubs his chin. "Well, it's getting late. I'll make it quick." He touches my shoulder, turning me in the direction of the car. "One Good Friday your dad walloped a home run, his hit as high as a rooftop. See that one right over there?" He points to a pink and red brick building holding a huge antenna. "Your dad ran the bases like a racehorse, slid into home, got right up, and boy, there was blood everywhere. He'd broken a bone. The radius, in his arm. He and I raced for the doctor's to get it fixed. Oh, of course, then Gramma found out and she wasn't at all happy about any of this."

I look past my uncle toward the Robin Hood trees, then turn and stare at home plate, the place where Dad slid and bled.

"What about Grandpa Patrick? Was he there?"

"No, I would say not."

"That's good."

"How's that?"

"If Grandpa Patrick was so sad, he couldn't have helped Dad. Maybe Dad would have been all on his own."

Father Jack whistles low as he opens the back door of the car.

"Why don't we see what Gramma Molly's got cooking for supper?"

• • •

Before we have a chance to unbuckle our seat belts, Gramma Molly steams out like a locomotive. She holds a rolling pin over her head. "Where in God's name have you been?" Behind is her brick house, tall and skinny, with barely breathing space between hers and the house next door.

"Don't worry. That means she is glad to see you," Father Jack whispers, shutting the car door behind us.

"Hello, Muth." Father Jack bends to her cheek and she makes a face like even though Father Jack's duty is to kiss her, she loves it more than anything.

"Hello, Gramma Molly . . ."

"Well, look at all of you." She studies us as if we are the

shimmering boats sailing in New York Harbor. "All right, get in now, get in. I thought you'd never arrive, good Lord."

We step up the back stairs and land in the kitchen filled with steam. Gramma Molly has four pies lined up on the kitchen counter. I wonder if she has made one for each of us. On her walls are several framed pictures of Jesus and the Blessed Virgin Mary, and a small wooden crucifix hangs above the kitchen table, which is covered with a red and white plastic tablecloth.

Gramma tugs a blue apron around her waist that's thick as a tree trunk. Father Jack sits down and asks about her day, and the four of us sit around Father Jack, our hands folded in our laps, even Michael, who's twice as tall as Gramma now.

"I bet she's making some sort of Irish meal," Michael whispers to me.

"What was that, now?" Gramma Molly must have eyes on her back. Her hands dart to her hips.

"Muth, the children were wondering what lovely meal you are preparing for dinner."

"We're starveded," John pipes up. "We had cotton cand—" I throw my hand over his mouth.

"We're starved, Gramma Molly. We saw the Statue of Liberty."

Gramma turns her back swiftly. I listen to her say, "Oh, dear Lord," and watch her scoop up bottles to her chest as if they hold her secret potions. Into the bowls she throws in a dash of this, a dash of that, then chops, sifts, rinses, while water goes whistling out the kettle.

I tiptoe forward and lean to smell what is cooking on the stove while Gramma's not looking, but she zooms around and my head almost knocks into her bosoms, her red cheeks coated with perspiration.

"What in God's name are you doing?"

"Um."

"What is this, *um*? Good heavens, where are you learning that?"

"Gramma, um. What are we having for, um, dinner?"

"Shy, this one, humpf! Enough so you won't be going to bed hungry, dearie."

I smell her damp freckles, hoping my legs will quickly drag me back to the table.

"Italian spaghetti. That is what is for supper tonight." Gramma Molly leans her body into the stove, prods fat, sizzling sausages rolling back and forth in the frying pan.

I race to my seat, whisper into Michael's ear. "We're having an Italian dinner."

"As if I could not hear."

"Muth, did the children tell you they saw the Statue of Liberty?"

She waves, like there's an invisible bumblebee buzzing around her ear. "Aw, Jackie, ah, yes, I know all about that now."

"Why don't you tell them! You know they love hearing stories . . ."

"Ah, stories, I see. Well, we all like it best when you tell the tales."

I sit and watch Gramma marching this way and that in the kitchen, the four apple pies steaming on the metal racks, and I wonder why Gramma Molly, who came all the way from Ireland on a boat to see the Statue of Liberty, cooks Italian sausages and not Irish ones.

Father Jack starts to tell us more stories. He says how Dad used to be a paperboy and how after his route he would sneak in baseball games in the afternoons. "Remember that Jimmy McNally, Muth? He'd come by every day, begging Joe to show him how to hit," Father Jack says, shifting his chair toward Gramma.

"Who could forget the likes of him? He tried to steal the pies I had lined up cooling on my windowsill."

"Muth, I think that was actually Joe and me." Father Jack looks at us and winks.

She turns around, a spatula against her chest. "Jesus, Mary, and Joseph, you're right, then, and what kind of children were you anyhow, I raised you to be so good!" Her eyes scowl just a bit as I try to imagine Dad and Father Jack as young kids, sneaking up to steal the hot baked desserts cooling under the surveillance of Gramma Molly.

"Well, anyhow, your dad played ball right until the time he was shipped off to the war, all the way to China," Father Jack says, leaning toward us, his hands folded.

"Did he play when he got back?" Michael asks.

"No, it was off to college and then to law school. And, soon enough, the FBI snagged him. Hoover was looking for good men, just like your dad." I imagine J. Edgar Hoover riding through Queens in his black, shiny car, his binoculars spotting my father whopping home runs, and hiring him on the spot.

"Excuse me," I pipe up. "Dad says that J. Edgar Hoover—"

"Ah, that Hoover man boss of his, transferring my Joe so far—"

Just as Gramma gets that tragedy look on her face, there's a loud knock on the kitchen door, and I wonder if Gramma Molly knows J. Edgar Hoover personally, but I am afraid to ask.

"Those must be the aunts." Father Jack gets up to show them in. "Excuse me," he says.

I sit in the chair and nod as aunts I have never met climb the stairs with loud thuds, laughing so hard they sound like the church ladies who make you wonder how they could have so much fun selling cupcakes to the men at the bake sales after mass. They see the four of us Conlon kids sitting around the table listening to Gramma complain about J. Edgar Hoover, and they throw their arms out.

"Come kiss us, all of you!" Their brogue leaps out like a frog. We go and kiss them, the mysterious aunts who are sisters of Gramma Molly, both of them short like her, and with the names Fiona and Brigid. They kiss our cheeks twice on each side. Each grabs my shoulder and stares deep into my eyes. "Ah, we've been waiting so long to see all of you, and here you are now." I have never been held so tight in all my life, so tight that my lungs flatten. "Well, tell us how you are and how is your dad, our Joe in California, and how do you like New York? And where is Mary, and will she be coming over or is she still down at Jetty Point? Oh, your mother loves the sea, she does."

The great-aunts sit down and Gramma Molly pours tea. Aunts Fiona and Brigid fold their hands when they speak, say how handsome Dad looked in his uniform when he left for the big war, how Molly worked as a seamstress in New York and counted each day he was gone after telling him if he didn't come back alive, she'd come over and kill him herself.

"My dad's a special agent for the FBI." My voice quivers.

"Oooh, yes." The aunts hold their tea, nod to me, to each other, and back to me. "He's an important man. We watch that production on the television set—concerning all those inspectors. Oh, your father's just as handsome as they are. And he's even more hardworking. Why, when he was just a lad, he bought his very own mother an icebox!" The aunts lean closer, their stockings baggy at the ankles, and then point: "An icebox just like that, and Molly so proud for having such a good son." Then they shake their heads. "And your Grandpa Patrick—a fine man, but oh, he was a quiet one—and falling flat right in front of the icebox with a heart attack. What a shame to die that way!" They lean in closer again and ask, "Now, how is your

Mom, Father Jack, and my grandparents in the olden days.

mother—and how is she doing with that baby Joey? Is he doing okay, God bless him?"

Gramma Molly interrupts, slow moving is her voice. "Ah, how could such a thing have happened . . ." Her Irish brogue simmers, and for the rest of the night, I remain silent, staring at the walls, thinking Gramma's got ghosts in hers too.

• • •

Father Jack drives us home late that night to Jetty Point, where salt air is as thick as oatmeal. He tells us to get our rest because tomorrow is another big day. He is right, for a whole new batch of relations comes down to see us at Jetty Point. Our Aunt Anne teaches us Irish songs, even French ones. Second and third cousins come too. We sit under bright umbrellas at the beach all day and take turns comparing accents. We say *hot dog,* they say *hot dawg.* Mom shows us where she and Dad courted in the summers. Gramma Molly twiddles her thumbs, says how Mom and

Dad took walks in Forest Park and Dad was always coming home late for dinner, and then she gives me a quarter for an ice cream cone and winks when I say thank you.

After the relations leave, I walk down to the Sweet Zone at the end of the row of bungalows and step sideways past all the people smoking and drinking beer, listening to "I can't get no satisfaction." I wonder if anyone can tell I am from California, if my green eyes and tan legs give it away.

I ask for a mint chocolate chip ice cream cone and try to speak like my cousins, with that New York accent. The man behind the counter wants to know where I come from and who are my folks.

"My father can't be here now because there's criminals on the loose and he has a case to crack for the FBI," I tell him.

The man with the cigarette behind his ear says I have a cute face. He gives me the ice cream for free and says I can bring my father here when the case is cracked.

The next day we fly all the way back to Los Angeles International Airport. Dad holds his black fedora and stands at the exact same spot where we left him waving good-bye. I can see by his big eyes that he has cracked the case.

Scheming about future escapades as a real live special agent.

chapter 9

B aby Face Nelson, Pretty Boy Floyd, John Dillinger, Al Capone, Alvin Karpis, Ma Barker and her bad Barker sons. By the time I'm in sixth grade, I've got it all down in my FBI log. I can answer any question about these criminals: where they came from, what crimes they committed, and most important, how the G-men nabbed them.

"G-men" is code for "government men." They got that nickname in the year 1934, when J. Edgar Hoover and his agents were closing in on Machine Gun Kelly in Memphis, Tennessee. The Bureau was just getting famous, and when the agents inched toward capturing the criminal, he yelped, "Don't shoot, G-men." The name stuck.

My most recent reading includes *The Bad Guys, The FBI Story,* and *The Gangster Film,* which I check out at the Jacaranda Public Library. Wearing my St. Bede school uniform, I approach Mrs. Remidian, the librarian who also doubles as the leader of our Girl Scout troop, number 2362. I keep my getaway vehicle, my stingray with its wire basket, parked outside and ready for the arrival of my next stash. Mrs. Remidian, her glasses sticking to her wide nostrils, reviews my book titles and shakes her head, not pleased at all.

"You are *still* reading this criminal genre?" Mrs. Remidian asks. "I don't know—we have a wonderful collection of new home-economics titles in. These might help you obtain more Girl Scout badges."

"I'll look at those titles the next time," I say, wondering if she can tell that I am lying. The only books I want are those that will help me learn to crack the FBI code.

When I was ten, I wrote the word "evil" in my FBI log twenty times, staring at every loop and slant, and after I studied the word for hours, I realized "evil" was just a cover-up—a code word for "devil." "Evil" is "devil" without the *d.* So far, this is my secret.

I have not mentioned my discovery to Dad, even though I learned about evil from his metal FBI car radio. The sound of evil goes like this: *sssssss.* This is what I listen to when Dad drives me to St. Bede on his way to work. My class starts earlier than my younger sister's and brother's, so Dad and I get to travel alone in the car. *Sssss.* Evil flies in like a dart. It hides in the static infiltrating the car. *Sssss.*

The low voices of FBI agents on the car radio are husky and echo a ping and a pong and a pong and a ping. I close my eyes when I hear them, imagining them like pilots in the sky, lassoing wide nets as they track all evil below, then bellowing calls to FBI radio dispatch headquarters.

When I travel, sitting next to Dad, I fantasize about an emergency call breaking through, beckoning us to the scene of a crime or a high-speed chase. I set my book bag firm between my knees, tighten my black seat belt, ready for action.

"Dad, those voices we keep hearing, they belong to fellow FBI agents, huh?" I want Dad to notice how observant I am.

He is dressed in his usual black suit with the stiff, white-collared shirt. With eyes straight and narrow, he analyzes the road ahead. He is on the lookout. He shifts his eyes to the rearview mirror and they lock in, scouring the road behind, then back again, to the street ahead.

"Huh, Dad?" I repeat.

"It is not proper English to end a question with *huh*."

"Huh? Oh."

I am getting closer to cracking Dad's code. When he corrects my English, he is really saying I should not be asking further questions. So I remain quiet, like I usually do, and go back to listening. *Sssss.* I listen until the next call breaks through. I can barely hear the words.

"Yeah, we got a 1490 at Lompoc and Sixth."

"We read that. Roger."

Code 1490. That could mean a bank robbery, a kidnapping, a bomb threat, a suspicious character on the loose. I suck in my stomach, tighten my seat belt again, forgetting about the per-fect pleats Mom ironed on my brown-checked uniform.

"Dad, did you hear that?"

He looks ahead, still scouring the boulevard as we pass alongside other cars and rows of eucalyptus and palm trees.

"Dad . . . Code 1490? Code 1490?"

He turns up the volume, listens to the voices of the agents rattle the green metal box.

"Lompoc and Sixth. Lompoc and Sixth. Sssssss. We're approxi-mately five blocks away."

"Roger. Ten-four."

"Dad. Lompoc and Sixth. How far are *we* from Lompoc and Sixth?"

His eyes surely calculate the miles as I start biting my nails, trying to decipher the code so I can be prepared to provide required backup, assist at any shoot-out, crawl with Dad through basements filled with rats, if necessary.

"Dad, we just gotta be close to Lompoc and Sixth." My voice squeaks as I notice we roll along at only thirty-five miles per hour.

"Dad, how—"

He snaps off the FBI car radio. *Click.*

"But—"

"You shouldn't listen to this." His voice is flat.

"But how will I ever know anything if I can't hear the code? What if—"

"That's downtown L.A. Out of our range."

• • •

My father hates Los Angeles, which he thinks I should hate too. I figure Los Angeles has a few criminals—that may be why the only time we ever drive into L.A. is to pick up our New York relations, and even then, Dad tells us to stay in the car. But Dad goes there all the time, probably even meets Mr. Zimbalist for bologna sandwiches when the show is low on story ideas. How else could Dad watch *The F.B.I.* and wear that face that says he knows how everything's going to turn out.

You have to drive through Los Angeles to get to Hollywood, where all the television shows are filmed. The Castrillos, our new neighbors who moved with their five kids from Peru, are my informants. One night when Dad is cleaning up after our lamb and mashed potatoes dinner, I ask him if we could visit Hollywood.

He squeezes the water from his dishrag, then leans over to each corner of the Formica kitchen table, swiping to the right, then the left, then in circles until all the crumbs accumulate in a tidy mound.

"Dad, couldn't we go up, just once?"

"Bring me the wastebasket, will you?"

I bring it to his side, set it down next to his hard-soled shoes. With the side of his hand, he pushes in the crumbs, which come mostly from Joey. Because of his thick tongue, Joey ends up not chewing all his food so well and crumbs fall around his chair and onto the floor. Dad never gets upset when it's Joey's mess, but when it's my turn to pick up after his crumbs, when they're smashed flat and I have to crouch on my hands and knees to unearth them, I hear myself muttering like Dad does at the rest of us.

"Dad, do you think we could go to Hollywood?"

He lights a cigarette, then hands me the red wastebasket to return under the sink. He unfolds a checkered dishcloth, starts drying the table. His cigarette ashes fall on the Formica, but he is not so quick to wipe up those.

"Nothing but a bunch of crooks in Hollywood."

I step back. Dad mustn't have heard me. How could there be nothing but crooks in Hollywood? That is where all the movie stars live.

The next day I see the Castrillos leave in their purple station wagon, license plate 423 TXY, to tour the Hollywood movie star mansions. When they return, I run down the sidewalk and knock on their door.

Juan Castrillo, who is nearly my age, answers.

"*Hola.*"

"*Hola.* Did you guys really go on the Hollywood movie star mansion tour?"

"*Sí.*" His eyes bend like Gumby's.

"*Sí?* Did you get to see Efrem Zimbalist, Jr.?"

"*Quién es ése?*" That's what he says, with his black wiry hair swimming around him. "Who's that?"

"Who's that?!" My head drops, and I look at the donkey piñata with a bright pink hat on the Castrillos' front stoop and I wonder if it's filled with chocolate bars and gum. "Who's that?!" I say, shaking my head.

"Who—who's that?" Juan repeats, an owl on a little branch.

"Efrem Zimbalist, Jr., is the star of *The F.B.I.*, and, you know, J. Edgar Hoover's the boss. How can you live in America if you don't know these things?" My hands tug on the edge of my orange T-shirt purchased in J. C. Penney's boys department, which I see is just like Juan's.

"We saw Lucy and Ricky's house. Lucy and Ricky's mansion—as big as this!" Juan stretches his hands out like an accordion. I look into his pretty eyes and realize Juan is too young to understand evil. Still, I love the Castrillos. They speak Spanish all day. Once they called up and asked if I would like to go to Mexico with them—just like that—and Mom said sure, that would be a great adventure, and there I was one hour later in the purple station wagon, license plate 423 TXY, with the Castrillos heading down to Mexico where you can buy statues of Jesus and the Virgin Mary for twenty-five cents apiece.

• • •

Dad flicks the silent FBI car radio back on again. He drapes one hand over the steering wheel, his eyes boring holes into the road ahead, then the rearview. I look out the window, squint my eyes, then turn around to inspect what lurks behind. I see nothing but innocent car exhaust.

"Dad?"

He turns the steering wheel, and down the street I see station wagons lumbering into St. Bede's school ground, and kids piling out of cars.

"That way you look with your eyes? Back and forth? Is that FBI code too?"

I count the seconds. Eight go by.

"You have lunch money?"

"Yeah . . ."

"*Yeah?*"

"Yes. Mom gave me hot dog money last night."

"I see." He reaches into his pants pocket and I hear coins spill around in the secret cloth. "So, you're sure you have enough?"

"I'm sure." He hates the idea of us ever going without food. If only he felt that way about words. "Dad?" I repeat.

Five more seconds.

Our FBI car approaches the statue of St. Bede. She is one statue I never pray to. I don't think St. Bede is a genuine saint. Not with a name that sounds like a piece of jewelry. Once I dreamt I told this to our principal, Mother Perennial, and she warned I'd be burned at the stake for speaking like a heretic. She pronounces it *haratick,* speaking in a brogue of flames, like Gramma Molly.

Dad's FBI shoe slaps on the emergency brake—and that is the only emergency we will have as the car rocks safely on the school parking lot. He fishes a Lark 100 from his left shirt pocket, lets it dangle, unlit, from his lips, like the gangsters when they smoke and talk about dirty rats. I can tell he is getting ready to say so long.

I grab my bag, feel my stomach go in knots when I see all the kids hanging around the busy school ground. This is the worst part of the day and still it's only morning.

"Bye, Dad." I reach for the door handle.

"One more thing."

"Dad, I really do have enough mon—" He stops me.

"When you're driving, do not turn when you look into the rearview mirror. Keep your head perfectly still." He lights his cigarette, tosses the match outside, and speaks as he exhales. "If you keep your head still, the guy behind won't know that *you* know you're being followed." He rolls up the window and smoke fills the car, making the wheel and the dashboard and the radio with its *ssssss* all hazy as I watch him demonstrate the technique.

I straighten the pleats on my uniform, tugging them past my knee, trying to stay calm, repeating to myself over and again that Dad has just told me a code. I hear his words echo, and they slowly fall down my throat, like the sweetest apple pie in the world.

Dad stares out the window. I wonder if there's more to the story. I try to count the particles in the smoke he blows out and imagine what it's like to be followed and what you do once you spot the guy in the rearview and how you just can't keep driving all day with some guy on your tail. But just as I am about to ask Dad this question, he turns, like he is weary from this long conversation.

"So long." He pulls his jacket tight.

I pull taut one more pleat.

He reaches for the brake, then looks at my door handle, as if wondering when I will make use of it.

I lean to kiss his cheek, which smells of Old Spice cologne. "So long, Dad." I slam the door behind me and wave good-bye as he drives away, wondering if he peeks into his rearview and sees the sparkle in my eyes. I barely notice the shiny blue 1972 Cougar, license plate 390 KHD, that pulls up, the door swinging open, Elizabeth DuPoint sliding out. When she sees me, she wiggles her shoulders, raises her hand to begin a hello, then drops it, remembering I am not one of the popular girls. Elizabeth opens her mouth, which is the color of a plum, watching me drop my wave to Dad.

"Your father—he drives such a bizarre car," she says.

"It's a special car."

"Special. Oh. I see," Elizabeth says with indifferent shoulders as she starts walking away.

Elizabeth DuPoint heads straight for the inner school ground, where each morning all sixteen classes at St. Bede line up, boys in one line, girls in the other, all lines going from shortest to tallest person. I am always three girls from the tall end. Elizabeth DuPoint and all the other popular, midsize girls stand in the middle of the line. The boys never stare at us talls, only at the midsizes, especially Elizabeth, who has a posture like Miss America. I pretend not to watch the boys noticing her.

During our first recess, I run to the bathroom and stand for five minutes waiting for a stall to open. Ever since we reached the sixth grade, girls take so much time in those stalls. I look up and down the bathroom walls made of bricks painted ugly green. The temperature is as frigid as the frozen food section at Hydro's Supermarket. The green bathroom is dark too, dim like church before the altar boys light the candles.

The nuns don't like it when the girls come to the bathrooms just to chat—maybe that's why they try to freeze us out. The nuns must know girls talk about strange things, like, you know, all that female stuff, staring at themselves in the mirror like their looks have changed since the time they left their house. I don't know why they even bother with the bathroom mirrors in the ugly green St. Bede bathroom. They only show you from your shoulders up, so you have no idea what you really look like in your uniform, not that I care.

Elizabeth DuPoint pushes through the swinging bathroom door. As she saunters in, all the chatting girls—Adele Romero, Miriam Daniels, and Jane Fitzgerald—shush, turn around, and look at Elizabeth wide-eyed like she is some kind of movie star.

"Hi, Elizabeth." Everyone chimes in except me.

Elizabeth leans into the mirror and coats her eyelashes with mascara, then puckers her lips for some illegal, grape-smelling lip gloss.

"Hi, Adie. Hi, Janey. Hi, Miri," she says, parading around the frozen bathroom. She thinks it is cute to put a *y* on the end of everyone's name as she pushes her face up to each girl, like they are dying to see her brown eyes. Then she comes to me, standing alone in the corner, still waiting for a stall.

"Oh, hi, Maur-uh," she says. "Or is it Maur-*duh?*" Elizabeth's head swivels to look at the girls, then back to me like a siren on a police car. "You have anything to say today?" She puts her hand like an oxygen mask over her mouth, as if she wants to say something but can't or won't let herself. When I hear the girls giggling, I realize she is making fun of me.

"Well, *I* have something to talk about." Elizabeth swirls around and I wonder what she will do next. She leans back into the mirror, then reaches for her waistband and rolls up her skirt, running her palm down her smooth, freshly shaven leg.

"So, girls, I've been meaning to ask—have you thought what you're going to model in the upcoming Girl Scout fashion show? It's *only* six weeks away, you know. I'm wearing a powder-blue polyester pantsuit with red high-heel shoes."

"We go to Sears at Vista Park Mall to be fitted next Thursday after school," Jane says. "I'm wearing an evening gown."

"My mother's taking me to a beauty parlor."

"My mother's ordered special net hose with a seam up the back."

"My mother has invited all five of my aunts. Two of them live in Arizona."

"My mother's ordering a black limo to take me," says Elizabeth.

"She is?" the girls chime in unison.

"Well, maybe . . . it's a distinct possibility."

Elizabeth gets to wear hip-huggers and high-heeled sandals to mass on Sundays, with her hair cascading in waves down her small back. I wonder if she notices me, but I realize I am hard to miss with Joey standing next to me, dancing as Father McKinley sings the Our Father. He sings like a sick elephant, but Joey's arms fly up, as if he's a member of the audience on *Let's Make a Deal.* Joey waves his arms, swings his hips. I feel sorry when I have to ask him to stop, but it's embarrassing when the whole congregation, so straight and serious, stares at Joey having so much fun.

"Maura, what are *you* going to wear?" Elizabeth pulls her hands under her tight breasts.

I don't know what to say. I open my mouth, my lips parting, my jaw moving, but nothing comes out. I just silently wait to use the toilet as I see a stall finally open up.

"Maura, you are *so* queer and *so* quiet."

Elizabeth throws her braids behind her shoulders, joining the huddle of three girls. My knees lock as I watch Elizabeth's mouth open again.

"You must get it from that queer—no, that mentally *retarded*—brother of yours."

The bathroom goes silent, but I can hear my face flushing red, a pounding, cold sweat underneath. Elizabeth stands with her nose in the air. I stare at her, my eyes growing big like they always do when I wish they could speak for me and yell out whatever is stuck in my throat. I look to the other girls. Now their hands are on their hips too. They shake their heads as if I am a retarded girl who can barely make it to the bathroom.

I race into the open stall and lock it and wait for them to forget where I am and to start talking again, but there is only the sound of bathroom faucets dripping water, *splat, splat, splat.* I try to hold my pee, but I can't because it stings. I let it go and quickly flush the toilet and wait for the girls to start talking, but all I feel is silence strangling me like a thorny vine. I sit on the toilet, dressed.

"You have problems figuring out how to get out of there?" Elizabeth's voice is like a snake.

I make a fist and rub my cold knee and open my mouth, and even though my head goes dizzy, I start talking as loud as I can.

"I bet you don't know about my dad! I bet you don't know my father is a special agent with the FBI. He investigates crimes like sabotage, espionage, grand larceny, federal robberies, kidnappings, forgery, communist activity . . . and cold-blooded murder."

I stop, my heart racing as I listen to the cold silence on the other side, hoping they'll gasp with awe and then just leave out of respect, but they don't.

"You have anything *important* to say, Maura?" Elizabeth starts whistling.

I open the stall, step in front of them, feeling like a brown dithering weed. "We have letters from J. Edgar Hoover plastered all over our house—everywhere. Hoover congratulated my dad when I was born."

Elizabeth lets out a huge giggle and then another. "Well, fine. That's so quaint about your father—but *please.* Who cares?"

"Yeah, really!" Even Adele Romero joins in with Elizabeth.

"All I asked was what are you wearing to the fashion show. Gawd, such a simple question." Elizabeth turns for the door and the others follow her out, snickering before the door closes with a thud.

. . .

I kiss Mom on the cheek when I arrive home. She asks if I'd like to go with her to pick up Joey from the Long Branch Mentally Retarded Children's Center, where he has special speech lessons. The last time I went along to pick up Joey, he took off his shoe on the way home and threw it out the window, and we had to spend two hours driving up and down Cottonwood Boulevard, slow as ketchup, looking for a small white leather object on the side of the road. I tell her not today.

After I watch her leave in our new Ford LTD station wagon, license plate 240 DWT, I head for my bedroom and lock the door. I reach behind my shoe rack for my FBI log, flip past my surveillance notes, and begin sketching.

I draw one outfit after another for the upcoming Girl Scout fashion show. My drawings are from the life of intrigue, action, suspense, and power—all those exotic things that make the world go round.

Sketch number one: a black velvet crime cape with my initials monogrammed in red on the shoulder seam.

Sketch number two: blue jacket with five pockets for badge, handcuffs, pistol, direct phone to J. Edgar Hoover, and stun darts.

Sketch number three: overcoat—a reversible parka, fake fur on one side for when I am investigating in Yugoslavia, changing into a cool, rain-silver silk for late night meetings with informants.

Sketch number four: red suede boots with a small square pocket for my stash of applied scars and a small one for poison lipstick.

I draw seven outfits in total, filling in the lines using crayons I've borrowed from Joey's box. I imagine the face of Mrs. Remidian, our Girl Scout troop leader, when she goes around the circle at the next troop meeting and asks each girl her choice of wardrobe to model in the fashion show. Sleepwear, Formal Dress, Casual Day Wear, Barbie Doll attire—I just know that's what those girls will say.

When Mrs. Remidian gets to me, I'll watch her face worry as she remembers my criminal genre reading habit, but she will understand after I pull out my log and page through my sketches. "Career Wardrobe," I will proclaim.

"Career Wardrobe?" she will say, dumbfounded, as all the others gasp, jealous that they didn't think of my idea first.

"Yes. Career Wardrobe, please—for the first female agent, the one and only FBI Girl."

Playing piano during my off-hours.

chapter 10

The living room in our house feels like its own continent, with only a white hallway, illuminated by a lonely pink bulb, connecting it to the rest of the house. In the living room, I crawl on my bare knees in front of the blond stereo cabinet where Mom stores her albums, feeling the scrape of the green shag carpet. I examine her records as if they're the Ten Most Wanted, tracing my finger over names like *Camelot; Hello, Dolly!; The Music Man; My Fair Lady; and The King and I.* We also have a Trini Lopez album. Joey loves dancing to *Bye Bye Blackbird,* where Trini sings all about being sugar-sweet.

All these lyrics are about this thing called love. Love is what adults feel. I am supposed to feel love when I become an adult, but I don't think I will. I will be much too busy. Even if I am on a break from fighting crime, I still can't imagine feeling love. To feel love, you have to say love words. To say love words, you have to strike up a conversation, which is not my specialty. When I try to speak, my heart races like a dogsled and my head lightens like a hot air balloon so that I don't know which way to go. Fortunately, this will not be a problem in my chosen career.

If I ever had to have a partner in the FBI, it would be Matt Hershey—though I'm not sure he could handle being a special agent, even though he is the most mature boy in our class and has a hairy wrist with a fancy silver wristwatch. I think his father must run the Hershey chocolate company and that is why Mrs. Hershey drives Matt to school in a chocolate-colored Cadillac, license plate 348 CHC. His hair is dark as a Hershey's Kiss. All during the seventh grade, I have been trying to practice walking up to him, to ask him for the time. So far, I've yet to make a move in real life. I am glad my thoughts about Matt Hershey have nothing to do with love, because love seems complicated. Furthermore, I have confirmed from reading the lyrics in the new songbook Mrs. Eveready gave me that being in love makes people unhappy.

Every Monday I walk over to Mrs. Eveready's garage after school. She still keeps the door open, so all I have to do is wait on the piano bench for her arrival. I plunk my dirty fingernails down on the keys, start off playing slow. The garage is as cold as a refrigerator for hanging sides of beef, cold as the frigid green bathroom at St. Bede. Sometimes the light over the piano flickers, making the notes look like flashes of dancing ink, loose on the page.

One afternoon after I finish a slow version of "Spring Song," Mrs. Eveready stands up and begins pacing around the cold garage, rubbing her hands together.

"Honey," she says, patting her large brunet bun sprayed so

high it looks like cotton candy, "you have any dream songs? Any songs you'd just die to play?"

I don't understand Mrs. Eveready. I have never had a dream song in my life. Dream songs are for adults who feel love—complicated love. I just stick with whatever is in my *John Brimhall Beginning Songs for Piano* book and receive my gold adhesive stars. I've peeled off all my stars and used them for my own personalized FBI badge, which I keep in my wooden box.

"What exactly is a dream song?" My tongue dashes around my closed mouth. I feel molars in the back, a piece of potato chip lodged in between.

"It's a song that makes your heart sing, honey. A song you just can't get out of your head!"

Abigail Eveready's arms spread like magic wands. I look around for the magic dust and then notice James Dean and Gary Cooper staring down at me. Maybe every month that Mr. Eveready does not arrive from Texas, Abigail Eveready hangs up a new poster of a movie star in her garage. There must be about seventeen posters now. Maybe she thinks those movie stars will lure Mr. Eveready to California, being that we are kind of close to Hollywood, which she says he loves so much.

I bend down, tie my sneaker shoelaces, then stand up again, hoping some movie star poster will inspire a dream song. I glance around, but no song comes to mind. Then in the corner I see Jimmy Cagney with baggy trousers, a straw hat, and a revolver with a fat cage tucked in his hand.

My eyes open wide as ideas start to churn.

"How about the theme song from *Dragnet*?"

The eyebrows of Mrs. Eveready arch upward.

"*Dragnet*? You mean the *television* show? Good God!" She says *tsk-tsk* and I think maybe she doesn't approve because it's on reruns.

She waits for my next idea, but I can't get *Dragnet* out of my head. In my mind, I snap my fingers, waiting for another dream song, then *poof,* one slides in.

"*Get Smart.* How about the theme from *Get Smart?*"

"What?" Mrs. Eveready's eyebrows fall like a collapsed bridge.

"You know the song that plays when Maxwell Smart keeps going down one long hallway, through a ton of doors, and then he finally finds Agent 99?"

"Listen, you know I was just kidding when I called you my little spy!" She adjusts her jaw right to left and back to center.

I take another gulp, remembering how I like the words "my little spy," although it does not have the same ring as "FBI Girl." I scratch my head, looking again at her movie star posters.

"Do you like the theme from *Mission: Impossible?*"

Mrs. Eveready blows out hot air. "It looks like you've got some real thinking to do. By next week, come back with your dream song all chosen and we'll be all ready to go, okay?"

I leave her garage and walk back home. Joey stands on our corner, waving as he usually does each afternoon to the cars stopping at one of our three stop signs. Some people pretend they don't see Joey. Some smile and wave back. One or two will roll down the window and yell, "How ya doin', Joey!" I have no idea who they are, so I write down their license plate numbers, just in case.

Joey sees me and starts running like one of those slow-motion people in the Breck commercial that says the closer you get, the better you look. He gives me a huge hug.

"Joey, it's getting dark. Let's go inside."

"Yeah, sure." These words he says almost for everything.

I bend low and look into his eyes. "I need some dream song, okay? You gotta help me. Okay?"

"Yeah, sure." He grunts, hugging me again, tighter this time.

That evening I sit in my room, studying my mathematics. The textbook is wrapped in a slick, glossy book cover with printed business advertisements on the back. Every year we must sit in class and wrap our books to protect them from wear and tear. I stare at the advertisements for Nagle's Donut Shop, Romero Jewelers, Mr. O'Hara's Happy Plumbing. Mr. Nagle and Mr. Romero and Mr. O'Hara all go to our church and have kids enrolled in St. Bede's.

I think of Matt Hershey and I wonder why his father, the president of Hershey Chocolate Company, does not print an advertisement on our textbook cover. I think of Matt and his deepening voice and how he looks so important when he uses his nose to point to things while the rest of us have to use our fingers.

"Excuse me, do you have the time?" I mutter this inches from the donut ad. "Excuse me," I repeat, "do you have the time?" The donut ad stares back and I can no longer stand to see my reflection in its picture of jelly rolls. I twist around in my chair and sigh, eyeing my bedroom walls. Simon and Garfunkel stare from their poster toward the sunset scene Mom gave me that says *Follow Your Dreams,* and then I look and study the crucifix of Jesus Christ hanging over my bed. I wonder if Jesus Christ would mind standing in for Matt Hershey.

I close my eyes and pretend I am on the school yard, standing alone on the black asphalt, surrounded by the basketball hoops and schoolkids racing during recess. I see Matt Hershey standing there, dropping one hand in a pocket, staring down at his other hand with its watch that is the grooviest in the world. My mouth relaxes and my eyes remain shut long and hard. I try to stay calm, then open my eyes and stare at Jesus Christ and pretend he is Matt Hershey. I smile, like Dad would, in code.

"Excuse me, sir, what time do you have?" My voice is like a barbecue grill heating up. "Pardon me, what time do you have on that shiny watch?" I say it nice, so no one could refuse giving me a straight answer.

I get up from my desk and approach Jesus hanging on the crucifix. I move with a sure foot, like a cunning agent stalking the school yard, each step grabbing a patch of ground, closer and closer, trying to stare at Jesus without him noticing. "What a handsome watch. Uh, what time might it be?" My palms sweat together.

I peer into Jesus's lowly eyes. He does not look up, just studies his wounds, like I am not the first person to approach him with a question. "Excuse me, sir, but do you know the hour of the day?" I squeeze in closer, kneel on the bed, and with a firmer voice, whisper, "Could you *please* tell me the time?"

Just as I ask Jesus Christ to give me the time of day, I hear the hall clothes hamper clank outside my bedroom.

"How was your piano lesson today?" It is Mom's voice through the door.

I look at my hot breath over the crucifix and back away, shooing the bangs over my forehead as Mom comes in.

"Fine."

"Did Mrs. Eveready like the way you're playing 'Spring Song'?"

"Yes." I look up at Mom, noticing the dash of tomato sauce on her apron. "Mrs. Eveready wants me to choose a dream song."

"A dream song?"

"Some song that I've always wanted to learn."

"Well, do you have any ideas?"

"Not really. Not ones that she'll approve of."

"Why don't you look through the albums? Maybe something will strike a chord . . ." Mom chuckles. "Get it, strike a chord?"

I don't laugh. "Yeah, but all those songs are about love."

Mom watches as I sit down on my bed, my head just under the crucifix.

"Maybe you will find a song about, hmmm, adventure . . ."

My eyes widen. "There are songs like that?"

"Well, you'll have to find out. Now, in the meantime, would you mind . . ."

"I'll wash Joey's hands."

"Thank you."

•   •   •

During dinner, night after night, I have lots of time to think about my dream song, since no one says much. What we all do at dinner is watch Joey eat. Mom cuts up his food into small sections so he does not choke. Dad ties a bib over Joey's shirt, as he is the messiest eater alive. Joey points to the cupboard where his ketchup is housed, and waits for one of us to bring it to the table. Dad likes to give Joey bread with butter right away, but Mom says Joey must eat his meat and vegetables first. Dad scowls, making Mom seem like the bad guy.

After Joey begins to eat, Mom looks around the table, then back to her own dinner. She always has a little less food than the rest of us, but she always makes sure no food goes to waste. Julie and John try to stick a few peas underneath their plates, but Mom catches them, her expression saying *that's not such a nice thing to do.* After a few bites of ham croquettes, Mom then lifts her eyes to Dad, who sits across from her.

"Anything new with you today?"

Silence.

Mom asks this every night, and still she doesn't seem to understand that FBI agents can answer only in code, with some completely unrelated comment.

Dad looks up from his plate. "I need to run up to the pool store to get more chlorine."

That is a perfect example of how the code works. Dad shines his shoes, mops the floors, pours chlorine in the pool, one thing after another, on specific nights of the week, as if doing all these chores helps him concentrate on keeping his cases straight. Similarly, his code forces you to think of the real meaning behind his words and actions. Mom's still trying to figure it all out. After she asks a few more questions and Dad answers back with news about floor cleaner or shoe polish, she puts her fork down and stops chewing.

"Joe, will you answer my question, please?" She asks nicely because she knows dinnertime is a happy time.

Dad puts down his fork, like if she can do it, he can too. He gets up and walks into another room like he forgot something, and then comes back a few minutes later and sits down and continues eating.

"Somebody say something?" He gives that quizzical look. He counts the peas on his plate like they are little bullets, laying them gently on his tongue.

"Dad?" Since Michael is now away at the university and I am the oldest at home, it's up to me to figure out what to do. I watch John with his downcast eyes and Julie, who keeps wiping her nose, then take a few gulps of milk because I don't know what I will say. What comes out is this: "I hate to tell you, but I know you're talking to Mom in code."

His eyes dart like fire at me, like who do I think I am saying this, telling him about code, because if anybody is going to say anything about that, it will be him. "Who asked you?"

My eyes fall to my plate like parachuters out of an airplane— twirling, downed. Sometimes I feel tearful, but tonight I whisper to myself instead that Dad just loves Mom in code.

"What did you say?" he asks.

"Nothing." The teeth in my mouth freeze. "Except to say this is the best dinner in the whole wide world." I look across the table to Mom, her face flat and pale. Joey watches, his eyes dart-ing from Dad to Mom to Julie to John to me. I am forced to wink at him, to let him know he should just keep eating his dinner.

I am sure Dad's words work great on criminals because they can feel like daggers tossed by a knife thrower, entering your heart and puncturing something inside. I can feel it, but Mom is the one who slams down her fist, gets up from the dinner table, and runs into her bedroom.

We sit there. The food tastes like mud now, and no one can eat except for Dad, who spoons one helping of mashed potatoes after another into his mouth. Joey keeps looking at me to fix things. He stops eating and takes one gulp after another, the terror on his face looking like we're having a loud thunderstorm.

"Dad, aren't you going to go see what's wrong with Mom?" I ask this after a few minutes, when the silence at the table blows like the wind in a lonely seashell.

"You think I can help with what's wrong with her?"

That is an example of the code and how it can rip you open.

"She is upset, you know."

He looks at me, startled, as if I were asking him what year he signed the Declaration of Independence.

"Did I say something?"

"Maybe you should go in after Mom and make sure she is okay."

He waves his hands at the invisible bees in the air. He looks over at Joey, who still does not eat a thing, just cranes his neck toward my parents' bedroom, where the door is shut halfway, not all the way, just halfway.

"Mom-ee?" He has ketchup all over his mouth.

"Here, Joey." Dad pulls out a slice of bread and butters it with thick, hard wads. He cuts it in half and serves it to Joey on top of the knife. Joey takes it, runs his mouth all over the butter.

"Excuse me," I say. Dad does not turn his head, but I hope he is using the rearview-mirror technique. I hope he is watching as I go into the master bedroom, where I know I will hear Mom's sobs coming from the bathroom. I hate that sound. I just stand outside and listen, waiting for her to catch her breath so I can say something. I know that an agent's partner can sometimes break under the strain.

"It's okay, Mom," I whisper into the crack of the door. "Dad does not mean it . . ."

I say that line every time, standing outside her bathroom, gently tapping on the door as if it were made of silk.

"It is a great dinner, Mom, the best dinner in the world. You are the best mom in the world."

She does not like me having to worry about her problems with Dad, and I wonder why he never follows her into the bathroom like I do. Soon enough, Mom opens the door. She has brushed her curly hair and applied her lipstick, and she tries to smile. Her tears are wiped, but her face is red, as if hot bricks from the desert had just heated the bathroom. I see three soggy Kleenexes at the bottom of the white metal wastebasket.

"Daddy can be difficult sometimes," she says. "Who knows why he's this way?" She hugs me. She wants me to know everything is okay. I hug her back.

"Maybe it comes from fighting crime all day," I say. "It must be draining—it must be extremely tough."

She says nothing. We just hold each other. Her skin smells like carnations. She lets go and marches back to the dinner table because she knows Joey will be alarmed. I walk behind her. We both smile as if we have just won the Academy Award for Best Actress. Joey's face is full of butter as he watches me and Mom. He gulps, his eyes wiggling. Julie and John chew hard, pretending they love their peas. We proceed to eat in silence, just like before.

• • •

I practice piano in the evenings. Sometimes when Dad uses his confusing words and the air gets heavy, I push my foot hard on the pedal, sending loud music throughout the house. Sometimes I get Dad's attention and he walks into the living room to lock the windows and shut the drapes. Sometimes Joey comes in to dance. He likes "It's a Small World" and the Beatles song "Ob-la-di, Ob-la-da," which Michael taught me how to play.

I sit on the piano bench tonight and stay quiet when I hear Mom and Dad at the kitchen table. Their voices are calm, like gray dolphins sliding in circles through waves. They must be talking about Joey. They are always talking about Joey when their voices sound sweet, without the storms rippling underneath. I sit perfectly still so I can hear those dolphin words slip all the way down the hall, into the lonely planet of our living room.

"How is his new schedule at school?" Dad asks.

"He's got square dancing now three times a week—Tuesdays, Thursdays, and Fridays. Joey's catching on quickly. And he enjoys that sign language class."

"Any problems with the bus this week?"

"No. The bus driver was sick just that one day."

"Yeah. Well."

I hear them slurp their coffee after each question. Mom loves her Sanka, Dad, his Folgers instant regular. Dad likes his cup half empty so he can add milk and sugar. Mom likes hers black, piping hot, poured all the way to the top.

Dad lights up a cigarette, and the smoke travels down the hallway.

"Where are those new pants you bought for Joey? I'll take up the hems tonight," Dad says. I can hear his inhalation a mile away, and then his cough, which has become so predictable.

"That's okay. I finished the hems this afternoon." Mom sips

Joey's wet kiss extinguishes his birthday candles.

as if she is drinking from a bottomless cup. "I appreciate you doing all that paperwork, by the way, for the foundation."

"Hmmm-mm." Dad spends his extra time working to raise money to help people like Joey. He meets with the church leaders in Los Angeles to get them interested in the cause, which is to build group homes where retarded people can live if they don't have parents to take care of them. Mom says it is slow going. I tell myself this will never happen to our Joey, and every night I pray that God will back me up.

I hear Dad's chair as he pushes it away from the table. The conversation for this night is finished. That's how it is. Dad leaves, and Mom's coffee cup goes back to the table and stays there, far away from her pretty lips.

I play "Spring Song" with my eyes closed again. I start out low, then get a little louder, repeating the song three times until I am so sick of it I stop right in the middle. Joey comes in and puts his arms around me.

"Hi, Joey."

"Fe-eh," he says. That means "funny" in Down's syndrome talk.

"Who's fe-eh?"

He points to me. "You fe-eh."

"Me fe-eh? I say *you* fe-eh."

I reach out to tickle him. Joey is extremely ticklish, laughing even before you touch his side.

"Joey, I need a stupid, totally stupid dream song by Monday."

He wiggles his shoulders and says *la la la*. He does this whenever he hears the word "song."

"It can't be a square dance song, though."

Joey wipes a kiss on my cheek. "Ah, Waah." "Waah" is his name for "Maura."

Sometimes I wonder what I'd do without Joey. It's almost as if he takes the kisses Dad gives him and distributes them to the rest of us.

I turn off the lights in the living room—sometimes that's how I think best. Joey sits next to me. Julie and John wander in soon enough. I tell them not to touch the light switch. We sit in the dark and watch the reflections of passing car headlights splash on the white walls. Mom somehow senses we are in the living room. She comes in and sits down in the dark too, and we all remain quiet. It is hard to find the first thing to say, but Mom always thinks of something.

"How about we play the bouncing light game?" she asks.

"Yeah, yeah," we say. Joey grunts, "Yeah, sure."

Mom made up this game all by herself. This is how it works. You sit silently in the dark and watch the approaching car headlights bounce from wall to wall in slow motion.

"Very good. So remember how we play—each time the headlight hits the next adjacent wall, call out your favorite word." Mom explains the directions, as if we could ever forget.

Mom and me, we call out majestic words. Julie and John, they call out food words. When it's Joey's turn, he just says, "Coke." Joey loves *Coke*. Each time Dad drives to the liquor deli for his cigarettes, he takes Joey along for his soft drink. Mom says it gives him too much gas, making him burp and fart more. But when it comes to pleasing Joey, Dad does not like to be told what to do. "Poor Joey, poor Joey, your mother won't let you have Coke." He says this as they walk out the door on their way to buy a bag full of it.

A car slithers down Margaret Rae Drive; its headlights hit our faces, then bounce onto the first of the living room walls. We start calling out words.

"Searchlight," I say.

"Lasagna," says Julie.

"Happiness." That's what Mom says.

"Cream-a-ling donuts," John yells.

Mom turns to Joey. "Joey, what do you say?" Joey leans his head on Mom's shoulder as if this game is wearing him out.

"Joey, come on!" Julie and John yell together.

He smiles and gulps, holds his hand like a traffic cop, as if he needs all his energy just to say "Coke." We sense Joey's smile in the dark.

We keep playing as the next five cars roll down Margaret Rae Drive.

Pistol. French fries. Fox-trot. Cream-a-ling donuts! Pillows go flying when John repeats himself for the third time. "You can't keep doing that," Julie yells. Joey laughs and opens his mouth. "Coke, Coke!"

"Okay, enough pillows. It's getting late—this is good for tonight." Mom stands up, reaching to take Joey by the hand. Dad appears in the doorway with a towel. He is in the middle of the laundry. He folds towels in a specific way, putting the left then the right sides together. He squints down to the pillows thrown on the floor. Nobody says a word until Dad turns around and walks in the other direction. Mom asks us all if we have finished our homework, reminds me of my upcoming lesson, and asks if I have practiced my piano.

"Mom, I still need that dream song."

"Well, you better look at those albums tonight."

I get back on my knees and put the pillows in their proper place, then inspect all of Mom's records. She comes back to the room after Joey's in bed and sits in the chair, watching me thumb through one album after another. I pull out one I've never seen before. "How about this, Mom?"

"That's one of my favorites."

"Not about love, right?"

"Well, how about you listen, and you can tell me what the song is about. We could even dance to it." She stands up, holds out her hand.

"Mom, I can just sit here and listen to the lyrics."

"Fine, if that's what you want to do."

"You can ask Dad if he wants to dance." I already know that FBI agents don't dance unless the job is undercover and calls for it, but I hate the idea of Mom dancing alone. I realize that she is not about to call Dad into the living room, so I force myself out of the chair to join her.

I hear long beats of silence and then the scratching from the record going round after Mom drops the needle. Then violins swirl, and the singer's voice slips open like a rose. She is singing about people who need people—but I think this may be different than a real love song.

Mom and I stand in an official dance embrace, and I can feel her large breasts above my small ones, soft like blankets that keep you warm at night. She steps into the music and takes me with her. I look at our white drapes that are like tweed and imagine them breathing in and out with the violins.

Mom leads us around in a small circle, holding my hand loose in hers as she moves with confidence. "When I was younger, I used to ballroom dance, and as a little girl, step dance too," she says.

"What is step dance?"

"Dancing from Ireland, lots of fancy leg work. I loved dancing."

We keep our heads perfectly still as we go round, and I feel Mom's cheek near my own.

"You're so good, Mom. You could have gotten a part in one of those big-time musicals and danced onstage."

"Well, when I was your age, I almost did dance onstage—at a big AFL-CIO convention."

"You did?"

"Grandpa Hogan was president of the stereotypers' union. Labor unions were big in those days. Anyhow, Nana drove us all up, going thirty-five miles per hour the entire way from New York City to Buffalo!"

"How long did that take?"

"Days."

"Then what happened?"

"Here, let's try this." Mom holds my hand tighter and spurs us in a different direction, taking four steps, not two, as the singer fills the living room with lyrics about how once you were half and now you are whole. While she swirls me around, Mom tells me how the emcee at the convention took the bullhorn and asked if there were any young ladies to perform Irish step dance onstage.

"You raced right up there?"

"Not quite. George Meany's daughter—Mr. Meany was the president of the AFL-CIO—she got up and ran to the stage."

"But you could have—"

Mom squeezes my hand a little tighter and looks me in the eye. "I was too shy then. I stood up, but only halfway out of my seat. Oh, it was terrible being so shy." Mom then looks up to the cathedral ceiling and hums along.

I never knew Mom was a shy girl. She can't be as shy as I am. If it was me at that big conference, I would have never stood up at all. I would have paid that Meany girl twenty dollars to beat me to the stage. Mom swings us around as the singer's voice falls deeper, the lyrics talking again about all those feelings deep in your soul. Maybe that is why Mom loves this song. Maybe shy people need people even more than talkative ones do. I keep stepping on Mom's toes, but she has such a flair, she does not seem to mind.

"Does Dad think people who need people are the luckiest ones?" I ask. "I don't think so. When you are a special agent, you have to rely on yourself."

As soon as those words are out of my mouth, I spot Dad walking past the living room hallway. He tries not to show he sees us dancing. I figure he will not come in because the living room windows are shut and locked, already checked twice tonight.

Mom spots Dad too and twirls me around. "This is what you'd call the fox-trot. Once upon a time, I nearly taught this at a dance studio."

I hold on to Mom's shoulder as we go round another time, my feet starting to get the rhythm. "You did?"

She nods. "Holdstadt Avenue in New York, but the owner wanted me to take off my wedding ring." Mom's face turns red, and so does mine. She does not say any more. I cut my eyes down the hallway, but Dad has disappeared.

We turn around the room slowly, Mom in her orange apron and me in my white corduroy pants and blue Los Angeles

Dodgers T-shirt. I think of how Abigail Eveready's husband has yet to arrive from Texas, and I wonder if he ever will. I think maybe it's a good thing if people *sometimes* need other people, and I tell Mom that I think Mrs. Eveready will approve of this selection for my dream song.

As we turn once again, Dad returns to the edge of the room. He sticks his hands in his front pockets as if he's ready to give a speech.

"Hi, Dad. You wanna dance with Mom?"

"No thanks. Mary?"

Mom turns to face him, and her legs loosen like wind abandoning a flag.

"Do you have Joey's lunch money for the school week?"

Mom's eyebrows tense and she does not say a word.

"Should I put aside Joey's lunch money for the week?" Dad cocks his head, rephrasing his question. I try to decipher the hidden meaning.

Mom looks at Dad as if his words are scratches on the record.

"It's—already—taken—care—of." She talks like an actor on *Dragnet,* saying it like "Just the facts, ma'am."

Dad turns and walks away. Mom's eyes follow him, like a wolf.

She holds my hand tighter, and even though the music has stopped, we dance in one more slow circle.

"When you get older," she says, "don't let anyone interrupt when you are dancing. Do you hear me?"

Swinging like they do in the big leagues.

chapter 11

The experts have labeled Joey severely retarded because he scored low on the I.Q. test, or whatever they give to the Down's syndrome kids. We get the Iowa Basic Skills test at St. Bede, which comes with choices A, B, C, D for each question and strict instructions for how to use your number 2 pencil. I never score superhigh on these exams, as I'd rather design FBI costumes in my mind than worry about my pencil mark fitting tight in the right circle.

Maybe it's the same for Joey too. Maybe he imagines himself kissing everybody in the world instead of worrying about displaying his skills to the experts. Anyhow, because Joey has the label "severely retarded," he sits there with all the other severely retarded people in his classroom at Long Branch School. Mom disapproves. She believes Joey should be in a classroom with normal kids, because he acts more normal when he is with the normal kids and more retarded with the retarded kids. She writes letters to the officials at the school board, but so far, they think she is just another crazy mother.

Mom writes letters to everybody when she thinks something could be improved. One Thursday she came home from Hydro's Supermarket with a box of Cream-a-ling powdered donuts that turned out to be stale. That was disappointing because on shopping day, our stomachs growl with visions of dunking donuts in our hot chocolate. Mom marched immediately to the corner desk in the dining room and pulled out the gray typewriter. Fingers up, fingers pouncing down on the keys—*wham!* Ring-a-lings from the typewriter bell clanging as she pushed the carriage back and forth.

I asked her what she was doing.

"I'm writing a letter to the president of Cream-a-ling Baked Goods. Spending good money on a box of stale donuts . . . that's not right!"

The executive must have heard about Mom from the president of the maraschino cherry company, because two Saturdays later, when Dad was sweeping the leaves down the gutter, a man in a big white truck pulled up to our curb. He stuck his head out the window and asked Dad if this was Mrs. Conlon's residence.

Dad didn't answer because first he had to stare the guy down, and his white truck too, as if the guy might be part of a communist operation. After a few seconds of tightening his jaw, Dad set his rake down and tossed his cigarette into the gutter. "Whatcha got there?" he said.

The man in the white truck handed Dad eight jumbo boxes of Cream-a-ling donuts.

"This is for Mrs. Conlon—with our apologies."

I saw all this from my corner bedroom window, which I pushed wide open. I took a whiff of that bakery smell from the truck and immediately dashed to find Julie and John, who were hanging blankets over chairs to make tents.

"Dad's got huge boxes of donuts and he's headed for the front door!" When the door opened, we all stood ready to tackle him like Dino the Dinosaur from *The Flintstones.*

"Get out of the way, will ya, so I can get this to the kitchen."

We sucked in our guts, watching Dad hold the precious cargo as he said to the wall, "I've never seen a house like this in all my life."

I don't know if that's good or bad. With the code, it's hard to tell. I think he is secretly proud of Mom that she wrote the president of the Cream-a-ling company. Dad likes donuts more than any of us do. When I go to the bathroom at night, I see him sneaking in an extra donut as he sits with his coffee, his lips quite pleased. Sometimes I think Mom and Dad are worlds apart but not all that different—like two halves of the same whole that got separated: Dad fights against what's wrong, and Mom stands up for what's right. The one place they come together for sure is when it's about Joey.

· · ·

Dad sometimes drives Joey up to the St. Bede field, where I work in the snack shack in the summer selling Sno-Kones, licorice, Milk Duds, popcorn, soda, and hot dogs. They arrive during the seventh-inning stretch, the busiest time, Joey with his red junior mitt, walking on tiptoes, his eyes speckled with excitement as Dad, in his old work shirt, scans the crowds. He escorts Joey to the snack shack, which is like a zoo full of monkeys, kids pounding the counter demanding candy.

"Got any specials today?" Dad calls from the end of the line, towering above the army of kids, his eyes going around in big circles like how they do when he feels silly. "How about a Sno-Kone for Joey?"

I don't see Joey in the screaming crowd, but I can tell he is there, because kids are staring. Some of them back away, or their parents come over and pull them closer. I want to tell them that Joey appreciates kindness, but I can't say this because I must serve hot dogs and candy, and besides, my voice gets locked in my throat and I can't release it even when I think I might have something to say. And so I make for Joey an extra-special Sno-Kone with cherry syrup all over the frozen ice, then grape, then lemon-lime. I look at the Sno-Kone, admire its colors of dancing lace. I can't wait to hand it to him.

Dad gives Joey a coin. "Here, now you pay Maura."

Joey smiles wide because the quarter feels important in his hand. Even though he is almost six years old, he has no idea what money means. Still, he loves exchanging a coin for anything in return.

A chubby kid with a red baseball cap stares at Joey. His eyebrows are angry. *Stop staring,* I want to say. *Just tell me what kind of candy you want and stop staring at my brother,* I want to say. After Joey bows and pays me the quarter, I stand up tall like I am in a beauty contest, and turn to the kid. "Can I help you?"

Dad lights up a cigarette as he tucks a napkin into Joey's shirt. He looks at the kid with the angry eyebrows and then Dad crouches low so he can meet the kid eye-to-eye.

"What is your name, young man?" Dad wears that face he must use before arresting a criminal, the look of sizing him up.

The kid pouts while Dad reaches for Joey's waist.

"Robert." He wipes his nose and points to Joey. "What's wrong with him?"

"Nothing is wrong with him. His name is Joe."

Joey's face is buried in the Sno-Kone, turning purple and cherry red. "Hi," Joey says with his Down's syndrome accent.

Dad takes Joey's extended hand and puts it back on his dripping Sno-Kone. "Hold your cone with two hands, not one." He reaches for a few napkins, tucks them inside Joey's pocket.

"Robert, where are your parents?" Dad's eyes go like Superman's with that X-ray vision and there is no escaping their power. The kid falls into a trance, raises his arm, and points to a pudgy man stuffing popcorn into his mouth, yelling louder than anyone else on the bleachers.

"Robert, you can tell your father, when he decides to sit still and enjoy the game, that you just met a very nice young fellow named Joey. Do you understand?"

Robert's face is white.

"Now, would you like to order something from the nice young lady at the counter?" Dad points to me as if I am his secret partner in crime. Robert shakes his head no and without even looking at Joey again, runs back to the bleachers.

Dad stands up and grabs a few more napkins. You can never have enough napkins for Joey's face, which now resembles a finger painting. Dad sucks on his cigarette and the smoke trails behind him, away from the snack shack, filled with steam from the cooking hot dogs.

"Where were we?"

I shrug my shoulders. Dad orders himself a root beer and gives me a quarter. I make a perfect root beer while looking out the back window and watching the pitcher wind up. I wait for the foam to settle as the pitcher throws the ball so hard it smacks like a BB gun into the catcher's mitt. "Strike two," the umpire roars. I think how nice it must be to throw a ball so fast, to hear that loud, satisfying smack—the kind of sound that says there's nothing to worry about. Maybe that's how baseball is supposed to make you feel.

I hand Dad the root beer and he and Joey leave for the car almost as fast as they came up. I turn around and go back to watching the game, thinking of the St. Bede field and how girls are not allowed to play in these leagues and how the closest I ever get is working in the snack shack. The other ladies who work there couldn't care less about baseball. They stand around and chat like hens about recipes and their extra-talented children and all the latest gossip infiltrating the parish church. I bet none of them have ever held a bat.

· · ·

Things change the summer before eighth grade, the year I am to graduate from St. Bede, when the Jacaranda Highlands softball league makes its debut and Mom suggests I try out. I am drafted to a team called the Groovies. Our coach, Bill, must be one of those hippies because he wears leather thong sandals to practice and sometimes goes barefoot. He keeps his long brown hair in a ponytail and leaves his first three shirt buttons undone so we can see the hairs on his chest, although I try not to look at that.

Bill tells me that with the muscles I have in my legs and my arms, I will be a powerful player. I go home after the first practice, look in the mirror, and think of Dad when he goes for a swim in the pool at night and how his muscles bulge in his legs and arms. Mom doesn't have the same natural muscle. She is tall, with slender legs like the women in fashion magazines. I must take after Dad, which means someday I'll be hitting homers like him.

I show up at our next practice, hoping Bill the hippie coach will stick me on the pitcher's mound and teach me how to do one of those windups. Bill's eyes are sometimes bloodshot, but alert. He keeps looking at my height and muscles and thinks *hmm, hmm,* I will be the power girl who'll hit the grand slams. First he puts me at shortstop, but I can't fire the ball fast enough to first base. He tries me batting fourth on the lineup, and although I am good at swinging, I shut my eyes with each pitch.

Bill puts a scratch next to my name. Now he sends me scuffling out to the lonely grasses of right field, just two innings a game, and I start praying to God no ball will ever come flying out to me. I think I'll transform into a tree with a sign that reads *Hit it to center field—not to me!* I am always the last to bat, and when I walk out to the plate, all the fielders sneak in closer as they know I can't hit a thing. Even the bench sends out a sigh because in all our practices and in four games so far, I've never made it to first base.

Dad and Michael and even John are powerhouses, so I think I should be too, whamming the ball out past the center fielder, making her run, fetching the results of my spinning might. But even before I swing, the pitchers smile like they know ahead of time I'll be striking out again.

•   •   •

Angela Larson, the retarded girl who is in the religious education class Mom teaches at St. Bede, starts to show up at the ball field. She impersonates a cheerleader, yelling, "Go, girls! You can do it!" She stays at the girls' field for hours, rooting for all the teams. By the end of the day, sometimes you can hear her hoarse voice.

I tell Mom about Angela Larson.

"Her grandmother lives just four blocks away. How could she resist coming by to watch the games?"

"But she should *watch,* okay? She can be as loud as a tuba."

"Well, I know you're already into your season, but maybe

Angela could become a ball girl or help out in some way. That would make her feel special—and it never hurts to have a cheerleader on board."

"A retarded cheerleader?"

"Just a thought. Maybe you can talk to your coach and see what he has to say."

Mom does not know about Bill our hippie coach, and I'm not sure I could explain to her why a retarded girl could never be part of a team called the Groovies.

"Maybe Angela can cheer you on to some good hits."

"Oh, God. Mom . . ."

Mom does not say anything else, because that's how she is. She presents an idea, then leaves it up to us to decide. This is a terrible thing, especially if you think she might be right. Still, I'd have to become a saint before I ask a retarded girl to join my team.

Angela continues to stop by our games on Saturday. I keep to myself, pretend like I'm not so familiar with her. I am, after all, still getting used to wearing cleats and feeling how they dig into the soil, like they're telling me I really do belong out here in the field with its smell of clean-cut grass. Sometimes I keep my cleats on for hours after I return home because they double as good tap shoes, and I dance away while making myself a burger, until Dad tells me to knock it off.

This is my first softball season and I want it to be just me and my cleats and my yellow Groovies uniform and my new mitt and my position, two innings in right field, assigned to me by my hippie coach.

Angela can find her own team.

• • •

Being a good agent, I am starting to recognize the pattern here: there are no breaks from the mentally retarded in my life—not at church, at Hydro's Supermarket, at Disneyland, nor at Bobo's Big Bulge restaurant.

We walk into Bobo's and proceed to the waiting area. With my eyes, I plead to the waitress that she find a table immediately. Meanwhile Joey attempts to spread kisses around to everybody, saying hi in that clumsy way, like he thinks he's some politician. Some people say hello fast, like that is enough for now. Others smile, trying not to look sorry that we have a retarded child in our family. Some must think Joey has leprosy, because they back away as if our air might contaminate them. After this torture, the waitress finally calls: "Conlon, Conlon. Party of six." We sit there, Dad with his X-ray eyes, Mom in her orange lipstick, me with my muscly legs, Julie doing tic-tac-toe, John sucking his thumb, and retarded Joey.

Conlon, Conlon. Party of six.

We get up from the polyester seat cushions and go walking single file down the restaurant, past one booth, then the next, heading for the back room. I wonder if we go there to avoid upsetting the other customers. Mom says no, that's just where the big tables are. I grab Joey's arm, escort him like I am a movie star and he is my leading man. I take his arm in mine because I don't think he should be trying to shake everyone's hand as we walk like snails for our table. After all, the people are eating their burgers or fried chicken and it's enough already just to see Joey. But I smile anyway. Like I am lucky. Lucky to have Joey in my life. And all those people who don't have a retarded person in their life, well, they just don't know what they are missing.

• • •

Bill works extra hard with me during practices, telling me to keep my eye on the ball when I swing, and I keep trying. He hits extra fly balls to me in right field, and soon I can throw it all the way to the catcher. "You're developing a good arm. Before long, you'll be playing all nine innings, I swear it." My teammates look as if they can't wait for the day.

Soon Angela starts appearing even before our games start, joining the other spectators, and finds her favorite spot. I hang out deep in right field, close to the eucalyptus trees, and watch Angela stand behind our team's bench with her spaghetti sauce red hair and glasses with lenses the size of grapefruits.

"Go, softball girls! Hit good hits!"

All of the other softball players with their cleats and their new mitts and just the right pink lipstick and polyester shorts look at Angela like where did she come from, like who invited the retarded girl onto the field? Most of them don't pay attention, but some of them stare.

At first, I try to ignore her too. Well, not ignore her. But just never be in the exact same spot where she is. I know that if she sees me without my baseball cap, she will recognize me immediately and start telling me about all her favorite television shows. One day I must be in a daydream, for I take off my cap and sure enough she walks up, finally catching me.

"Maur-a? I saw *Flipper* two times yesterday. Flipper's so great." And then she makes that loud dolphin noise she's so good at. "And I watched *The Partridge Family* and Keith is so cute I could just pinch his cheeks. And *The Brady Bunch*. Cindy has new braces. But I like *Flipper* the best." Then the dolphin noise again, and without trying I see Flipper in my mind as Angela pulls her head backward in a Flipper imitation.

"Okay, Angela. That's great you know so many shows." I get ready to go on deck, taking a few practice swings and speaking in a low whisper, trying to get her to do the same.

"I told Mrs. Conlon that now I wear Kotex pads."

My teammates gawk.

I look away, swing some more, just waiting to get to home plate so I can belt one out of the park.

"Mrs. Conlon says now I am a lady." Angela puts her hands on her small hips, then rocks back and forth.

It's finally my turn to hit, so I walk to home plate, holding my bat, quiet, knowing that everybody, including Angela, is watching me. I bend over the plate, face the pitcher, and think that true ladies, retarded or not, do not talk about Kotex pads. True ladies climb trees or play softball, even if they play only two innings, even if they hunt down vice in Jacaranda Highlands by stockpiling evidence in their FBI logs. True ladies are on the lookout. They listen to no one but themselves. They are invincible, just like Helen Reddy says, but then I remember that Angela is retarded and that she needs people to be nice to her, which I know I have to be.

"*EEEEeeek. EEeeeek. Eeeeek.* Do you think Flipper is a man or a lady?" Angela's voice echoes as I swing a third time, striking out again.

• • •

I have listened to Angela talk about Flipper for a while now at St. Bede, where Mom convinced Father McKinley that the developmentally disabled—that's the new term for mentally retarded—have the right to know about God, and got herself trained as their teacher.

Every Wednesday when I arrive home from school, I help Mom load poster paper and a portable chalkboard, Magic Markers, the statue of baby Jesus, and construction paper into the station wagon. Then I brush Joey's teeth after his afternoon snack while Mom's making sure Julie and John are doing their homework and the meat is defrosting for dinner; then off Mom and Joey go for the one-hour lesson. Sometimes Mom asks if I will come up to help her with the lesson plan. I've said okay a couple of times.

Father McKinley always arrives to unlock the parish library, but then dashes away quickly, saying, "Good day, now."

One afternoon last year, though, Mom got ahead of him. "Father, would you like to stay and observe class today?" She asked with her hands folded together, her skin sweet as the roses Father McKinley planted all over the parish grounds.

"That would be a kind offer, but I've parish business to attend to."

"Maybe some other time, Father. Well, I hope you remember our upcoming Christmas play."

"Christmas play, Christmas play?" He scratched his thin graying hair. "Yes, that's right, of course. And who might be appearing in this Christmas play?"

Mom, wearing a red blouse with a light, flowered scarf, stepped to the side. Behind her stood six mentally retarded kids in a huddle. Father looked at them one by one, almost losing his balance as Angela curtsied and Otto, rotund as a wrestler, smiled and Ralph raised his droopy eyelids and Carlos jumped up and down and Leroy clapped as he does when he's excited and Joey put out his hand to shake Father McKinley's.

"I see," he said.

"December fifth," Mom said, rounding up the kids back in their seats as Father McKinley flew off, wind gusting up underneath his priestly robe.

When the time arrived for the Christmas play, Father McKinley was among the last to appear. He stood in the back of the dimmed school hall next to Dad, who came straight from work. They both were in black, standing with arms folded. The rest of us parishioners sat in metal folding chairs.

Angela played the Virgin Mary and Ralph with the eyelids played Joseph, her husband. Otto, who has Down's syndrome like Joey but is older and higher-functioning, played the innkeeper. For months, Mom and the St. Bede music teacher, Mrs. Flavin, coached the actors as they learned the lines.

"Remember," Mom told Otto the Innkeeper, "Joseph and Mary will knock. They will ask you if there is room at the inn. Your job is to say, '*No. No room at the inn.*' Okay?"

Otto nodded okay.

"That way, Mary and Joseph go find the stable. Remember the stable and the manger? For baby Jesus to be born in. Okay?"

"Okay." Otto swallowed, then repeated his lines. "No, no, no room in the inn."

On opening night, Joseph and Mary walked onstage, on cue, and recited their lines. They trudged along, step by step, until they found the inn and knocked. Otto, in his innkeeper costume, a purple vest with macramé belt, opened the door.

"My wife, Mary, is having a baby. We need a place to sleep. Do you have room?" Joseph executed his lines with precision. Then the spotlight shifted to Otto. Rotund Otto with his Tootsie Pop eyes examined Joseph and Mary as if they were Christmas presents. You could see his stomach filling. After moments of silence, he opened his mouth like he couldn't take it anymore.

"Yes, yes, there *is* room in the inn." He waved them in.

Everybody in the audience started to laugh, including Father McKinley. Dad cracked his smile, lifting his face to the stage. After the play, Father McKinley asked Mom and Dad if they would like to come to the rectory for a drink. Mom said that was Father McKinley's way of saying he was proud of the show.

•   •   •

On Saturday, before the game, I find Angela behind the backstop and decide to have a talk with her before she yells something about Kotex to the whole crowd.

"Hey, Angela. I wonder if *Flipper*'s on TV right now."

"No, he is not. Seven o'clock. Channel 6. KXLA."

"Yeah, today could be that special day when TV stations are doing a Flipperathon. Flipper could be on for hours. All day. Starting just about *now.*"

Her eyes light up behind her glasses as she claps her hands. "Oh boy, oh boy. Flipper all day, oh boy." And she takes off, running down the block.

I take a deep breath and head for right field. The pitcher throws a fastball and *schwam,* Adele Romero's hard hit bounces in front of me, then slips right through my legs. I scurry into the eucalyptus trees to fetch it, thinking of Angela, how I fooled her with the Flipperathon and how sad she'll be when she realizes she's been tricked. Maybe she'll never come back, I think, but sure enough, our next Saturday game rolls along and there she is, sitting on the grass all alone, wearing her red elastic-waist pants, not saying a word.

When it's my turn to bat the next inning, Bill yells for me to take a deep breath and watch the ball. I say okay, then swing twice and miss. I sigh and stare back at the pitcher, who eyes me like a snake, then I step out of the batter's box, stretch my neck to see Angela leaning forward. I take a practice swing, then inch back. The pitcher fires another pitch, this one zooming right down the center of the plate, smacking right into the catcher's fat glove.

"Strike three, you're outta here," the umpire yells.

I rub my eyes, step away, dragging my bat behind me. Bill jogs over to the bench and suggests that I sit out a few innings, since I don't seem so focused today. I look over to Angela, who doesn't return my gaze as she sits picking blades of grass in front of her. She just takes the grass into her lap, playing with it as if it's a tassel of hair.

I stare down to my muscly legs and my white socks, which

look much too clean for a real softball player. I look back at Angela and then try to watch the game from my position on the bench. But for the rest of the afternoon, all I can think about is the conversation I know I will have to have with Bill.

When the game is finished and our team chants our usual *two four six eight, who do we appreciate* with me barely joining in, I go up to Bill and utter the first words I've said all season, with the exception of *hey, batter, hey, batter,* which I never say as loud and clear as my teammates. Bill's hair is up again in a ponytail and he smokes a cigarette. It almost seems like he will offer me one, but instead, he asks what's up.

"Would you consider letting Angela, the retarded girl, help out with our team? She could keep our equipment together, like one of those mascots." I take a large gulp and look at Bill's eyes, waiting for him to say no.

"Mascot?" He scratches his head, then takes his thin brown hair out of his ponytail. "I think that sounds groovy. Sure, we've got room. That's cool."

Bill looks at me and pats me on the shoulder and tells me to tell Angela she can sit on the bench with us from now on. Every practice, every game—even if we make it into the championships—she's welcomed to be our very own cheerleader.

"In fact . . ." Bill walks over to the huge canvas athletic bag where he keeps his mitt, extra softballs, tobacco, and other things. He pulls out an extra yellow Groovies T-shirt.

"Here, maybe she'd like this." He drapes it over my arm. "But that Flipper routine. You think you could persuade her to stifle those damn dolphin shrieks?"

I nod my head and take a full gasp of air that smells like acres of grass after it's been cut. I find Angela and tell her the news. She plunges at my cheeks with a wet kiss and runs off smiling, waving her Groovies T-shirt like a flag in the air.

• • •

That afternoon I find Mom in the kitchen. She is steaming rhubarb, the pressure cooker spouting at full force. I tell her about Angela.

"That was a very nice gesture. You should be proud! Are you?"

"I don't know. Maybe." I sit down and pick a few blades of grass from the bottom of my cleats.

"Well, you've given her a place. Who knows what will happen next?"

"Maybe I'll tell Dad."

I walk out the back door past the red bottlebrush flowers that stick in your hair if you get too close, and peer into the garage. I hear the California Angels game on the radio. I prefer the Dodgers uniforms over those of the Angels, and I love the sandy voice of Vin Scully, who broadcasts games from Dodger Stadium. Once I asked Dad why he listens to those Angels—every year for them is a losing season. "Someone's got to root for the underdog." That's what he said.

A cigarette glows in the marble-green ashtray. That's another piece of evidence indicating Dad is in the garage. I look behind the station wagon and see him in the corner, his head bent low. He is pumping up all the bicycle tires. He does this on Saturday afternoons. The black transistor radio is on the floor, next to his feet. The announcer screams, "Home run!" and the crowd goes wild, and in the background I can hear the organ play.

"Dad?" His head is down, but I go ahead and speak. "Guess what?"

He crouches by the tire, turns the volume down a notch.

"I got Angela to be invited on our team."

"Is that right?"

Even though he asks that question, I don't answer it—just

watch him switch to the rear tires, with his pump a *whoosh-whoosh-whoosh,* like wind into a hot air balloon, and soon my new blue ten-speed stands proud in the corner. I think the bike returns my stare, saying how it loves standing this tall and how, at any minute, it would be glad to take me as far away as I wanted to go, to see the relations in New York or even go someplace like Ireland or China.

Dad hangs the orange bicycle pump back on the hook.

"Would you like to go to Patty's Pantry for a tuna melt?"

Dad knows I like tuna melts because whenever it is a special occasion and we go to Patty's Pantry instead of Bobo's, I always order a tuna melt. I love how the melted cheddar cheese flows in and out of the caves of tuna and mayonnaise on rye bread. Dad says maybe Joey can come with us, that I should ask my mother if that is okay, and I go ahead, grabbing Joey's sweatshirt in the meantime.

Patty's Pantry is right next door to the liquor deli where Dad buys his Lark 100s. They all know him in there. "Hi again, Joe," they say when Dad strolls in. It's the only place we go where people say anything to Dad right away. He buys his pack of cigarettes and also a Coke for Joey, who now knows the sign language for "Coke," which is making your finger look like a needle and pressing it into your arm.

Inside Patty's Pantry, I look around and notice all the palm trees and how high the ceiling is and how it is filled with gold speckles. Dad sips his coffee, looks at Joey, and never says a word about my getting Angela on the team, although I know my being nice to her must be why he takes me out to lunch this day. Instead, he just bites into his plain hamburger with no ketchup or anything, watching who walks in and out.

The restaurant blasts its air-conditioning, sending gooseflesh up my legs, and I start to rub my hands together. Dad chews and keeps his eye on the people sitting around us. A few of them have already started in staring at Joey. Dad uses his look of X-ray vision in revenge, returning their stares, piercing into their insides, his expression saying he doesn't like what he sees. He puts his hamburger down, sips more coffee, watches Joey, whose face is practically engulfed by his cheeseburger, then looks over to me as I tear off the bread crust, chewing the rye seeds slowly.

"They hold the keys to heaven, people like Joey," he says to me. "They are the little lambs—they hold the keys to heaven."

I pick up a french fry as I try to imagine heaven requiring keys for entry and wonder why God would station the retarded at the gates. People would arrive, stare at them, then probably not even want to enter heaven. I picture Otto holding keys, saying "Yes, yes, come on in," and then I laugh and Dad looks at me like what am I laughing about, and so I stop.

This must be a serious thing Dad is saying, maybe as serious as all FBI matters, because he repeats what he just said. He never talks about heaven or religion except when he's on the phone with Father Jack complaining about the church and the terrible changes, like how dare they take away this thing called the Latin mass. Father Jack always seems to say the right thing, because eventually Dad stops arguing.

I look at Joey, whose face is still plastered with food. He says *um um um* after every other bite. I reach for a napkin and dip it into the ice water and wipe off the ketchup, and as I do this, Joey tries to kiss my arm.

"What about the people who *aren't* retarded?" I look at Dad, because I like my question. "Normal people would never hold the keys to heaven?"

"Normal people are really the retarded ones."

Dad lights up his Lark. He leans back in our booth and chis-

els out a few crumbs lodged in between his teeth. He looks at
Joey and you can see his eyes warm like fire. Then he looks
around again, as if his pupils are shields protecting Joey from
the stares of those around us. I sip my root beer and sneak a look
around too and wonder if all the normal people sitting in the
restaurant know *they* are retarded. I don't think so. I think they
enjoy being normal, going to picnics, sailing on boats, having
beach barbecues, traveling through the stratosphere of normalcy.
Because of Joey, I may never know what normal means—I may
always be catching up.

Joey drops the last slimy, saliva-filled bit of his hamburger
bun on his plate. "Done," he says, motioning his hands like an
umpire, then burps softly. This time Dad leans over with the
cigarette still in his mouth and wipes off Joey's ketchup fingernails and the bits of hamburger bun sticking in between his fingers.

"That was a good meal, huh?"

Joey crosses his hands over his heart. That is sign language
for "love." Joey would rather talk in sign language any day. He
loves cheeseburgers almost as much as he loves Coke.

I think about someone like Joey, or even Angela, owning the
keys to heaven. Maybe that is like Jesus riding into town on a
slumbering donkey, and people laughing at him and throwing
tomatoes and celery stalks and telling him he is a fool, for how
could a real king ever be riding such a slow, dumb animal?
Maybe that means Jesus was Down's syndrome too, but I've seen
a lot of pictures of Jesus and never noticed a retarded one.

Dad pulls out his wallet, unfolds crisp bills—his bills are always crisp—to pay the waitress, Annabelle, that's what her
name tag says. When Annabelle stands at our table littered with
thirteen wadded-up, ketchup-soaked napkins, Joey crosses his
hands over his heart to make the love sign. Then he lifts his fin-

ger and points to Annabelle. The cheeks on my father turn round and red. He tells Annabelle what Joey is saying—that Joey is saying that he loves her.

Annabelle gives Joey a love sign back. Her brown eyes, with wide, blue paint around them, smile. Dad looks at her and you can tell he thinks she is something else. He reaches back into his wallet, leaves her an extra dollar tip.

I think of how I have a brother who is called special, how I have a father who is a special agent, and how both of them are named Joe. I wonder if Dad likes having a retarded son named after him. I think so, because it sounds like Joey will be the one to let Dad into the kingdom of heaven, and not the other way around.

• • •

Dad, Joey, and I drive past the Jacaranda Highlands girls' softball field on the way home. The sun is hot but low in the sky; still, the afternoon games go strong, and it seems there are more crowds than ever sprawled on the sidelines. I look for Angela in her usual spot, but she is not there. Maybe she's with her grandmother, trying on the Groovies team shirt and getting excited for our next game. Or maybe she will forget about us altogether and I can be a normal softball player, just like everybody else.

Joey sits in the backseat. He repeats my name softly, *Waah, Waah.* I don't turn around like I usually do. I know what he wants. He wants to kiss me on the lips, although our family is trying to teach him to shake hands instead. I just sit in the front seat next to Dad and watch the trees go by.

My father turns the car into the driveway. He looks at our front lawn. The grass is never as green and smooth as all the neighbors'. Ours looks dry, like desert grass, with patches of bare spots and weeds where we kids have run it into the ground.

When he steps on the brake, I turn to him and think that maybe he will say I did a nice thing for Angela, but instead, he just looks away toward the garden hose coiled tight. I push open the door and say to my father the only thing that comes to mind:

"Thanks for lunch, Dad."

He says, "You're welcome."

Dad on his mission.

chapter 12

I record predictions on the same pages as my FBI surveillance notes, then mark the upper right corner each time I'm correct—which is most times. When Dad pulls into the driveway, I look at my silver wristwatch, write down the time, then scribble that in four minutes he will light a cigarette as he heads for Joey's room. I flick off my light, turn down my stereo, and listen.

Sure enough, Dad looks in on Joey, who still shares a bedroom with John across the hall from me. From the doorway of my darkened room, I watch Joey sitting against the wall, driving one of Mom's pie tins. He is addicted to steering everything round. If a pie plate is unavailable, he will climb a chair even though he is not supposed to, and reach for the paper plates. He then grabs a Magic Marker so he can draw crooked lines across the paper plate, as if that will somehow aid his steering.

I hear Dad place a kiss on Joey's red cheek, hear his crinkling knees crouch down as he asks, "How are you?"

"Aw, Dadeee . . ." Joey's arms go around Dad's neck. After a few seconds, Dad's knees crack again as he stands up, blowing out cigarette smoke, opening drawers, and laying flat the folded T-shirts he set on the dresser last night.

"I'll make you a chocolate cone after dinner, okay?"

"Chock? Chock?!" Joey says.

I jump back to my bed, in shadows from the purple twilight outside, and write that in fifteen seconds Dad will enter my room and close the curtains. I sit and wait, hearing the hum of the 605 freeway in the distance, the vibration of loud trucks shaking my windowpanes. Dad steps out of Joey's bedroom, peers into mine from the doorway. I wonder if he sees my silhouette, the log open on my lap, but he turns around and walks in the other direction, not venturing to close my drapes, after all. I shut my notebook, wondering where Dad's going as he lights another cigarette, smoking back-to-back. He never does this right when he comes home.

Joey walks out of his bedroom, driving the pie tin. He sees me in the dark and steers my way, plops down on the bed, and gives his pie plate a rest.

"Joey, what's Dad up to?" I ask, trying to decipher what the smoke is signaling.

"Dad-ee?"

Then I hear him lift the telephone in his bedroom. He pulls the dial around eleven times. This means he is calling long-distance. He could be calling J. Edgar Hoover.

"Joey, you stay here, okay? I'll come back and get you." I

hand Joey my log for safekeeping and sneak sideways down the hall.

The purple smoke wisps out like church incense, and through the haze I see Dad leaning against his dresser and holding his badge like he's forgotten to put it in his top right drawer. He sucks on his Lark 100, whimpering a little, then inhaling two or three times more on his cigarette.

"Aw, you can't be serious, now." His voice softens like a marshmallow. "If you keep talking about those Yankees, I tell ya—"

Yankees? I run the files in my mind. Dad would never talk to Hoover about baseball and it can't be Mr. Flanigan because he's not long-distance and it can't be Father Jack because Dad talks to him on Sunday nights. I listen, watch the Lark 100 crimped between Dad's thumb and pointer finger. I see the millions of freckles on Dad's arm. His back is slightly hunched, although his shoulders are so strong the whole world could rest there if it wanted. He nods yes, his hands motioning in the air, cigarette smoke trailing behind.

"Okay, enough already, Jackie. Listen, I got your letter. Sounds like things are changing back there, huh?" He sucks in. "New position? I hope you consider—things sound like they're getting—"

I run back to Joey, who waits for me in the dark, and flick on the light. "Joey, it's Father Jack on the phone! I gotta head back. Go steer to the TV room and I'll meet you there later, okay?" I grab my log, then race back down the hall.

Dad faces the wall and stares down. His eyes, like mine, always drop to his shoes when he thinks serious thoughts. He takes another draw off his Lark, then presses the cigarette into the ashtray with the red paisley print. He grinds it so hard I think it will melt the tin bottom and Mom will be upset because more than anything, except for when adults drink too much, she hates cigarette burns.

"—worry about me? Aw, come on, Hoover never lets us out of his sight. Yeah, right, right . . ." He takes another puff. "Listen, sounds like you could use a little vacation. I've got a proposal for—" Just then his thick waist shifts around toward the doorway, where I crouch. "Hold on, Jack, will ya?"

The receiver falls on the bed. I hide the log behind my back and gulp.

"What do you think you're doing?" Dad's face is beet red.

"You are talking to Father Jack!"

"This is personal business."

"But your door is op—"

"I've never seen a house like—"

He shuts the door, hitting my toe as I back away, and within a second Mom calls out because it is time to set the table and could I make sure Joey's face and hands are clean for supper.

I smell roast beef in the air and hear Mom's pressure cooker whistling as I find Joey in the family room. He sits so close to the television screen watching reruns of *I Love Lucy,* and I am always telling him to move back.

"Babaloo," he says as I pull him farther away on the carpet.

"Babaloo to you too."

During the next commercial break for Cal Worthington, who sells cars by standing on his head until his ears are turning red, I check Joey's hands.

"Clean," he says.

"Not clean," I report back, noticing smudges of pen ink. He takes my hand and kisses it as I inspect his light brown hair, which is almost free of dandruff. Mom uses special moldy green shampoo that is supposed to help people, like Joey, who have dry scalps. It's probably an underdog thing. Maybe the California Angels use the same shampoo.

"Come with me."

I take Joey's hand and go fill the bathroom basin with warm water. I hand him a washcloth and soap. "I'll come back when you are ready." I shut the door behind me, pass by Dad's room, and force myself to avoid the urge to kick his door open. Back in my bedroom, I sit and wait.

I check my watch. In five minutes, Joey will proclaim that he is ready for me to return to the bathroom and examine his hands and face.

The minutes pass and sure enough, Joey's voice wiggles with excitement. "Ready! Ready!" He giggles, almost hysterically. "Ready!"

"You sure you're ready?" I yell from the edge of my bed, wondering how many times he and I will go back and forth tonight.

"No—*not* ready!" he yells, then gulps, full of dramatic tension.

"Okay, then. Get ready! Here I come!" I start counting. "Ten, nine, eight, seven . . ."

Joey claps, so excited he almost starts choking. I wonder if Dad hears us through his closed door, if he thinks it was clever of me to create this little game to get Joey excited about washing up.

"Here I come." I get up from my bed, walk down the hall, and slowly push open the door, expecting to find Joey's arms raised in his usual victory pose. Instead, Dad hovers over Joey, drying each of his fingers, rubbing every last morsel of moisture.

Joey watches me. My smile says we will do our regular ritual again tomorrow night. I think I will just close the door—it's time to set the table anyhow—but before I do, I hear the gravel of Dad's voice.

"It's not appropriate—"

"Sorry, but I—"

"Yeah, you." Dad hangs the towel perfectly over the rack, then turns to look at me. "I've got something to tell you regarding your graduation. News from back East."

"News for *me?*" I start to feel like Joey, almost clapping my hands with excitement. "Do I get to go to Washington, D.C., and meet Mr. Hoover?" All during seventh and eighth grades, I've been dropping hints that there's nothing I'd like better than to meet J. Edgar Hoover after my graduation. Dad gives me a look like who do I think I am, at the age of thirteen figuring I can just go and meet his boss?

"Once I have confirmation, I will let you know." And with that, he walks out.

• • •

On Saturday, Dad prepares to mow the lawn again. He tows the dark, oily machine from the garage, its loud wheels banging *ka-phalt, ka-phalt* as I walk beside him on the hot driveway. I hope he says something, because it is not every weekend that I go trailing alongside my father as he mows the lawn, but he is faithful in ignoring me, reaching for the rope and, after one tug, starting up the motor.

"Dad . . ."

I try and push my voice louder than the lawn mower, but it is nearly impossible. Dad begins mowing the first stretch of grass. I keep pace, just inches away from his stern brow. "Dad?" I yell so loud. "Can you tell me how you got to meet Mr. Hoover?" I think if I ask him this, he will open up and confess it won't be long before I'll be heading to Washington, D.C., myself.

We reach the end of the first stretch and Dad turns the mower around 180 degrees, in sharp rotation. I loop around with him, as if we're connected by an axle. His jaw is tight, but finally, he speaks, as if noticing me for the first time.

"What?" Sweat drips from under his Angels baseball hat.

"How'd you ever get to meet Mr. Hoover?"

Dad has a faraway look, like Moses, parting the grasses, pushing the lawn mower through the wilds of our yard, as if talking to me would be the same as abandoning his mission. We skirt the junipers, then turn around again, still in unison. Dad looks at my sneakers as if they could hit the blades at any moment and I could lose my toes right there in our front yard, so I better be careful walking alongside him, amidst all the danger.

I repeat my question, my steps quickening to keep pace with him.

He gives me his look again, shakes his head like he can't be bothered. He must concentrate on the grass, but I scream as loud as I ever have, just this one time: *"How did you MEET MR. HOOVER?!"*

I know it might be more logical to ask Dad after he finishes the lawn job. Still, I imagine he just might have a change of heart and turn off the motor and answer me on the spot. Instead, he maneuvers in another U-turn, shaking his head. I fall back, watching splinters of grass fly up around his spotted white pants, a few grasshoppers leaping from the bushes. I stand in my shorts and tank top, my hair pulled back in a ponytail as I stare at Dad's firm shoes walking the cut grass as if it were a path to the promised land. He comes my way again, then, after ten more paces, opens his mouth.

"Go talk to your—" he says, yelling over the motor, but still I can't hear his last word.

"What?"

He snarls.

"Your mother." He shakes his head again.

I find Mom inside the house. She stands in the empty bathtub, hanging yellow fishnet curtains for the window above, sewing on seashells that we collected at Delphina Beach last week.

"Mom, can I ask you a question?" I wonder if she knows the secret Dad is keeping from me.

"Sure." She finishes pushing the netting through the curtain rod.

"I was wondering—can you tell me how Dad met Mr. Hoover?"

"Oh, goodness, that's so long ago." She steps out of the tub and admires the curtain, its shells in the fishnet holes hanging on for dear life.

"Those are nice, Mom. We'll be at the beach while sitting in the tub."

"That's just the idea," she says. "What were you asking about Daddy?"

"About J. Edgar Hoover. How'd Dad ever get to meet him?"

"Oh, yes. That's right. Hoover once asked Daddy to deliver his personal bag from L.A. to Washington. Daddy took the train back East."

"You're kidding. Dad *held* Mr. Hoover's personal bag—all the way across the country?! How old was I?"

"Well, this must have been, let me think—the same summer I was pregnant with you."

My heart skips a beat as I imagine Dad sitting on a train for days on end clasping the goods, staring out the window, counting the miles. I wonder if he thought of Mom being pregnant with me, as much as he thought about meeting J. Edgar in the flesh. "That timing's got to be more than a coincidence. Don't you think?"

"Maura, what on earth are you talking about?" Mom gathers up the scissors and thread, placing them in her rattan sewing basket, eyeing me with curiosity.

"Well, *you know*. What about the news from back East!"

"What news?"

"Dad's news about my graduation."

She looks at me, blinking her eyes.

I lean and whisper into Mom's ears. "I could be meeting the Boss this summer."

She raises her eyebrows. Mom doesn't understand my fascination with the FBI. Someday, when I am an agent flying in high-speed aircraft, she will understand. I'll even give her a ride.

•　•　•

A crisp envelope sits at the foot of my bed when I awake a few mornings later. Since the outside is blank, I figure Dad must have used invisible ink.

Inside I find a letter with Dad's regular handwriting. I read it slowly. At first, my heart sinks because I'll not be meeting J. Edgar Hoover, but then it starts racing when Dad asks if I'd like for Father Jack to come out and be the guest speaker at St. Bede's graduation ceremony this June. Father Jack would be honored, the note says, to attend this important ceremony.

I stare at the letter, read it three times, close my eyes, imagining Father Jack flying all the way from New York, standing at the podium with his hands raised, telling the whole congregation how special I am.

I look up and smile at my Simon and Garfunkel poster. "Groovy," I say out loud. "This is so groovy. Just wait until I tell Elizabeth DuPoint and all the rest of them. My uncle—talking to my whole graduating class!" I stuff the envelope inside my sweater pocket and hang on to it all day.

•　•　•

The following afternoon, I take out the envelope at school and let it rest on top of my science project. We are all lined up on the baseball field because Mr. Cutlass taught us the subject of aerodynamics last week and then instructed us how to build our own kites. Today we are supposed to fly them—our graduation kites. All the other kids in my class make regular, traditional, diamond-shape kites, most of them blue, some red, with perfectly cut tails. You can just tell they had help from their parents.

Mr. Cutlass, whose tie is as wide as a steak, helps each kite get airborne, one by one, so that soon there are twenty-nine kites soaring high above us as our faces glare up into the sun. I am the only one whose kite is still on the ground. I stand and wait for my turn as Mr. Cutlass loosens his tie and approaches my kite.

"What is this?" he asks, pointing. I pretend he is looking at my envelope about Father Jack and I am all ready to tell him about the big speech my uncle will make, but then I see it is my science project he stares at. I stuff the envelope back in my pocket and pick up my kite, constructed in the shape of an angel with a huge wingspan, painted green with orange polka dots.

"This is an angel kite." I lift it above my head.

"And how do you think it's going to fly? What about aerodynamics? Where is the tail?" He tugs on his mustache, and underneath I can see he is trying not to laugh.

"Well, see, she's got wings."

"Wings, wings? I don't think my science lesson covered wings."

I never get my angel kite off the ground, but Mr. Cutlass gives me an A minus for creativity, even though he says that applies more to an English class than to science. That night I nudge my FBI log way behind my shoes to make room for the kite. I position her so that her face is what I see first each time I open the closet. I will show her to Father Jack when he flies out. We'll head straight for the field. I'll hold the ball of string and Father Jack will run into the wind, whispering to my angel kite that it's time to sail for the sun.

Trying to say . . . something!

chapter 13

Mother Perennial marches into our classroom with permission slips for our final field trip, scheduled for three weeks before the graduation ceremony. "You'll be going out into the world as mature young adults," she says in her Irish brogue. She studies our faces as she hands out the slips, her eyebrows like fuzzy caterpillars. "You'll have your parents sign these, please, and return them promptly."

She flips the permission slip over on its back side to make sure we don't forget to read the most important part.

"The field trip will be a free-dress day. Please read the instructions about the appropriate attire to wear." The class breaks out in fast applause, but our eighth-grade teacher, Sister Hortense, rushes her finger to her lips, telling us to quiet down and be respectful of our principal.

"Well," says Mother Perennial, "it appears you would like me to read these instructions out loud."

We all fall silent, with a few of the girls beginning to sneer.

"Boys wear slacks, no jeans, a collared shirt with cardigan sweater, and hard-soled shoes. Is that clear, boys?"

Sister Hortense looks at all the boys and urges them on to answer.

"Yes, Mother Perennial."

"Now, girls . . ."

Girls always get instructions after the boys—that is something I keep noticing, but no one seems to think this besides me.

"Girls will wear dresses. Girls, remember, no more than three inches above the knee. And no open-toed shoes, please. Heels are not to be higher than one inch. Anyone violating these rules will be sent home. Is this clear?" Mother looks directly at Elizabeth DuPoint.

That night I go home and hand Mom my permission slip.

"I think we're a little old for permission slips," I say.

"You're certainly getting to that age." She signs it, not even reading all the specific instructions. "Have you thought about what you'll wear?"

"I have a pattern—McCall, sort of a Betsey Johnson style."

"Oh, which one is that?"

"Just a skirt, a basic skirt. I rode my bike to House of Fabrics Saturday. I got some purple corduroy."

What I don't tell her is that I have already named it Special Agent Skirt, Code Fieldtrip. It has an elastic waist and features a hidden pocket inside my hem where I can stash anything, from my badge to my discreet stick of Juicy Fruit gum. I designed the secret pocket myself.

"I think I'll wear my black boots too." I lean on the ironing board.

Mom sits nearby at the typewriter, nods, writing another letter. I look over her shoulder to see that this one is addressed to the pope. I'd be scared to write him, but it doesn't matter to Mom. She has no fear, and she always expects a prompt reply.

"What're you writing him about?"

"The church could offer better support for families of the developmentally disabled," she says. The typewriter bell rings. Mom returns the carriage, then turns to me. "Now, what was this about black boots? How high is the heel?"

"One inch." I was expecting that question.

"Sounds good. You may want to polish those boots. Dad just bought new supplies."

I like the idea of Dad's FBI shoes and my boots shined with the same official black polish.

"Okay, well, I'll get back to my sewing."

I leave Mom in her makeshift office and go find my boots sitting next to my angel kite and log. I measure the heel, exactly one inch, then cut out my skirt. It takes two nights, about six hours, to finish it. The skirt matches the sketch perfectly. I don't finish the seam edges the way Mrs. Helsinkola, my summer school sewing teacher, would have liked. She was a perfectionist. Once she had me rip out my zipper twenty times before she finally approved it. I almost gave up sewing after that.

Now I will have no choice but to sew even more after graduation because Mom has decided I will attend public school after I leave St. Bede—the first one in my family to cross over. She says I will overcome my shyness problem in public school, that those boisterous teachers will pull me out of my shell. Mom says it took years for her to overcome her shyness problem, and that I shouldn't have to wait so long.

The majority of my St. Bede classmates, about sixty-four in both eighth-grade classes, are signed up for the private high schools. They will continue to wear uniforms, the same uniform every day. The only thing good about public schools, as far as I can tell, is getting to wear what you want, but even that may not be good enough.

•   •   •

On the day of our field trip, Mother Perennial rounds us up in our classroom. The day is so warm you can smell the chalk on the board.

"Okay, children." I don't know why she calls us children when we are supposed to be going out into the world as mature young adults. "The bus has arrived. Boys first, please arise, and row by row, please walk quietly down the hallway and form one line in front of the bus door. Girls, you will do the same."

We file out of the classroom in our free-dress clothes. I tuck my white blouse into my purple skirt and make sure my piece of gum is secure in my hidden pocket, my log stashed in my black purse.

A school bus sits like a fat elephant in the middle of the church parking lot. I find a torn seat in the back. The bus driver gets up and turns his belly toward us after nodding first to Mother Perennial, our teacher, Sister Hortense, and four adult chaperons.

"Hi. I am Mr. Hornsby, the bus driver."

I hear Victor Pomeroy in front of me whisper, "Yeah, like as if we didn't know."

"I would appreciate you keeping your voices low. Please remain in your seats while the bus is in motion. And no bubble gum, please."

I reach down and feel my gum wrapped in its foil deep inside my pocket and hope it's not me Mr. Hornsby is noticing.

As we rumble down Jacaranda Boulevard, I look out the window, then down to the cars passing below, their drivers scratching their pant legs or hanging on to cigarettes. We drive past Bobo's Big Bulge restaurant, where a plump Bobo the Bulge statue used to stand—Joey used to pat his belly—until the public school kids stole him late one Friday night.

My classmates look so different when they do not wear the brown St. Bede school uniform. Jim Riley's collared shirt is made with such thin material you can see his undershirt underneath. Victor Pomeroy, the tallest guy in the class, wears cowboy boots that make him look like the Marlboro Man. Matt Hershey keeps his nose well above his shirt that's made of a fine weave. Elizabeth DuPoint is in a polyester pantsuit that she got special permission to wear, while the rest of us wear dresses or skirts. She looks like a model from *Seventeen*, but I am sure she has no secret pocket.

Mr. Hornsby pulls into a special bus parking space in Alamos Mall, where we are scheduled to see a movie, then afterward have ice cream at Farrell's, where they signal an alarm and run around like clowns if you tell them it is your birthday. Off we go, into the mall and into the theater, one by one, quiet as starved mice. The adult chaperons and the nuns walk in front of the class, in the back, and on each side. I wonder why they have us surrounded. What do they think we will do at Alamos Mall? Buy the sinful cinnamon pretzels at Mr. Twisty's? Dart off to Spencer's to see the latest lava lamps?

I sit down in the red velvet chair. Lillian Sardinia, the class genius with cat's-eye glasses, sits to my right. She does a crossword puzzle while waiting for the movie, *Sounder,* to begin. Richard Plomb sits to my left. Wouldn't you know I would get stuck sitting next to Richard Plomb, the quietest boy in the class? His shirt pockets are always stained with cartridge pen ink and his front teeth have Froot Loops cereal stuck in the cracks. Directly behind me plunks down Mrs. Sardinia, the chaperon— as if I, the special agent, or Mrs. Sardinia's genius daughter, Lillian, or geeky Richard Plomb would need a chaperon near *us*.

Mrs. Sardinia takes her job seriously, pushing up her horn-rimmed glasses as she leans over and taps Lillian's shoulder. "Now, you be good!"

Lillian puts down her crossword puzzle and pushes up her glasses too. "Yes, Mama."

I turn and look at Richard. He sticks something inside his shirt pocket that now has a cherry-red stain. I guess because it is a free-dress day, Richard decided to switch to a new ink color.

I wait for the theater to darken. It takes forever. Maybe the movie is stuck in the projector or maybe the theater is on fire and I should quickly look for the nearest emergency exit, which is straight up ahead and to the right.

I lean forward and touch my hem and feel my secret agent pocket. No one has found out about my Juicy Fruit gum. I will sneak it into my mouth once the movie begins. I look behind me and there is Mrs. Sardinia, her pearl skin staring at me. I lean back in my velvet chair, stare ahead, and count the seconds as I watch the flashing *Get Your Buttered Popcorn* advertisement. Just as the lights dim, the knee of Richard Plomb accidentally touches mine. I feel like throwing up, and immediately draw my boots together.

"Sorry," Richard whispers. I think that is the first time I have heard him talk all year, so I feel I have to say something back to him.

"It's okay."

Richard opens his mouth again. Then he closes it, then he opens it again. He looks like a turkey trying to gobble. Finally, something spurts up.

"Um, will you win—do you think you'll win a . . . award at the awards ceremony Friday?" I look at his teeth, and the cracks between them are red, matching the stain on his shirt pocket. He has such horrid breath. And he forgot to use the word "an"— *an* award. It is no wonder he never opens his mouth to speak. I would keep my mouth closed too if I were him.

"I don't know what you mean, Richard."

Just then Mrs. Sardinia breathes down our necks. "Shhhh. No talking. Watch the movie, please."

I sit like a statue in my seat, watching the screen. I wonder if *Sounder,* which is rated PG, will feature swearwords, including the word "damn," which makes me blush. All during the movie, I forget about "damn," though, and instead think about Richard's question about the awards ceremony. I almost had forgotten about it until Richard Plomb opened his mouth, and now I can't get it out of my mind. Win something at an awards ceremony? Me? There is no way I would win any award. I don't think they recognize Best Secret Agent. Still, still, still. A sick feeling, like I ate too much candy corn, overcomes my stomach.

• • •

Mother Perennial, the strict grand marshal of St. Bede, organizes the awards ceremony each year for the graduating eighth graders. Prior to graduation, we fill out forms, voting for the Most Intelligent, Most Neat, Most Beautiful, Best Athlete, Best Personality. There are other categories, but I forget what they are. I just hope Elizabeth DuPoint does not get more than one award. I don't think that would be fair. It's too bad they don't have an award for Most Snotty.

Mother Perennial corrals the entire school body into the assembly hall, which has been named after Father McKinley. Once we are all seated with our palms in our laps, Father McKinley breezes in. We stand up from our bleachers and metal folding chairs, all of us 450 students from first through eighth grades, reciting in unison, "Good afternoon, Father McKinley."

His posture is like a fence and he waves to the crowd. Then gallantly, he climbs the stairs to the stage, takes the microphone, and tells everyone to bow their heads and close their eyes for the blessing. I bow, but my eyes stay open, staring at my black and white oxfords, which Mom polished last night.

". . . and may you fill the hearts and souls of these graduating boys and girls with your most holy presence. May you make them eager soldiers of Christ."

When he says "soldiers," I think of Dad and how he always says *it's a war out there.* Then I decide I will close my eyes and ask the Holy Spirit to keep protecting Dad and Joey, to protect Father Jack when he flies out on the airplane, and to protect me as I must prepare to venture into public school.

Sister Eleanor, our religion teacher who keeps a folded handkerchief under her wristwatch, has already warned us that public school students are the equivalent of devils, since they insert drugs into the mustard and ketchup bottles in the school cafeteria.

"You better beware," she has told me, sniffling into her undone hankie. I am only one of three girls going into the public schools, and Sister never lets me forget it.

Father McKinley usually acts as if he has more important things to do, but today he seems slightly excited to announce the award winners. He leans close to the microphone, then pulls back a bit.

"Why don't we start with an Our Father?"

Our Father? At an awards ceremony? I fold my arms and barely mouth the prayer. Quite honestly, I would rather just get this whole awards ceremony over with. I'd even rather do math problems than sit here.

"The first envelope, please." Father McKinley clears his throat, twice, and adjusts his phosphorescent-white collar. Mother Perennial walks across the stage with a batch of envelopes, her habit swaying above thick black shoes. She lays the results on the podium in front of Father McKinley, who fakes a bow to Mother Perennial, who then bows back to Father.

"Okay, then, here we go . . ."

Our whole class starts fidgeting in the metal folding chairs. My heart starts racing. The backs of my thighs are starting to stick to my seat, which means I must be sweating. I keep my head perfectly still like Dad does when he looks in the rearview mirror, and peek around to my classmates. The ones who know they are going to win just sit and smile, just sit so casually like they have been receiving awards their entire life. Elizabeth Du-Point brushes her hair, again.

"And the first award is: Most Athletic." Father McKinley pronounces the word "athletic" in an Irish whisper as if the Holy Spirit would not approve of such an award category. "The Most *Aaathletic* awards go to . . ." He rips open the envelope gently. "Victor Pomeroy and Adele Romero."

Victor Pomeroy stands up immediately and saunters up to the stage, shakes Father's hand, and accepts his award certificate. Then Adele Romero, with calves the size of cantaloupes, runs up to the stage and does a cartwheel, wearing blue gym shorts underneath her skirt. Father McKinley's chest quakes and he shakes his head in disgust, signaling with his finger for Mother Perennial to scold Adele immediately after the awards ceremony. Meanwhile the whole school applauds because no one is accustomed to seeing a girl show off her gym shorts doing a flip in McKinley Hall, which is usually reserved for overflow masses, weekend basketball games, and special events like our upcoming graduation dance.

Father McKinley points his finger at us as if we are bad sheep for clapping, telling us to hush and be respectful. I never applauded, so I just let out a sigh and start staring at the red drapes hanging behind Father McKinley, wondering if they are made of real velvet. Two fans spin onstage behind where Mother Perennial and Sister Hortense sit. I look over their covered heads and watch the drapes sway. They are dancing like I was last March, practicing the box step at our girls-only religious retreat. We sneaked into the chapel late at night, lounged on the altar eating Fritos, and played Cat Stevens records. I practiced with Lillian Sardinia, because no one else would dance with her.

One thing I do know: if there is one boy I would definitely refuse to dance with, it is Richard Plomb. He still brings a Soupy Sales lunch box to school, the same kind I carried in the *fourth* grade. All day long, he sits at his desk at the back of the classroom surrounded by his battalion of leaky ballpoint pens as if he is preparing to launch World War III.

Just as I stop thinking about Richard Plomb, someone from behind slaps me on the shoulder.

"Get up there," I hear. "Your name's been called. Father McKinley's called your name. Get up there fast before he dooms you forever for making him wait."

"What?" I turn around, my eyebrows stern.

"You won an award!"

"What award did I win?" I ask, not wanting to hear the answer.

"Don't you know?" proclaims Elizabeth DuPoint from down our row of seats. "You won the *Most Quiet Girl award.*"

I gulp and turn my head to Father McKinley onstage. He stands frozen with the envelope ripped open in his hand, his eyes peering over his eyeglasses down to me. I shake my head slowly no, no.

"Get up there, Maura—come on!" Elizabeth DuPoint reaches over and kicks me in the foot.

"There's been some mistake," I say. "That's not for me, that award."

Mother Perennial stands up, as does Sister Hortense, and they cross their arms like steel and stare me down. My feet start feeling like they are on fire, and I wish I could be the Wicked Witch of the West who melts into the floor. Mother Perennial uncoils her finger, pointing me toward the stage.

I stand up and begin walking, surrounded by the awful dampness of McKinley Hall. At first, the only sound is the buzzing of the fluorescent lights high overhead, and then the whole school assembly starts clapping. Why do they clap for someone who won the Most Quiet Girl award? I drag my legs up the stairs, hoping not to trip. Father McKinley awaits, barely inching out to shake my hand, making me walk the entire way to him.

"Ah, Mary Conlon's daughter."

I look right at the small hairs escaping his ears, then look right through him, past the walls of McKinley Hall, and feel my cheeks burning. I tell myself to take my award and disappear instead of just standing there in shock.

"You may be seated now." Father McKinley's voice is exasperated, almost as if I am tiring him out, how I just stand there and stare.

This Most Quiet Girl award is a mistake, I wish to say to him. This award is a mistake, I wish to say to Mother Perennial and Sister Hortense and the entire school of St. Bede. Instead, I smile like Mom does when I can tell she does not feel like smiling. I descend the stairs of the stage as the audience claps, my stomach tense. As I take my seat, I see Richard Plomb look at me with embarrassed eyes, and then it is Father McKinley's voice again filling the hall.

"Most Quiet Boy . . . Richard Plomb."

That night I open my FBI log and write: *Severe crime committed. Special Agent Maura Conlon given erroneous recognition at awards ceremony. Procedure is to burn the certificate. Procedure includes asking my uncle to correct the situation.* I tear out a few blank pages from my log, then address a letter to Father Jack. I tell him what happened, ask if he could insert a few words in his graduation speech about how I am not a quiet girl at all, how I am like a volcano—full of ideas and thoughts and intelligence—and how I could explode at any second.

I sign the letter *FBI Girl,* then erase it, writing instead, *Your talkative niece—Maura.*

Joey loves to tear up the newspaper.

chapter 14

Joey awakens before anyone else on Saturday mornings. He pushes a dining room chair up to the front door, undoes the chain lock, and tiptoes to the driveway for the *Los Angeles Times*. While the rest of us are sleeping, he takes it to the living room and section by section tears up the entire newspaper, shredding it to pieces smaller than a pinkie fingernail.

I am the next one up after Joey. If I see the chain off the front door, I know he is already at work. I run into the living room, but by then it's too late: the room is blanketed, with Joey looking like a gift surrounded by ankle-high confetti. I want to get mad at him, but sometimes it's hard.

"Mo-waah. Hi, Waah!" He loves to see me first thing in the morning. It's like he's never seen me in his entire life.

"Hi, Joey." He can tell by the tone of my voice I've got more to say. Still, he looks around the living room, raising his eyebrows as if he is amazed with his level of detail work. Then he sees my stern face and takes a few gulps, saliva dripping from his lip as it often does.

I sit down next to him, bending to look in his eyes.

"Joey, why do you do this!"

He shrugs. *"Times?"*

"Yes, Joe, *Times*. We read a newspaper, not tear it up."

His eyes widen and he takes a thick gulp. "Why?"

"Because."

"Soh-wee . . ." He pats my back.

"You know—you say sorry every time!"

I look around the living room and bet nobody else in my class has to get on their hands and knees every Saturday morning, week after week, and pick up hundreds of pieces of shredded newspaper.

"Joey, I'm telling you, I am tired of this . . . Okay, please don't do this!"

I grab a paper bag and one by one toss in the shreds, tiny enough to get in *The Guinness Book of World Records* for smallest shredded newspaper. Joey rubs my shoulder as if to say shredding is his contribution to humanity and collecting shreds is mine. His stroke tries to say *isn't it nice we can sit together,* but I tell Joey by my firm posture this is not my idea of fun.

Maybe Joey tears the paper because he is frustrated that no matter how hard he tries to speak, his words hardly ever come out clear, unlike Carl Mowoski, who is in Joey's special education class and talks as fast as a dropping Slinky. With Joey, you've got to read his mind by looking into his eyes and studying his body language. Mom signed Joey up for another sign language class this spring. She takes it too. The two of them sign "Silent Night" together, but the only words I can sign are "crazy," "love," and "airplane."

Joey goes back to driving his pie tin. I raise my right hand, make the "crazy" sign in sign language, and point it to him.

He laughs, puts down his tin, and gives me the "crazy" sign back.

No, no, no. I shake my head, using both my hands, giving Joe two crazy signs back. "You are crazy!"

Most times I don't mean it, but this morning I do.

He laughs so hard he snorts, once again coming over to stroke my back, then brings his hands to his chest, signing the word for "love."

"Yeah, yeah, yeah, okay, Joe . . ."

• • •

I hear Dad's toes creak, which means he is awake and getting orange juice for Joey and himself, which is the first thing he does Saturday morning. He does not normally pour juice for me because he knows I can do that on my own. Sometimes, though, he will surprise me.

His creaking toes enter the living room, where I am halfway done picking up the shredded *Times.* I don't say anything to Dad, just concentrate on collecting Joey's mess. Dad appreciates it when I tend to my brother's needs. Joey points to his pie plate, then stares at Dad, who stoops to gather more shreds. Even Dad says, "Ah, come on, now."

Now that Joey has accomplished his weekly task of shredding the *Los Angeles Times,* he asks Dad about the next little item on his agenda for this Saturday.

"Drive. Drive?" Joey drools again.

"Yeah, okay, Joey. After breakfast. After I mow the lawn."

Dad takes Joey's hand. He places Joey's finger on the grocery bag full of shreds. "No more. You understand?"

Joey does not say a word, crouching lower, his mouth hanging open. He looks at me.

"Drive?" he says with pleading eyes.

"Yes, Joey! Dad'll take us for a drive. But no more shred *Times!*"

•   •   •

Ever since I turned thirteen, Dad takes me and Joey to the St. Bede school ground. Julie and John beg to come along, but I tell them they'll have to wait a few more years. Julie stomps off, grabbing John's hand, and out the door they go to play cops and robbers.

Once we regulars reach our destination, we drive on the very same asphalt where I line up each morning, the same asphalt that spreads from the school to the bleachers, to the snack shack and the baseball field. The school ground is vacant except for Father McKinley pulling his sleek Buick into the rectory garage, which has one of those automatic openers. He is nice enough to ignore us—perhaps because it is Saturday, we are off the hook. If it were Sunday, Father McKinley would be shaking his finger at us for scaring everybody on their way to church. He rushes into the secret interior entrance of the St. Bede rectory. Someday I'll sneak in there, although I'm sure it could never be as fascinating as where Father Jack lives.

Joey is at the wheel, and our car swerves wildly up and down the school ground. It is always Joey's turn first. Dad sets him on his lap, stretches the seat belt over the two of them. You can tell by Joey's face this is a million times better than tearing up the *Times* or driving the pie plates, Tupperware tops, and Frisbees around the house, which he does all week.

"Fst, fst!" That means fast. Joey points to the accelerator, asking Dad for a little more speed.

Dad, however, slumbers along at five miles per hour, just fast enough for Joey to have the thrill of swerving to the right and the left, rocking all our heads back and forth. For being only seven years of age, and for being Down's syndrome, Joey is quite skilled behind the wheel. He holds it straight before lunging the car into figure eights around the basketball poles, staying comfortably away from the St. Bede school building. *"Woooaaaahh!"* Joey's face looks like Santa's while he's driving his sleigh on Christmas Eve. *"Wooooaaaaah."*

I laugh. I look at Dad, who's in his orange cotton shirt with the round ribbed neckline and beige pants with paint spots, to see if he laughs too. His mouth is a straight line, but he must be laughing inside, because after he lights his cigarette, he lets it hang out the window the entire time Joey drives, not even taking one puff, until it finally extinguishes itself. I wish Dad would smoke all his cigarettes that way.

From the corner of my eye, I see Mother Perennial and Sister Hortense step down the convent stairs. One head swings toward us, then two. Mother and Sister are in their summer habits, made of cotton instead of wool, and through them it is easier to see the shapes of their figures.

"Well, what do you know, the sisters have arrived for your performance, Joey. One more figure eight, then let's say hello."

"Dad, you can't be serious!"

He keeps a poker face. "Good job, Joey—straighten it out now." Dad takes Joey's short arm, helping to steer the wheel, aligning the car with the position of Mother Perennial and Sister Hortense.

The nuns have white prayer books clasped in their hands. They drop the prayer books to their sides, pointing to us on the other side of the school ground. I slide down in my seat. I'd rather collect newspaper shreds than feel their torturous stare.

"What are you doing?" Dad says, noticing my body sinking low.

"Just hiding . . ."

"Hiding from what? Get right up."

I slither back up in my seat, twisting away from Mother Perennial and Sister Hortense, who must be drumming their fingers on their prayer books as they watch the Most Quiet Girl careen through the St. Bede school yard with her retarded brother at the wheel.

As our car approaches the sisters, Joey laughing like a clown and Dad guiding his hand, I watch the nuns shake their heads in disgust, then march back into the convent. I heave a huge sigh.

"Dad, what were you going to say to them?"

"Maura, the sisters have better things to do than talk to us." He coughs into his palm, hard, and rolls down his window, as if the heat conjures his rough cough. I realize that Dad knew all along the nuns would scatter before we drove over, and that this was just a ploy to claim the empty school yard again for ourselves. Maybe he uses some strategy like this in reverse to catch communists.

"Okay, Joey. It is Maura's turn. Time to stop."

Joey stretches his foot down for the brake, but he's too short to reach, and I wonder how anyone called severely retarded is smart enough to know to search for the brake.

I unbuckle my seat belt and jump around to the driver's position. Dad picks up Joey, sits him in the back, and buckles him up, then sits beside me, lighting his third cigarette for the afternoon, coughing hard like something is caught in his lungs.

I grasp the wheel and go slow, my foot gently pressing down on the gas, the car sailing forward in long, sweeping motions. As soon as Dad catches his breath, I glance into the rearview mirror, just like he taught me, not moving my head, and I can't believe what I see. Sister Hortense is back out of the convent, staring at our car like a bull ready to charge.

"Dad?" I try to hide my nervousness, like a good agent. "Sister Hortense is back out." I tug the wheel to the right, keeping equal distance between rows and rows of school picnic tables and the basketball poles painted yellow and green.

"Yes, fine. Keep driving."

"Don't you think I should stop? Maybe it's time to go home?"

"You're doing all right."

Dad looks past his arm resting on the window, his cigarette sailing in and out of his mouth as wind rushes through the car. He waves at Sister Hortense in the distance as I do a graceful figure eight, just like Peggy Fleming, around a basketball pole. The car glides as if it is on ice, as if we are on a field trip all day long and I am taking Dad past the Grand Canyon or the White House, up and down, back and forth and around again. I straighten the wheel, then curve into another figure eight, Dad quiet next to me and Joey asleep in the back. For a while, I forget all about Sister Hortense and her pacing muscles.

Dad then leans over, inspecting the gas gauge. I look down to the needle as well.

"Half empty," I tell him, knowing better than to say "half full." I know this means that it is time to go home, stop first at the Chevron station and breathe in the invisible gas fumes.

"I'll take the wheel." Dad stashes his cigarette in the ashtray, coughing as he exhales.

Just as I brake and shift into park, Sister Hortense marches toward our car with her prayer book. I reach to roll up the window, but Dad stops me.

"Hello, Mr. Conlon. Maura." Her voice sounds like cellophane crinkling in the wind.

"Good day, Sister. We sure have a driver here, don't we?" He gestures so that now all eyes are upon me.

Sister smiles, cool.

"Yes, and at the age of thirteen, I'd say a bit young, Mr. Conlon." The frame of her wimple shifts to Dad and back to me. Underneath her black veil, I see piercing eyes.

"Maura, might we have a few words together after school on Monday?"

I hold my breath, thinking that right before my graduation, Sister Hortense is going to suspend me, make me repeat eighth grade, force the Most Quiet Girl award upon me, humiliating me once again before the entire school.

"Yes, Monday after school, Sister Hortense."

"Very good." She takes a look at Joey in the backseat, then back at Dad. "And give my best to *Mrs.* Conlon."

"I'll do that, Sister."

Sister Hortense bows and hurries along, looking back to assure herself the crazy drivers have quit for the day at the St. Bede parking lot. Dad tells me not to worry, that maybe Sister is hoping I'll give her a few driving tips. I tell Dad I don't think so.

• • •

When we get home, I find Mom in the backyard. She has the outdoor speakers turned on, and music from *Camelot* fills the air.

I sit down on the grass beside her, watching her pry open a paint can with a flat wooden stick. I am to help stain the ash-blond dresser that will move from Mom and Dad's bedroom to mine. We will make it antique white with the paint Mom and I chose up at Haley Hardware. This is my first time painting furniture, and I worry whether I'll do a good enough job.

Mom's hair is pulled back under a pink kerchief, and her lips have the slightest trace of orange lipstick.

"It's hot today, huh, Mom?"

"Sure is—and probably too hot in the car, hmmm?"

"It's got to be extremely hot inside the convent, because the nuns were out watching us."

Mom does not approve. She tries again and again asking Dad not to take Joey up to the school yard, but Dad never listens. He says Joey gets too much pleasure out of it.

"Those poor nuns—they must be scared to death!"

"Yeah," I say, not telling Mom that I drive the car too. "Sister Hortense walked up to us." I pick up a small stick and break it in half.

"Ah-hah."

"She wants to talk to me Monday."

Mom puts her brush into the Fuller paint, swirling until the paint swims in circles all on its own.

"What does Sister want to talk about?"

I see a second brush lying on the newspaper awaiting me. I pick it up, feel its dry bristles, flip it back and forth. I don't have the nerve to tell Mom that as of Monday, I may be repeating eighth grade and winning Most Quiet Girl all over again, so I try to dream up another reason.

"Maybe it's about public school. She does not approve of us St. Bede kids crossing over to public school. Sister says public school kids are monstrous."

"Sister said that?"

"Well, Elizabeth DuPoint said that she said that." I stick my brush in the can and let the bristles soak, until the brush is thick and dripping with paint. I make a little dab with the antique white, thinking of those public school kids, like the paperboys who sit five doors down from our house, bundling the *Daily*

Branch Press Telegraph with rubber bands. Every time they see me ride by in my uniform, their voices erupt in a war cry.

"Catholic, Catholic—foreigner!" they yelp, and then the rubber bands come shooting at me like arrows, hitting me in the feet, arms, and legs. I pump twice as hard to get past the public school boys, skidding into our driveway dripping with sweat.

"It sure would be nice to go to an all-girls Catholic high school like you, Mom, where people are nicer."

Mom's lips tense up. I can tell she is tired of me begging not to be forced to attend Arbor Junior High.

"At my all-girls school, we wore horrible uniforms—terrible, terrible." Mom says the ugly uniforms made her feel more shy than she already was.

"You *stayed* shy, even until high school?" I lay my paintbrush down.

"Painfully."

"Painfully?"

"Dancing always saved me—fortunately. I lived for the school dances."

"But how could you be shy in junior high or in high school? You were the prettiest girl. And you were in a beauty pageant!" I say, staring at the long, thick lines of paint streaking the dresser like airplane trails across the sky.

Mom starts to dab her paint on faster, her strokes accelerating. "Sometimes people can hide behind their good looks. Sometimes you end up living in a dreamworld. What's important is what's underneath, what you have to say for yourself." She drops her brush and looks at me. "Besides, I am sick and tired of all this shyness in our family—it is a *problem*!" She takes a huge breath.

I think of everybody in our family, imagining all of us with the word "shy" painted across our foreheads, except for Dad. Because he is a special agent, he is allowed to be quiet—but I can tell Mom's getting tired of that excuse.

"Why are we all so shy?" I bite my lip. "Maybe because you and Dad are kinda quiet?"

Mom finds several small petals that have fallen from the jacaranda tree onto the dresser. She puts her brush down, picks them off, her fingers now blotched with spots of white.

"Shyness can be mixed with sadness—and *that* is a very long story."

I want to ask Mom to tell me the long story, but then I think it might stop us from ever finishing this dresser. So I keep painting, back and forth, trying to imagine how the story might go. Maybe Grandpa Hogan, the president of the stereotypers' union, would be in the long story. Mom says she learned to smile to cover up the scariness when Grandpa Hogan came home from work. Maybe Nana, who loved the light at Jetty Point, would be included too, coming in to sleep with Mom on her cot when Grandpa was drunk. Maybe Grandpa Patrick, who Dad's never talked about, and Gramma Molly, whose voice is filled with ghosts, are in the story too. But the rest of it, I don't know.

"How you doing?" Mom watches my nervous strokes.

"Okay. I guess I'm getting the hang of this."

I look at Mom and think how glad I am she's not shy anymore. I love how she always asks me questions and how she always has something positive to say. Every time the phone rings at our house, it is always for Mom. Even Dad knows. When the phone rings, Dad says, "Here we go again," like somehow it is bad for all this talking to be going on as people call Mom and she stands there scratching her lower back like she always does and laughing so loudly you have to stop whatever you're doing, whether it's homework or playing the piano, just to listen to her laughter that sends ripples through the house. At Christmas, Mom picks up the phone, and soon we are delivering a turkey dinner to the Benitos and Sanchez families who live in the small houses on the other side of Jacaranda Boulevard. Or the phone rings all summer, and everyone from the Mercados to the Potters comes over to swim with us in our pool. Or the phone rings and Mom goes to some kind of Catholic march, pulling Joey in our yellow wagon, which upsets Dad because he uses that wagon on the weekends for his weed pulling.

"Mom, if you please let me attend Joan of Arc—where I swear *all the girls* are going—I promise I'll dance off my shyness and I'll start getting lots of phone calls." I push my brush so hard into the can that white paint comes sputtering up.

"Maura, come on, now, how much longer do you want to worry about this? You're going to be much better off at Arbor Junior High."

"But—"

"There is a teacher there—people are crazy about him." Mom gets up from her knees, peeking through the screen door to check on Joey, who watches *I Love Lucy* again.

"But—"

"Why don't you see what Sister Hortense has to say. If you won't listen to me, maybe you will to her." She dabs on more paint, covering the small places she's missed.

"Yeah, Sister Horse Tense."

"What was that?"

"Nothing. I've already told you—Sister hates public school kids!" My voice is the worst whine.

Mom ignores me, but examines the first coat we've applied. The antique white paint sinks into the grooves of the thirsty wood. We have a ways to go and another coat to apply. Still, I take a break and pour turpentine that smells like a pine grove into my palm.

"So, what about this antique white—do you like the color?" Mom is much neater than I am, not an ounce of paint on her pants or her short-sleeved shirt, as her paintbrush always glides from a gingerly wrist.

"Yeah. It's okay . . . but the dresser would be happier if it knew it was headed for the room of someone attending an all-girls high school."

Mom breathes three heavy sighs, grimaces. She caps the turpentine, looks at my empty hand, then points her brush to the dresser.

"Are you ready to go again?"

"Huh?"

"Look. We could keep painting like this . . ." She applies a thick, even stroke of antique white over the first coat. "Or, if we wanted, we could make a pattern like *this*."

She turns her paintbrush up, then twists it around, painting one circle after another, crisscrossing the grain of the dresser so that it looks like a magnificent finger painting of dancing, ruffled loops.

I stare, my mouth open, as Mom draws another stretch of circles, wondering how you can do this, just break the rules and paint any design you want.

"Are you sure, Mom?" I lean over. "Circles, on my dresser?"

"Why not?"

"I like it!" I inspect closer. "Those circles set the dresser free."

She points to my paintbrush, sitting alone on the grass.

"Then let's set it free."

•   •   •

Monday after school, I run to St. Bede's ugly green bathroom for the third time, then return to my classroom. I can smell the empty desks, the smell of our skin that has stuck to them all day long. I stare at the clock. Maybe Sister Hortense has forgotten about me, but as soon as I get up to go, she sticks her head in the doorway.

"Stay right there—I'll be back."

I make sure my posture is straight and try not to scratch the new pimple sprouting on my chin. I look up to the class bulletin board. It is filled with poetry, our assignment last week. I wrote a poem about the sunset, and my poem was the first to make it up to the bulletin board with a glowing red star. If Sister will let me graduate, then my parents and Father Jack will see the poem when they come to the classroom after the graduation ceremony.

Sister Hortense moves through the door again, this time pulling a stern wooden chair so that it makes a scraping noise against the floor. I sit still in one of the desks at the top of the class, looking at my nails, which I keep short by biting them. Mom says I am old enough now to keep nice nails, but I'd rather have them short and full of dirt. Dirt is a good thing—it shows you are alive, masculine, riding your bike with wind in your hair, living the life of action and suspense.

Sister pulls out a white tablet from her desk. This tablet is probably full of detention menus, listing various ways to punish students for their transgressions. Since I have already been humiliated with Most Quiet, I hope God will inspire Sister to be easy on me.

"So, I have listed here that you—" She clears her throat, speaking as if her mouth is holy and designed to say only pure words.

"I am sorry, Sister. I did not mean to drive on Saturday."

She blinks her eyes several times.

"Oh, right, yes." She pulls her head back, her cheeks wide like a plate. "That matter, my child, is between Mr. Conlon and Father McKinley. I don't handle driving violations on school property."

"You don't?" My feet slip on the floor.

Sister shakes her head.

"O—kay."

"Now, let's get down to business, shall we?" She peers into her tablet, studying fine print so small she must squint to read it. "I understand you are to be attending public school, Arbor Junior High, in the fall?" She stares down, saying *hmmm* three times.

After the third *hmmm,* my mouth opens on its own and spews out a torrent of words.

"I am sorry. I tried to convince my mother to let me go to Joan of Arc, but she will not listen to me, and then I asked my father and he said it would be okay to attend Joan of Arc but that I would have to ask my mother, so I ask her, again and again, and she still says no, that public school is the best for me, but then I reminded her about Penelope Ratcher, who left St. Bede in the fifth grade for public schools and how she started wearing low-cut hip-huggers and developed a snotty attitude and started smoking and hanging out with the boys with those funny cigarettes."

Sister holds up her hand like she's directing traffic. I catch my breath and watch her hand rest back in her lap of black cloth.

"I'll try to convince my mom about Joan of Arc. I will! I know the public school kids are monstrous."

"Maura, I have a few words of wisdom to share with you. When you attend Arbor Junior High, I do recommend—and your mother and I have discussed this—that you enroll in the class taught by a Mr. Schlatter."

Sister's cheeks glow. I look into her eyes that are the shape of figs.

"What do you mean?"

"Exactly what I said."

"You mean I won't get poisoned if I go into public school? Surrounded by all those kids who've never been taught the difference between right and wrong?"

Afternoon sun spills into the classroom, and a few blue jays come to the open door, inspect what's going on, their heads bobbing stiff, like robots. I look back at Sister. Her face is full of sun and her eyes are wide open. She looks as if she is accustomed to having such visions.

"It is perfectly fine. This fall you will be a student of Mr. Schlatter. You'll be in his drama class. Someday you will thank your mother for sending you there. I promise." Sister then stands, ready to excuse me.

Drama? The word takes on claws as it goes down my throat. What do they mean, sending Most Quiet Girl into the public schools for drama? Drama is for people who speak loud, who are not quiet, who are not special agents, like me.

I cycle home from school, past the Romero house and the Sutherland house and the DuPoint house, all my classmates who I have known for eight years and all who will carpool together to attend the all-girls Joan of Arc next fall.

When I get home, I ignore Mom as she calls out hello. I bang my bedroom door shut and pull out my log, writing: *When I'm a special agent, no one will tell me where to go! This is the first topic of conversation when Father Jack arrives.*

Tough and elegant in my graduation dance dress.

chapter 15

I fill the tub with Mr. Bubble the night of our St. Bede graduation dance. The bubbles in the bath never bulge like those
advertised on the outside of the box. After I wash up, then
towel off, I snap on the bra that Mom had me especially measured for. I despise this measurement thing. I don't get measured
for pants or shirts or socks, so why must I be for bras? The ladies
manning that J. C. Penney bra and girdle department have been
there for sixty-five years. Since they look at you with those radar
eyes, they should be able to snap their fingers and call out your
size as soon as you appear.

After my bath, I slip on my new white seersucker dress purchased at Hydro's Supermarket—the only supermarket featur-

ing a clothes department. Dad and I went shopping a few weeks ago, and while he picked up bologna, Velveeta cheese, Wonder bread, and milk, I wandered into the clothes department and found the dress right away. I didn't even try it on. It just called out my name, with its flat pinafore smock, small pleats, and butterfly sleeves.

I tighten my dress waist-tie, then comb layers and layers of my hair, clipping it back with new barrettes with the same blue roses as on my dress. I roll on nylons over my muscly legs, then sniff the patchouli oil from Spencer's Gifts, the store that sells the lava lamps. I dab on a small amount so I can barely smell it.

I walk out of my room, down the hallway, and into the kitchen, where Mom sits at the table, waiting.

"Oooooh!"

Mom whistles as I appear in the dining room, that special kind of whistle that says *you are good-looking*. She also does this when I wear my conservative navy-blue one-piece bathing suit, which makes me self-conscious of my new figure.

Dad walks into the dining room. His hands are in his back pockets and his eyes pop out of his head. His lips curve upward, his grin hiding his little whimper of delight.

"Bee-utiful. Bee-utiful."

I love how my father says that word. I look down to my white sandals with crisscross leather straps, and place my hands on my thighs because I don't know what to do next.

"Did you brush your hair?" This is the question Mom asks me more than any other. I have hair that has a mind of its own. I could live without brushing my hair for the rest of my life because I'd just love to see which direction my hair would go.

"Twice. I brushed it twice."

"Here, let me brush it once more." Mom loves brushing my

hair. She thinks it is something mothers must do for their daughters. "How about a little hair spray?"

"Yuck, no way."

I usually say *yuck, no way* when Mom tries to introduce me to any of those feminine-type, womanly things. The fact that I am wearing nylons that came out of a plastic egg at Hydro's is achievement enough. I don't think nylons were created for tall girls who have strong legs like me. Nylons were developed for girls like Elizabeth DuPoint who slither around instead of plunking themselves down like "Just the facts, ma'am."

"Joe, did you get flash cubes at the store?" Mom says this as she runs to find her camera, which she keeps in her little office with the typewriter and ironing board.

"Did I get flash cubes at the store?" Dad rolls his eyes at me and I smile back at him. He returns from the master bedroom with a flash cube, snapping it on top of Mom's camera. Mom takes the camera, takes her time to get me in the frame.

Smile, smile. I stand, arms at my sides, hoping my small pleats don't make my stomach look like it is sticking out.

Smile, smile. Mom almost takes another photo, but then calls for Julie and John. "Come on! Get in the picture!"

John whizzes by, yelling, "Catch me if you can!" Julie trails behind and stops to grab Joey by the hand. He's ready to give a kiss, but since he has the flu, we tell him a smile is good enough.

Smile, smile. Mom lines up the next photo, which is one of me and Dad. He stoops over a bit, folds his hands, and smiles without exposing his teeth. Mom says he's embarrassed because they became yellow from all the tea he drank in the war. Sometimes, though, I catch a glimpse.

"Very good, you will be the belle of the ball! Have a great time!"

"Okay, I'll try."

Mom holds the camera, patting Joey on the back so he realizes it is time to get ready for bed. I look at Dad, who takes his hands out of his back pockets and folds his arms.

"The Royal Chariot awaits."

"Dad, can you drive me up in the FBI car?"

"As I said . . ."

Dad unlocks the passenger side and opens the door for me to get in. He lights his cigarette, coughs as he closes my door, walking slightly slower than usual to his side. I place my hands on my lap, feeling the pull and bubbles of the seersucker and how strange and excited my body feels to be draped in a long white dress, with blue roses that match my barrettes.

A soft rain falls. The drops slither down our windshield, collecting until they look like rose petals, or a field of stars. I watch them up close. Each is a different shape hugging and then falling down the slant of the dark window.

Dad lets the black car roll into the street and turns on the radio. *Crackle, crackle.* Some voices mutter low, sounding like astronauts with oranges in their mouths. They say the usual *ten-four, ten-four,* even though it's 7 P.M. on a Friday.

"Ten-four," I say to Dad.

He nods his head.

According to FBI law, we are not supposed to be in Dad's FBI car, especially on the weekends. Maybe because we drive it to St. Bede, it is not a sin. As we pass through the streets of Jacaranda Highlands, I press my face against the window glass, wondering who lives in these houses. Sometimes I dream I will go and knock on everybody's door, flash my badge, and ask, "What is your name and how do you live your life and do you know any of the big secrets yet?"

We drive up Margaret Rae Drive. We have lots of female names in our housing tract. Mr. Flanigan says the developer named them after his daughters, wives, and former girlfriends, but that may just be a story. The lights are on and the curtains are open in the corner house on Linda Ann, and right in the front window, a man and woman embrace. The rose petals and stars on our windshield vanish. I see the embrace just for a flash, but it sends chills up my back. I wonder how long they've been standing there, if they are dancing, or if they are feeling that adult thing called love.

I want to ask Dad if he saw what I saw. I shouldn't, because it is so embarrassing, but I can't stop myself.

"Dad, did you see those people?"

"What people?" he says, keeping his eyes on the road.

"Back there, those people back there, in that open window?"

"What open window?"

My shoulders drop. "Never mind."

I look out the window that has cleared from the rain. Dad must have seen them. He sees everything. He just never lets you know.

We pull into the church parking lot. I can see Father McKin-ley and Mother Perennial outside the hall, quietly gesturing, and my stomach goes into roller-coaster mode.

They look to Dad and me. Dad ignores Father McKinley, but Father McKinley stares nonetheless. Maybe he's envious that Father Jack will be giving the graduation speech. Mother Peren-nial glances over, watching the Most Quiet Girl step out of the car. Even though I have this award, no one, not even Mother Perennial or the high holy priests, will ever know Most Quiet travels in an FBI car. No one except me and Dad.

I walk into McKinley Hall. The fluorescent lights are off. The basketball hoops are drawn back. Tonight it is filled with soft spotlights. The boys are all huddled in one corner, the girls in another. I trudge into the bathroom filled with hair spray smell, then walk out as soon as I can. Meanwhile Mother Perennial, the grand marshal, has taken the stage and motioned the disc jockey to turn down the music for a second.

She turns to face our graduating class all decked out and standing in the semidark below her. She purses her lips, holding on to the crucifix necklace, which hangs low on her flat chest.

"Now, boys and girls."

It is always boys before girls.

"Welcome to the graduation dance at St. Bede School." She stops, then continues like she's found a pound of fresh air. "In a short time, you'll be graduating from this school as mature adults, and we hope you will behave accordingly tonight. Now, this is the first mixed dance the school has ever held, and we have special instructions for you."

Adele Romero nudges me. "What does she mean by mixed?"

"Boys and girls. I mean, girls and boys, you know—mixed."

Mother Perennial pulls the microphone closer to her thin lips so we can hear all her *ppp*s as they *pp*ound the insides of McKinley Hall.

"Now. You are to maintain substantial distance between yourself and your dance *ppp*artner. Sunlight should be able to *ppp*ass through."

I chew on my gum and look around the room filled not only with my classmates, but an army of parent chaperons.

Mother Perennial speaks again. "We will begin the graduation dance in this fashion, boys and girls." She pulls out a piece of paper from some compartment in her habit, then adjusts her bifocals. "For the first dance, I will call out names of the award recipients." She calls out to the semidark hall, then looks again down her nose. "*Ppp*lease come out to the dance floor when your name is called."

My seersucker dress starts feeling like it is twisting around my waist. I glance over to the pay telephone by the bathrooms and think of calling for a ride home. I would rather go home and put on Trini Lopez and dance with Joey, who has the flu, than follow Mother Perennial's directions.

"Are you ready now, Mr. Klingler?" Mr. Klingler is the disc jockey, but he is really the father of Katy Klingler, the new girl in our class this year. He takes off his black leather jacket, which looks controversial, since all the other chaperons wear simple cardigans. Mr. Klingler flashes an A-okay sign to Mother Perennial and lowers the volume on his first song, "Morning Has Broken."

"Okay, then . . ." The hall is silent, the buzz of anticipation rushing in like bees. "First we will have Maura Conlon, winner of the Most Quiet Girl award, on the dance floor. Maura will be joined by Richard Plomb, winner of the Most Quiet Boy."

I gasp, then jump behind Irene Bauser, who is three inches taller than me. Even though the other kids call her the Jolly Green Giant and ask her what's the special of the day, frozen corn or peas, I hope she will be kind enough to hide me.

"Maura Conlon. Maura Conlon, *ppp*lease?"

"Duck, duck. She's looking this way."

Irene pushes me down, then folds out her arms, covering my width perfectly.

"*Ppp*lease, Maura Conlon, don't be shy." Mother Perennial's voice echoes throughout McKinley Hall as if through a canyon, and all sixty-four heads from our eighth-grade turn and ten chaperons in cardigans search for me through yellow and green hanging crepe paper and white balloons. I crouch lower, praying Mother Perennial will forget she saw me step out of the FBI car earlier, and instead believe I am sick, home in bed, sick with the flu tonight.

And then a tug, my arm almost yanked out of its socket,

sparks flying out of my elbow. "You've got to go out there, Maura!" Elizabeth DuPoint towers over me, her golden hands now bending to her thighs. "It is your dance. Even if you really *aren't* a quiet girl, it is still your dance." Maybe since Janine Rawlins won Most Beautiful instead of Elizabeth DuPoint, Elizabeth is becoming more human like the rest of us. She smiles at me, her eyes without the usual flares.

I look up at Elizabeth with a tear that escapes down my cheek. She smiles again, turns away, then comes right back as I stay crouching.

"I bet you are a great dancer. You can show 'em!"

She takes my wrist as the sound of scratches and piano music bounces off the walls. Elizabeth and I walk in the dark as if we are in some ocean, wading. The crowd of girls parts as we slip through. Finally, Elizabeth releases my wrist and I am forced to walk alone, landing on the dance floor, where pockets of boys clear away. Just as I arrive, Richard Plomb tumbles in front of me.

Mr. Klingler turns up the volume even louder. And soon all I hear is the voice of Cat Stevens singing about new mornings and sunlight and blackbirds. Richard Plomb's shoulders slope, but as soon as he reaches the middle of the floor, he straightens up, facing me like a peacock. I look at his shirt. It has no pockets and therefore no ink stains.

Richard Plomb reaches for my hand as we stand there, alone, surrounded by pillars of spotlights cascading to the dance floor, crepe paper swaying slightly. We start the box step without discussing which particular dance we will do. Around we go, slowly, smoothly, as precise as the big hand on a clock, 360 degrees, his hand on my seersucker waist, my hand on his cold nylon shoulder, as our classmates, chaperons, and Father McKinley and Mother Perennial and all the nuns, on tiptoe, look on.

I know I must say something to Richard Plomb before the

dance ends. I know I'll never see him again after graduation, just like I won't see the rest of my classmates who are lucky to be sent to private schools. It is strange to be thinking these thoughts now, as I am dancing and everybody in the world is looking at us.

"So, Richard . . ." My mouth reaches up to the quiet boy's ear. This causes a stir in the room and I can feel the whispers.

"Yeah?" I recognize his grunt. It is like Joey's—in it I hear a hope for release.

"I'm just curious."

"About what?" He slows down our dance.

"Are you looking forward to going to St. John the Baptist next year?"

"I don't know. How 'bout you, and public school?" His breath is measured.

"I don't know." I smell his open mouth. Richard has brushed his teeth. I even smell a trace of Listerine. "I hear the publics sneak drugs into the cafeteria ketchup and mustard bottles. It may not be safe to go there."

He smiles, exposing his one bicuspid tooth, slightly fanged. "Oh. That sounds kinda—I don't know. I guess you'll find out for yourself."

"Yeah, I know . . ."

We continue in our tight circle, allowing sunlight to come between us, and I can hear him breathing, in and out, just as our box step moves neatly forward, backward, sideways. I hear his heart thump through his shirt. It is a deep heartbeat. It starts to warm his shoulders where my hand is stationed. He then clears his throat, making a chomping noise with his teeth, like he is trying to gather enough saliva to say something.

"Maura, I wonder . . ."

"Oh my God, the song is almost over!" I have listened to

"Morning Has Broken" on my stereo so many times that I know every word. "I am sorry, what did you say?"

More of his saliva chomping noise.

"I wonder, are you, um, *really* quiet?"

His question feels like cold water pouring down my neck, freezing me like a winter icicle. "Only on the outside. My uncle's gonna make that clear to everyone." My voice sinks into my chest. We step round and round in our smooth box step, soft air falling like snow.

"You're lucky."

"I know."

For one second, we draw ourselves closer, microscopically so as not to alarm anyone. I hear both our caged hearts pulsing with the music. I hear the mouths of chaperons smiling, whispering *how sweet* in the shadows, the rustle of girls and boys loosening their huddles, turning faces to one another in the dim light, waiting to place their paws on one another's backs.

When the song ends, Richard Plomb takes my hand and leads me off the dance floor. When we reach the edge, he kisses my ring finger, then fades into the dark, and the rest of the night, I can't remember.

Looking for fresh angles.

chapter 16

The paperboys from the Tiglios' house are lined up once again as I cycle by. They've positioned their bikes like cannons this time, hiding like pirates behind them, and start shooting sharp rubber bands at me, high and low.

"Catholic! Catholic!"

Their voices and snapping weapons scream like firecrackers. I push my bike pedals hard, my skin sizzling as I think of their faces when Father Jack has a talk with these hideous boys. They are evil personified. They have a million mortal sins to confess, I tell myself, riding so fast I almost choke, like Joey when he's had too many Cokes, or Dad with his cigarettes.

John opens the front door, then dashes away as I walk into

the kitchen, where Mom is on the phone. She bends down, her hand covering her mouth as she hangs on to the receiver.

I don't know who is on the other end. Maybe Father McKinley. Maybe Mom is talking to him about the graduation ceremony, which takes place in ten days, taking a message to give to my uncle. Mom nods, keeps repeating, "Yes, Father, yes, Father."

I rub my leg because it still stings from the rubber bands, and I am all ready to tell Mom again about these less-than-ideal boys from the public schools, but then I stop when she begins to cry on the phone, her body turning away from us. Julie, who gets home before I do, sits and taps a glass of milk at the kitchen table. She wears her fifth-grade St. Bede uniform. Behind her, the kitchen is yellow with sunlight and waves reflecting from the pool. A bird outside sings in high pitch, its chirp echoing inside the house. Julie does not touch her milk. She looks at Mom, who crouches over the phone so we can't see her face anymore.

"Something's happened," Julie says, turning to me. "It's going to make you sad."

She holds on to her milk, not downing it like she usually does in two seconds flat. It sits there, as if her hand is an instrument holding on to something that belongs to nobody.

"Where is Joey?" I ask Julie.

"He drove his pie plate into the living room."

I run into the living room, like a referee who hasn't seen the play, blowing his whistle nonetheless. The pie plate is at Joey's feet and his face is covered by his little fat fingers.

"Joey?"

He drops his hands and looks up. When he sees me, his face crinkles like a raisin, his lips in a pout.

"Joey, what's wrong?"

He points to the kitchen.

"Mom-eee." His voice aches. I sit close and hug him.

"It is okay. Everything is just fine," I say, not knowing what I am talking about.

"Ah, Mo-waah." Joey grabs me tighter. He gets upset when he sees Mom cry or even before she starts to cry. He's got this radar for sensing things in the air.

"Okay, Joey . . . let's go find out, okay?" I give Joey his pie plate. "Okay . . . let's drive back to the dining room." Images of Dad rush in and I remember the time the Butcher banged him up and my heart starts racing and I think, *Oh, no, this cannot be about Dad,* about the Ten Most Wanted hurting Dad.

Mom looks up from the phone and sees me and puts her finger out to say something, I don't know what, maybe just that she knows I am home. Her cheeks are wet, clenched tight.

I swipe my glance to Julie, who gulps her milk.

"Nothing happened to Dad, right? Right?!"

She finishes and looks down to the table. "You're gonna be sad."

I sit down at the edge of the chair and look out to the pool, wondering what is going on, what all this chatting and these stares are about. A small windstorm picks up outside: the surface of the water skids back and forth, and green leaves fly up in a twister, then drop to the pool. Those little twisters almost never happen. I can't remember the last time I saw one.

"Thank you, Father McKinley. We'll let you know. Thank you very much."

Mom hangs up, wiping her entire eyelids with Kleenex, then wipes her cheeks and the bottom of her chin. She turns to speak to me. First her head. Then her chest, then her arms, then her legs. Then her lips open, and though I sit with my hands in my lap, I want to raise them and cover up my ears, because instead of sad news, I want Mom to ask us how our day at school was, just like she always does.

"Something horrible's happened—back in New York."

"New York?" My eyelids begin to twitch. I look at Julie, who unwraps a Cream-a-ling cupcake, then lets it sit there, next to her fist. My cheeks are numb. It seems for so long that nobody says a thing.

Mom inhales, holding back tears to free up words. Joey walks over, touches her shoulder. He lifts her chin, looks into her eyes. I sit still in my chair, trying to hide my terror.

"Ah, ba-bee . . ." Joey strokes Mom's curly hair three times before her tears fall again. She takes Joey's hand and kisses it and says everything is okay, then she turns to me.

"There was a robbery in Father Jack's rectory last night— sometime after Sunday mass."

Joey pats Mom's shoulder as she gasps for more air. I think of Father Jack's rectory and all the photographs on the wall and the stained-glass window on the rectory front door that made the light look so orange. Mom's voice comes up again, hard, as if it's pushing out of the ground, as if she is trying to force words out.

"Father Jack was shot."

"Shot? Father Jack was shot?! What do you mean?"

"Dad flew back to New York—"

"Oh." That is what I say. Julie looks over to see my reaction and I look back at her, then to Joey, and then to Mom, who bites her lip before raising her hands over her mouth.

"Maura, Father Jack was shot in the heart . . ."

I turn to the window again. A hummingbird lands on a red hibiscus, then flies away. For the smallest second, I wonder how Father Jack will travel to California for my graduation ceremony if he's been shot in the heart. Maybe Father McKinley will have to say his speech because Father Jack may be low on energy by then, but at least he can hold my ball of string as I run in the field with my angel kite, the winds taking it up.

When I look at Mom and see her white cheeks, it occurs to me what she means, what it means, to be shot in the heart, and how that means when you are shot in the heart, you are killed.

You are dead.

Cold, dead, on the floor.

You are murdered when you're shot in the heart.

I sit there. It is four o'clock in the afternoon. It is the time we usually have cookies and milk and watch *Batman*.

Instead, we sit as the phone rings. No one moves. Joey's arms go around Mom. Julie starts to cry—and then I can't help it either, as I sit, tearing into the hem of the tablecloth, kicking the base of the table, its hardness shuddering upon impact. The phone rings and rings, but we sit in the gray room, locked in, like there's a flood at the door, like we're already in the flood and the waters are rising, and they are taking us far, far away.

Julie wipes her nose and cheek, pushes her cupcake away. "Maybe we should say the Rosary."

Mom lets silence hold us. Tears and snot slide down my face. My legs tremble and my throat shivers.

Joey lets go of Mom's hand and it falls to her lap. I think of Father Jack calling her Mare, how Mom smiles so much when he is here, how Father Jack is the best uncle in the whole world. I feel myself shake. Maybe it is the Holy Spirit attempting to calm my heart, because right now my heart races like wild horses. It does not belong to me. It belongs to someone else, some shadow gasping for air.

"We will pray for Father Jack and for Daddy," Mom says low, getting up, taking my hand and Julie's and Joey's. "We will pray for the man who committed this horrendous act."

"No. I will not pray." I jerk my hand back. "I will not pray for that criminal. He is evil. He is the devil." Something sharp rips inside. It is like barbed wire scraping my throat, so hot all I can do is sink into Mom's shoulders, crying, "What about my Father Jack?"

• • •

Once, while we kids were sitting in Murray's Celestial Shoe Store on Alameda Street, Mom talked to us about evil. I was just glad to have arrived safely after Mom drove us through the Los Cabrillos traffic circle, where people lose their lives every year, including the man who designed the traffic circle and his son.

Murray's Celestial Shoe Store has nine illuminated planets painted on its black ceiling. I liked Neptune the best. I wondered if the astronauts who walked on the moon glimpsed a planet as blue as the one painted in Mr. Murray's shoe store.

"What is your favorite planet, Mom?"

"Hmm." Mom looked up, scanning all the way around. "I have never thought about a favorite planet before. Well, how about Venus?"

"I know why you chose Venus. Because it is red, the color of love."

Mom scooted Joey back in his seat as he sucked on the Tootsie Pop the salesman handed him. Then Mom opened her mouth and told me something she hoped I would remember forever. That is one thing about Mom: it does not matter where you are or what you are doing, she always finds a lesson about the big things in life. This is what she said: "You should always love people even if you don't like what they do."

Mom's face sweetened as my gaze drifted upward toward the solar system. I looked at Venus painted so red you could almost hear it beat. I thought about her words, until the important question popped up.

"What about the Ten Most Wanted? Are we supposed to love them?"

"You should love *them,* but not what they *do.*"

"Dad would not agree. He's gotta look at their faces and smell their armpit skin. Criminals can be devils. Do you expect us to love the devil?"

• • •

Mom spends the rest of the afternoon answering the telephone, all the way past dinner. The sky goes dark purple that night. Even the stars seem to ache, their chests punctured, their points wrapped around their bellies. I listen to Mom talk about the details of what happened in New York, then when I can't stand it anymore, I go into my bedroom and lock the door. I don't know what else to do.

I take out my FBI log and turn the pages, past the section listing the unrecognized vehicles parked in our neighborhood, their makes, models, and license plate numbers, past my sketches of Mary's crowns, past all my special agent wardrobes, past my secret letters I've been writing to J. Edgar Hoover, past all of Dad's code words that I've cracked.

I find the last empty page in my log. It stares at me. I've never felt a page stare, so lonely, or maybe it's just me, so lonely, looking at it as I sit, howling inside like a coyote on a warm May night.

I uncap my cartridge pen and press down. I stitch big, looping letters. I hope they will take this ache in my chest and squeeze it onto the page. I just let the words fall out, watch them flow, like blood.

Father Jack was murdered on Mother's Day. He said mass, then had supper at Gramma Molly's. After that, he returned to his rectory in Queens, New York. Someone shot him for a few hundred dollars. He was alone in his rectory home when he got killed. The other priests re-turned late after dinner and found Father Jack dead on the floor. My Uncle Father Jack was so, so full of flowing love.

Then my hands go cold. I hear a knock at my door.

"Who is it?"

Joey's voice is soft, like a purr. "Me come in?"

"Wait a minute, okay?" Then I realize this is too sad a day to make Joey wait, so I let him in and he sits beside me on the edge of my bed and he holds me as I cry, and then I tell him there is one more thing I have to write.

How could anybody shoot my Uncle Father Jack in the heart? I love my Father Jack. I love him so much.

I close my log. The rest is silence, until Joey rests his head on my shoulder, says as gentle as the flutter of a dove, "Dad-ee?"

"Dad had to fly in an airplane to New York, okay?"

"Why?"

Sometimes I wish Joey would outgrow the "why" word. How can I explain something I don't understand? Joey doesn't even know about the presence of evil in the world, let alone how it could kill Father Jack. I can't explain to him what happened. It's like his heart does not have the language to understand these things. Then I remember Dad saying how it's the normal people who are really the retarded ones and how people like Joey hold the keys to heaven. I remember the special way Father Jack always looked at Joey. Maybe Father Jack felt the same way as Dad.

I think about whoever killed my uncle, whoever he is—he is the retarded one. Before I go to sleep, I kiss Mom good night for a second time. "Do you think Mr. Hoover's sending all agents to New York, to help Dad catch the killer?"

She just looks at me, eyes deeper brown than ever, and kisses my cheek good night.

• • •

Almost one dozen flower baskets have arrived at our house in the last two days, so when the doorbell rings, I expect to see the flower man with tulips or roses or mums or lilies. Instead, I look up and see Mr. Flanigan with a stack of newspapers under his arm. He usually calls before he comes to our house, but not today.

"Hiya, kid." His eyes are red and a handkerchief hangs out of his right hand. "Will you give these to your mother?" His voice is low.

"Okay." I take the bundle from Mr. Flanigan.

"There's a bunch of 'em. The story's running in papers in New York, D.C., Boston, Chicago, Detroit, all over. Will you make sure your mother sees these?"

"Okay."

"You'll read about your Father Jack in 'em, kid. God bless his soul. You can tell your mother Lindsay'll be at the funeral."

I just stare up at him, my cheeks squared as my eyes well up, imagining for the first time Father Jack's funeral and Dad in his black FBI suit standing next to the casket.

"Lindsay's the mayor of New York. Tell your mother the papers in Ireland are covering the story. Okay, kid . . ." He gives me a soft tap on my forehead. "St. Jocko was a fine man—the best."

"Do you wanna talk to Mom?"

Mr. Flanigan waves his hand no, no, and takes a step back because maybe he thinks that would be too much.

"Ole FBI Joe will have the bastard locked up in no time."

Joey joins me at the front door.

"Flan! Flan!" Joey loves Mr. Flanigan because he always roars like Santa Claus when he sees my brother, a *ho ho ho Joey* swirling from deep in his belly.

"Hey ya, Joey." Mr. Flanigan's voice is soft as steam as he pulls his white handkerchief to his eyes, trudging back to his green sedan.

• • •

Mom keeps a church calendar by the pink kitchen telephone. I sit down with my pencil and mark off the days. Dad has been gone eight days, thirteen hours, and twenty minutes. I ask Mom when he will fly home. She says he will let us know when he is ready.

So I wait.

I wait forever for Dad to come home from New York so he can tell me everything. He will sit me down and close the door and report on all the events related to the murder of my Father Jack—he will describe the guy's past record, weapon used, and how they caught him. First, though, I will hug my father and hold him the way Mary held Jesus after the crucifixion, because Dad will be in tears and will need to know how much we all love him.

I don't need to tell anybody at school. All the nuns, Mother Perennial, Sister Hortense, the lay teachers, and even the school janitor stop me in the hallway and clasp my hands.

"We were looking forward to Father Conlon's visit. We're praying for your family during this time of tragedy."

"Yes," I say, trying to hold back sharp tears.

• • •

I hear that word "tragedy," which I learned from Gramma Molly, and think of how Dad writes a letter to her every Sunday at approximately 7:30 P.M. On every fourth Sunday, he calls up Gramma Molly on the pink telephone. We kids line up and wait for our turn to talk to her. It is like preparing for confession when you can't think of any sins to say. I am always the last in line. With Gramma Molly, I don't have to talk too much, just listen.

"Hello, dearie." She always starts out that way. "Have you been good to your parents?" I listen to her dancing brogue.

"Yes, Gramma."

"And have you been good for your gramma?"

"Yes, Gramma."

"Well, it was nice to see you in Cally-fornia."

I want to tell her that seems like so long ago. "Yes, Gramma. Maybe someday, when I get older, I can come again to New York."

"Yes, dearie."

Joey is sitting at the kitchen table. He points to his chest, saying, "Me, me." He wants to have a turn to hold the phone too, which is what he does, just holds the phone and says hello over and again.

"Gramma, would you like to say hello to Joey?"

There is silence on the other end.

"It's nice to hear your voice, dearie. Now, would you get me your father?"

Joey keeps pointing to his chest, pleading with his eyes.

"You wanna say hi to Joey first?"

Silence. Then she says the same words, every time, her voice sad and fierce:

"Such a shame it is, a tragedy."

•   •   •

On Wednesday night, Mom rouses me from my sleep at eleven o'clock, saying it is time to load up in our station wagon.

"Where are we going?"

"LAX. Daddy's on his way home."

Julie and John jump in the back of the station wagon with pillows and blankets, and within minutes after we leave, they are back asleep. I sit in the backseat next to Joey. I buckle his seat belt and place Gramma's beige blanket over his legs, telling him he can rest his head on my lap. I hold his hand all the way to the airport, watching the cars on the freeway sending sheer light into the night air.

Mom drives as fast as she can without getting stopped by a policeman. When she turns off on Century Boulevard, she glances back at me, seeing me wide awake.

"When Daddy arrives, he will be very, very sad and very tired. So just let him be quiet if he needs to be."

I look at Mom. I already know this. Dad will be very sad and very quiet, and I should save all my questions for a later time.

When we arrive at the American Airlines terminal, Dad in his black fedora is already standing outside under nervous yellow lights, smoking a cigarette. He chats with a Chinese man who is trying to sweep up the sidewalk with a metal contraption. Dad turns as we pull up. I want to bolt out and hug him, but I remain still, covert, not even waving from the backseat. Dad turns back to the sweeper, starts chattering again as the Chinese man smiles, says something back to Dad, and bows, then takes his sweeper inside the terminal. Mom says Dad learned a little Mandarin in the war—I wonder why Dad must speak his few words in the oddest moments.

Mom turns off the motor and we wait for Dad to come to our car, but he is so slow. He takes two long drags on the cigarette before throwing it in the gutter. Mom gets out of the car to greet him. I see their torsos—Mom in her bathrobe and Dad in his FBI jacket—touch as Mom kisses Dad's cheek for longer than I can ever remember.

I nudge Joey's shoulder. "Daddy's home."

Dad returns to the curb, takes off his hat, and bends down to pick up a box tied with twine. His arms look heavy and the hairs on his balding head spread this way and that. He lays the box in the front seat, glances back at all of us, his eyes locking into Joey's. I wait for Dad's eyes to lock into mine so he can see how much I've been worrying about him, but he just looks at Joey, reaching back to cover him with the beige blanket before sitting down as Mom starts the motor.

Dad? I want to say. *Dad?*

Dad is very sad. Dad is very quiet.

Silence takes on needles. It infiltrates the car, poking like a worm into an apple. Julie, John, and Joey fall asleep. I stare at the back of my dad's head the whole way home. He has eight horizontal wrinkles, deep grooves, at the back of his neck. I lean forward and smell the tweed and tobacco stench of his jacket. I open my mouth to let air out, even though it is my voice desperate to escape, like a criminal. I close my eyes, dreaming Dad senses me right behind him, that he detects my breath and that he is silently telling me through the airwaves that he is okay and everything is going to be okay and I should rest and go to sleep, and be patient.

• • •

I am very patient. For days and days, Dad does not say one word about Father Jack. Not one word about the murder. Nothing about what happened in Queens, New York, on Mother's Day.

Finally, he walks into the living room and stops in his tracks, looks at me sitting on the piano bench as I play so loud "Carry Me Back to Old Virginny." I play that song loud because I know it's one he likes. Once, long before Father Jack was killed, Dad walked in and sang a few lyrics as I played, then walked out. He's never done that since.

My foot falls on the soft pedal.

"Hi, Dad."

He just stares at me, switches his jaw from one side to the other with a wild look, and tightens his lips.

I know he is not going to sing.

"Why did you leave the bathroom faucet running? What do you think I—"

I stare back at the whites of his eyes that are now yellow as he turns around and walks out.

The next evening he grabs John by the hair, and I scream inside watching Dad drag John into his bedroom like a caveman almost on his knees. I run behind them, wanting to know what is so horrible that John must be dragged, yelling in tears.

Dad's face is red as fire, a cigarette in his one palm. He lets go of John, who shakes underneath streaming tears.

"Look at your clothes hanging out of your dresser—fold your clothes and shut your drawer the proper way." Dad walks away murmuring, "I've never seen a house like this in all my life."

Dad is very sad. Dad is very quiet.

Roast beef, pork chops, ham patties, lamb, potatoes, macaroni, fish sticks, beets, creamed corn, carrots, spinach, sweet potatoes, apple pie, cherry pie, homemade chocolate cake. Everything Mom cooks Dad stares at as if the food is the moon. He says nothing to Mom, not even saying anything to make her cry. She asks no questions, but is sure to look us kids in the eyes to tell us everything is going to be okay. Out of respect, we learn to listen to the sound of our mouths chewing food, slow.

Mom wipes off Joey's mouth with a wet paper towel. When Joey's hands are clean, he reaches out for Dad.

"Hi, Dad-ee." Joey gulps.

Dad swallows his roast beef like it is Jesus Christ on a Communion host going down his pipes. He sets down his fork, takes

Joey's hand, and smiles, strict, just the way a good FBI agent would.

"Hi, Joe." Their hands are like a bridge. Dad's are five times the size of Joe's. Still, Joey's hand looks the strongest. Finally, Dad lets go, and even though we are still eating, he pushes back from the table, stands rocking back and forth on his heels, and addresses Joey.

"You want to go to Thrifty's for an ice cream after dinner?"

Mom gives Dad her look like can't he see Joey is still eating roast beef and potatoes and besides maybe he shouldn't leave the dinner table like that.

Joey drops his fork, his eyes bulging blue. "Cream?"

"After dinner. Now, have some vegetables." Mom squeezes more ketchup on Joey's plate, enticing him to keep eating.

After dinner, I tag along with Dad and Joey. I don't ask. I just climb into the backseat. Maybe "ice cream" is the code for Dad finally telling me about Father Jack.

From the backseat, I watch him keep his head perfectly still, his eyes roving to the rearview mirror. His stare is hard, like plaster of paris. He turns to Joey, sitting next to him in the passenger seat.

"Joey, what kind of ice cream would you like?" Dad switches his eyes, ignoring Mr. Flanigan, who waves from his car as we pass by, as if Dad is having a more important conversation. I don't know why Dad asks this question. He knows Joey says chocolate every time.

"Chock, chock!" Joey rubs his hands together.

I stare at Dad's thin lips in the rearview. I wait for his eyes to find me, his mouth to open, move to the right then the left, to tell me about the code, about Father Jack, about the sadness. I wait for him to tell me what I should know, now that I am soon to be an adult, graduating from St. Bede in only two days.

We stand before the ice cream counter at Thrifty's, the sound of coins tinkling in Dad's pocket. His voice is as soft as that Irish tune "Too-ra-loo-ra-loo-ral."

"You can get a double scoop if you like."

I peer through the clear glass. I look past my own reflection, down into the wide containers of ice cream, so many colors, like the tide pools at Laguna Beach, where you can stand forever staring at pink starfish, coral, green anemones, as the waves rush to your ankles, leaving traces of salty froth behind.

"No, a single is okay." I speak in something other than code.

•   •   •

Father McKinley solemnly officiates at the St. Bede graduation ceremony, casting fresh incense throughout the church. I breathe it in, sitting in the front church pew in my white dress with small blue roses, the one I wore to dance with Richard Plomb and all the other boys I will never see again. I look at the spot on the altar where Father Jack would have stood to give our graduation speech. It is empty, except for a bouquet of white roses in his place. I think of life, how you never know when it's going to end, how it can end just like that, with a gunshot, and you are dead, and having connections to the FBI or being an agent doesn't mean anything, after all. Maybe it just makes things worse.

After the ceremony, I take out my log. I have not touched it since Dad got home from New York. I turn to the very last page, the one where I wrote about Father Jack. I cut out that page, lay it flat in my new spiral notebook featuring a cover of angelfish swimming freely. I Scotch tape it down, sign my name below, and the date.

I start to tear out the rest of the pages in my FBI log, one by one, shredding them into pieces, like Joey with the *Los Angeles*

Times, then toss them into my trash can. I close the empty book for good.

The day is so humid, crickets come out early, not in the evening like they are supposed to. They sound like a hundred lawn mowers cranked and running at high speed. Outside, Dad hangs up a load of wet towels on the clothesline. He snaps wooden clothespins, one after another. A cigarette hangs from his lower lip. On a day like today, a cigarette should explode, I think, fumes triggering flames in this heavy air.

"What are you doing?" he asks as I walk past him, my log tucked under my arm.

"Nothing." My lips are shut tighter than his.

I am like an angel kite, going step by step, still dreaming of flying a million miles an hour—so eager to fly but never lifting off. I stop near Dad, feel knives in my throat, trying to carve out my voice.

"I miss Father Jack. Do you, Dad?"

His eyes snap back to release another clothespin.

"You always told us to play it smart—but look at where it gets us. What good is—"

Another click of the clothespin.

And another.

I walk past Dad and the clothesline, unable to finish my sentence, and reach for the garbage can. I lift the metal lid and toss in my FBI log. It lands between cut grass and empty milk cartons. I throw the lid back on, my hand rushing to my mouth because my lips are shaking like mad.

Dad pulls a towel taut, its sound shrieking in my ears. He looks at the trash can, its lid hanging half off.

"Would you mind putting that back correctly?"

He reaches for the next wet towel, his cigarette sizzling as it touches the damp cloth. My shoulders drop. My mouth opens.

Nothing comes out except for a silent scream. Blood leaves my body, taking oxygen so I can't breathe, so I have to hold on to my waist to keep myself standing. I am dying right there before my father, and he does not see me, does not see how I am dying.

"I would appreciate if you would do things properly so I don't always have to follow and correct them."

I nod, like of course, of course, like of course I should place the trash can lid perfectly. I take the metal lid. It is like helium in my hand. I raise it higher, higher, oxygen slowly creeping back into my arteries and veins and muscles. I close my eyes, raise the metal lid even higher, then in a downward thrust smack it down—loud enough to make all the sheep in Ireland scamper.

Dad wipes sweat off his neck, the sweat culled in the palm of his hand. He takes out his cigarette, opens his mouth, but this time I get to the words first.

"Why—don't—you—just—tell—us—Dad?"

He lifts his chin, as if I am about to tell him something he doesn't himself already know.

"Tell—you—about—what?"

His high cheekbones freeze, and for the first time, I see it— the wild animal in his eyes boring through, something wrecked, in pain all over. The animal is like a ghost caught in a well for centuries, its cry a soundless wail clenched so deep that it shakes you to the bone.

I back away, one step, two, three, nodding as I do, as if to say *I see you, Dad—and I am so, so sorry.* I turn, leave him standing there. I go to my bedroom and pull my door shut, and tears stain my cold pillow the rest of the afternoon, uninterrupted.

Practicing the immigrant's lines with fire in my heart.

chapter 17

I have been cast in the play *Twelve Angry Women,* by Mr. Schlatter, the drama teacher at Arbor Junior High. I play the part of juror number eleven, the immigrant, even though I am not sure what country I come from. Each day my accent changes. One day it's German, the next Swedish. One day I tried to do Italian, but it came out Irish.

Juror number eleven sits on the jury to determine the fate of a young man accused of murder. The play is quite tense—we have to wrestle with our emotions, wade through all the conflicting evidence, and try to obtain the truth. According to the script, the killing takes place just as an El train in New York City zooms by, its rattle clouding the details of the actual murder. The play does not explore matters like how law enforcement caught the accused and all that—but I don't care about such things anymore.

When it is my turn to recite my lines, I stand, walk around to the other side of the juror table, and land right in front of the audience—the area called the forestage. I look up into the spotlights, take a breath, and begin a small speech about how lucky we all are to live in this country. In my speech, I remind the jurors, and the audience, that not all countries can boast of the liberties in America, that in some places you are persecuted for expressing your opinion, and that we should never take our freedom to speak for granted. This means we jurors must work from our hearts as we investigate this accusation of murder.

Several of the jurors don't get along, however; some have clashing personalities and conflicting beliefs. For example, juror number three, played by Gretal Heisecker, pounds the jury table with such fury that she intimidates all the others. She tosses her arms around as if nobody will stop her from getting the accused guy convicted. She is opposed by juror number eight, played by Pamela Paulson, who walks with excellent posture and speaks with grit. Pamela has tons of lines to memorize. She plays the knight in shining armor, fighting with passion and logic, questioning the truth of the accusation. Me, I am mostly silent as the immigrant juror, with my few lines, but I get to watch the story unfold until it's my turn to speak.

• • •

The spotlights on opening night make the stage feel hot as a furnace. Sweat fills every pore on my face. I drink so much water my stomach sticks out and snaps open the zipper on my plaid skirt, which used to be Mom's. I keep my skirt zipper fastened with a safety pin, which I hope no one in the audience will notice when I stand up. My hair is tied back in a bun, and the clod of brown makeup on my face makes my character look older, more mature, even though Mr. Schlatter says I'm mature beyond my years. My shoes have thick straps, and my shawl is of black crochet. I think of my juror number eleven as a Gramma Molly who would have made her own shawl. That's how I get into character. I imagine escaping starvation, sailing rough Atlantic seas, then spotting the Statue of Liberty in New York Harbor, just like Gramma Molly did.

As I prepare to give my speech, I imagine looking right into Gramma's heart, seeing the blue breath of ghosts. I hear the tick of her clock, smell the white votive candle, taste the rain blowing across a distant, desolate land. That's when I feel the ghosts go down my own spine, speaking in tongues, no brogues, no speaking in silence, hurtling, landing here, now, begging for release.

I remember the time Gramma was spreading butter all over her toast, dipping it in coffee, the butter spilling like oil. I told Gramma someday I'd like to go to Ireland and do farm chores. I waited for her to say that was a wonderful idea, for her to tell me stories about growing up with animals and so many brothers and sisters. All she did, though, was chew.

"Someday I would like to go to Ireland and learn how to milk a cow," I repeated as Gramma slipped into her silent stare, her eyes getting misty.

"Like I said, Gramma, I'd love to milk a cow in—"

"Enough talking about cows. Do you hear me?" Her eyes turned red.

"But, Gramma, don't you see? I am talking about *Ireland*!"

Her fork flew down with a thrust. "Ireland's a damn poverty-stricken, godforsaken country! I'll be hearing nothing more—do you understand?"

When jurors number three and five cue me with their brawl, I take a deep breath because I know I must remember to project my voice, and do what Mr. Schlatter told me: "Say your lines fierce from your heart, as if they're the most important words in the world." When I hear my cue, I push myself up, walk with thick, slow legs, my hands folded tight, as if holding a rosary, and open my immigrant's mouth. I try not to pay attention to the sound of my voice—the voice of juror number eleven—though I can't help but think it is lovely, especially with the accent, and even if I didn't have an accent, my voice would still sound lovely. My lines are beautiful. They roll off my tongue like sweet hay, as if I have been waiting my entire life to say them:

"Please. I would like to say something here. I have always thought that a person was entitled to have unpopular opinions in this country. That is the reason why I came here. I wanted to have the right to disagree."

I am so happy that Mr. Schlatter no longer has to roar *Volume!* from the back of the school auditorium, as he did during weeks of rehearsals. I think that maybe, for once, my voice carries so strong that the entire audience hears me, so absorbed, as they secretly wonder just who I am.

When I finish my first big set of lines, I hold my hand over my chest and lower my head, feeling as if I've thrown a humble shell into the hungry ocean, sensing nervous excitement from the black cavern of space, which is the audience.

The lights fade to black, then brighten for the beginning of act three, when all the jurors' tempers are pitchfork-hot and flaring. I stand up, shuffle to the forestage, to that special spotlight reflecting the moon on my face. I tilt my head, gesture, my knees calm. I look up to the flag in our jury room and draw a long breath for my final inspired lines:

"We have a responsibility. This is a remarkable thing about democracy. That we are—what is the word?—ah, notified! That we are notified by mail to come down to this place—and decide on the guilt or innocence of a person; of a man or woman we have not known before. We have nothing to gain or lose by our verdict. This is one of the reasons why we are strong. We should not make it a personal thing."

For a moment, I truly believe I am this immigrant. That I am new to some country, new to the United States, new to the land of the speaking, to the land where you get to have a voice. I close my eyes and huddle back to my wooden seat, a voice inside rising and saying softly, *I am onstage. I am in a play. My voice matters.*

• • •

A voice.

I sing this, to myself.

I have a voice.

I sing it as I ride my bike to Arbor Junior High School; and when I come home at the end of the day and see Joey get out of the special school bus, I say, "I have a voice, Joey," and he gives me a hug. I look at him and tell him that he has a voice too, but we just can't hear it yet. "Yeah, sure," he says, and points toward the front door because he would like his afternoon juice, as he knows I won't give him Coke.

Dear Father, I have a voice.

I sing this the same way Neil Diamond sings "Dear Father, We dream . . . we dream." This is a song from the *Jonathan Livingston Seagull* sound track, and for the first three weeks of drama class, we listened to that song almost every day during fifth period, which is just before physical education where the girls shave their legs in the locker room showers except for me, and also before sewing with Mrs. Planer, who seems thrilled that I am an expert with zippers.

I bet Mr. Schlatter could be directing movies in Hollywood and maybe make a million dollars and drive a fancy sports car, but I am glad he is here with us in the public schools. Mr. Schlatter's blue eyes make a beach, inviting us to comb magical sands. His class feels like a place from Camelot, some place mystical, where your imagination counts, where it can soar, so different than most of the other classes. Mr. Schlatter, whose jackets always seem a couple sizes too small, tells us we can learn a lot from *Jonathan Livingston Seagull,* especially the importance of holding on to our dreams.

Tom Oates, who is the major fox in our school, sits behind me and mutters, "Yeah, right, let's learn from a bird." But I try to ignore Tom, even though he is so cute with his blond hair to his shoulders.

"Jonathan Livingston Seagull was someone who had a dream," Mr. Schlatter says, raising his hands as if there actually were a seagull resting in his palm. "Jonathan saw possibilities beyond the limits set by his fellow birds. He knew he could fly more beautifully than any bird had ever flown before, if he would just challenge himself to soar into higher skies, to take the risk and follow his heart."

Mr. Schlatter, whose voice can unwind, then rev as fast as a high-pitched whirligig, walks over to the cabinet by the classroom door and turns on the record player. He shuts the door to the outside lawn, slightly dims the light in the classroom, closing the blinds just a tad, so we can understand better what he is trying to say.

"You can close your eyes if you want, and let yourself imagine . . ."

A lot of the other students look dazed, like they don't know what he is talking about, or they roll their eyes as if they'd rather be out smoking or doing bike flips or anything but sitting in a classroom with a freakish teacher playing the sound track from *Jonathan Livingston Seagull*. But not me. I close my eyes and think to myself that I love drama class. That I love the lyrics and Neil Diamond's voice and the pacing drums and fleeting violins, where the music sings about reaching for dreams. By the second week of class, I buy a silver Jonathan pendant, and I wear it every day.

• • •

Drama class. That is how it all started, listening to the music, then talking about the meaning of drama, techniques of acting, and all that. Sitting in the classroom the first three weeks, I think if this is what drama is, I'll take it. But something tells me we won't be sitting and just listening for long. Something tells me that Mom did not place me in the public schools, and specifically in Mr. Schlatter's drama class, to stay quiet.

One month into the fall term, our teacher announces our first assignment.

"Now it is time for all of you to stand up where I am." I look at his feet and glance around to the thirty of us students in jeans and tie-back blouses and ponytails, and I think no way am I going to stand up where Mr. Schlatter is and speak to all these faces.

"What I'd like for you to do is memorize a small speech, a soliloquy. Remember, we discussed those last week. Or a part of a scene from a play would be fine. Memorize the lines and you'll have about ten minutes or so up here to perform your work. And we'll do this, well, let's see—how about starting ten days from today? We'll keep going until we get everyone up here. Sound good?"

My stomach falls to my feet, and for a second, I want to grab my angelfish spiral notebook and run back to St. Bede and into Sister Hortense's class, where I can sit happily like a statue, under the protection of the Virgin Mary. I think to myself, *How could Mom send me here, to this public school, where we have to get in front of an entire class and perform alone?*

"And don't forget," Mr. Schlatter continues. "Gestures are going to be just as important as your voice when you perform. So be thinking of how movement of your head, your arms, your legs, can support your words."

Gestures? I am hoping the next time I go into Arbor cafeteria for my hamburger that I find the mustard laced with drugs, and that I will have such a serious mental reaction that I will be put in an insane asylum for two months.

Day by day my stomach anxiety increases. I can feel ladders and ladders of nervous saliva building, so that when it comes my turn to perform, I know I'll just vomit. I thank God Tom Oates sits behind me instead of in front, where Peter Norden once was stationed.

Just in case I keep it down, though, I figure I better go to the library and find something to memorize. I look at some plays by Shakespeare and think there's no way I can memorize that ancient type of language. Then I look at some Greek plays like *Antigone* and I don't feel up to that task either. I think maybe I can just recite some of the lyrics from the *Jonathan Livingston Seagull* sound track, but then I know my classmates will yawn, because they are tired of him. Then I think I can find some passage from one of the books on our living room shelf.

I sit down one afternoon and remove practically every title, looking for one that grabs me. *Two from Galilee. Mary of Nazareth. How Far to Bethlehem. I'm OK, You're OK.* Since I have to find a dramatic performance, I don't think any of these will work. So I think since we're all Americans, I can recite something patriotic, like my father will sometimes say out of the blue, "Four score and . . . ," although I forget the rest of that speech.

For days, stretching into a week, I still can't find what I will memorize, and each fifth period in Drama, I pray that Mr. Schlatter will not call on me to perform.

"All right, who's next?" He scans the quiet room, looking for a volunteer.

I am the queen of keeping my eyes to my feet. So I hold my breath, look at my shoes, notice the weave of the brown shoelaces, and then fall into an unblinking trance, staring at my unblemished Hush Puppies in such a holy manner that no teacher would dare interrupt the vision this student must truly be having. Meanwhile I am sitting in my own damp sweat. Some voice tells me I better find my piece. I better get it memorized. I better do it now. Sooner or later, I won't be able to look at my feet for even one second.

My day arrives the last week of October, just the time when Mr. Schlatter is about to begin casting for the upcoming school plays, which is something I won't have to worry about. Still, he catches my eye when he makes this announcement, and my cheeks rush immediately to fire.

Mr. Schlatter must know I am one of the few kids who crossed over from St. Bede. He must think I am uncharted territory, that perhaps I am like those religious types, with visions and ferocious prayers and statues and incense. Maybe he feels that I am different than all the publics, who are preoccupied by other things, although I've no clue what those might be.

"Maura. I believe it is your turn today . . ."

My look says to him *does it have to be?* Can't I just be the one student who gets to sit this assignment out? Then I try to remember how far away the nearest bathroom is, because all of a sudden I realize I really have to go.

I look over to the phonograph. The *Jonathan Livingston Seagull* record is tucked back into its jacket and lies on its side, almost as if it is tired of all this exposure to public school kids and it would just like a little break, please, and besides, isn't it someone else's turn to perform and inspire?

"Yes, I guess so." I pull my perspiring body out from my desk and smile, because that is something Mom has taught me to do whenever I feel out of place. She has never taught me this in a formal lesson, but I've watched her in these prickly situations and I think somehow you can prevail if you just act like you have waited your whole life to be in this predicament.

Besides, I think, if I smile, everybody will think I am calm. And maybe somebody besides Mr. Schlatter will smile back at me. But no such luck. The rest of the kids, Annette LeBarre, Liza Reynolds, Tom Oates, Barry Rodgers, Fred Martinez, and the others, hold faces slumped into their hands, and all of them look like they are ready to go home. So I decide to look out the window and out to the sky, as if I'm inspired by a cloud. And when I do this, I imagine I see Jonathan soaring out there up high, and I forget about my audience. I clear my throat.

Silence. The soft purring of the overhead lights. A tractor off in the distance cutting grass on the football field. There are sounds. My voice creeps up somewhere amid all this. The words carefully placed inside flow out now like syrup, and something feels sweet all over. I feel I am speaking to someone whom I've never met, to someone who listens, someone with ears everywhere, almost like I am taking a bath in ears, and my voice is okay and not so nervous. It is almost like my voice isn't coming from myself, but it is, because when twelve minutes are up, I look to my gesturing hands, and look to the kids in the class, then over to Mr. Schlatter, who has tears streaming down his cheeks. I think it must have been me talking, for I am the only one standing up here.

Then I hear a gasp. Did I? I didn't see anyone gasp. Nobody gasps in my classroom, that is only something you do in a movie theater, like when we watched Vincent Price in *House of Wax* and we spent the entire movie ignoring our popcorn because we could not stop gasping.

The class applauds just like they do when everyone is finished with their performance, but this time Mr. Schlatter jumps from his seat and marches directly toward me at the front of the classroom. Am I supposed to sit down? I wonder. Is he going to tell me my gestures were awkward? Why does he take my hand like he is going to shake it, and why are his cheeks wet?

"That piece was lovely . . . lovely." He looks down into my face with his blue-lagoon eyes and I think to myself, *My piece was lovely. It was?*

"The words went straight to the heart. I've never heard this selection before. You forgot to tell the class where it came from." He looks deeper into my eyes, deeper than anybody ever has in my entire life, as if he is finding something that's trying desperately to get out.

"Where did you find this piece, Maura Conlon?"

I look out the window again and bite the edge of my lip. Before I can think to answer his question, I try to remember what it was that was so lovely and what it was that went straight to the heart. It was just a piece about wondering about the meaning of life, wondering why we are put on this earth, wondering if heaven really is a place out there and couldn't heaven really just be here on this planet, and that if we truly learned how to love one another, each day we could feel joy, here, in our human lives.

"I'm sorry, Mr. Schlatter. But I couldn't find any speech or monologue or soliloquy I liked." I am hoping he will not be angered to find out that I wrote the piece myself.

So I tell him I wrote the piece, that I wrote it four months ago. I don't tell him that I wrote it right after Father Jack was murdered, because he does not know Father Jack, or that I wrote the piece less than one month after winning the Most Quiet Girl award, because Mr. Schlatter doesn't know that either—although I'm sure he wouldn't be so surprised.

Mr. Schlatter shakes his head, then scratches it.

"Say that again. You *wrote this piece?*" He says those words very slowly so he's sure I understand his question.

I look at him and don't say a word. I let my eyes tell him. My eyes have always told things best anyhow. I shake my head yes, yes, I wrote the piece.

That day I never attend sixth-period physical education or seventh-period sewing. Mr. Schlatter asks the principal for permission to take me out of my afternoon classes so I can repeat my performance for the rest of the drama students that day.

I appear the opening night of *Twelve Angry Women* seven weeks after my nervous speech in drama class. I feel my hunger for more lines, more lines to fill my mouth like grapes. I want to stand on the stage forever and speak the words of the immigrant, juror number eleven. I want to perform the words that inspire the lonely person in the audience who I know is just like me. I have always been the lonely person in the audience.

Until now.

My red sizzler dress made of 100 percent polyester.

chapter 18

It's not for sure, but I think I'm in love with Marco Scarpelli. It was never my intent to feel this weird feeling, but there he is in church, walking up to Communion with those shoulders, his swimmer's hair battened down to his head, and his big eyes lovely like a puppy's. There I sit in the pew, wearing my red and white polka-dot sizzler dress with the matching undershorts, trying to look disinterested, gazing in the other direction like I do every Sunday.

"Hallelujah. Amen." That's what the whole congregation sings, but I pay no attention as Father McKinley bows before the wall where the brown crucifix holding Jesus hangs. I just watch Marco until the services come to an end, which is always way too soon. I am already counting the days until the next time.

The Sunday I wear my sizzler dress, I walk out of church heading toward Jacaranda Boulevard, where Dad and Joey are to pick me up. I see a small daisy growing from a crack in the pavement and bend down to pick it, nearly shrieking when I see Father McKinley's purple face as I come up again.

"And whose daughter might you be?"

I jump because I figured by now, Father McKinley would be back in the rectory, sitting down for a warm meal prepared by the priests' housekeeper, but here he is, three inches away, breathing fumes down my neck. I'm well aware Father McKinley knows whose daughter I am, but that's not the point of his question. Still, I look at him, pursing my lips.

"Who is your mother?" he repeats, his voice like sandpaper.

"Mary Conlon—that's who my mother is." And proud of it, I want to say to Father McKinley, whose pointy finger emerges from a black pocket.

"She should be ashamed."

I step away, watching the veins bulge in his neck as he comes closer.

"She should be ashamed for letting you out wearing *that*." He points to my sizzler dress, which shows more leg than he is used to seeing at church. "I never want to see that, er, sinful lack of clothing again in my parish, do you understand?" I stand still, waiting for Father McKinley to call me a *haratick*.

I glance down to the dress that Mom bought me as a surprise for my birthday. She said the dress could be a little longer, but with its matching shorts I could still sit like a lady. I wear it each time we have company for dinner and no one has ever complained. Sometimes I slip it on when I am alone in my room, modeling before myself in the mirror.

I fold my arms, refusing to nod and agree with the pastor because this is my special gift and it is the first red dress I've ever had, and I love how it falls so flatly down my body. So I say nothing to him, just act like a shocked little animal, like a squirrel that's scurried in front of a car and is too dumbfounded to talk, or run this way or that.

"I am assured you shall sin no more—"

Just as Father McKinley's stomach begins to growl and he turns, then walks away, I see Marco Scarpelli drive by seated in his parents' sleek convertible, leaning to change a tape in the deck. I want to wave, to see if Marco noticed my red sizzler dress, which he may never have the chance to see again while Father McKinley is still the pastor. But I don't. I just walk down the block, find Joey and Dad sitting in the car with the motor running.

• • •

The following Sunday I wear a maxiskirt that I made in sewing class. It features eight panels, each one of a different, wild fabric—red poppies on one panel, yellow and orange firecrackers on another, green and pink stars on another. It swirls like mad and you just can't miss it. I made a matching jacket with lemon-yellow lining and a brimmed hat as well. I wear my new outfit to the evening services. Anyone who feels tired, they can just look at me for a boost, including Father McKinley.

I sit and search all the rows of the congregation, waiting for the reflection bouncing off the lights onto Marco's bronze hair, and finally I spot him. This time he wears a white pullover sweater that makes his tan look deeper than ever. The choir sings, and soon we join in with "Kumbaya," which is the musical cue for Communion. I am at least ten rows behind Marco and must wait in my seat for my turn.

Marco Scarpelli goes up to receive the host from Father McKinley, turns around, his body swaggering from shoulder to shoulder back down the aisle. I lean to the left to get a better view of him, brush my walnut-colored hair behind my shoulder, and smell the patchouli rising from my skin. I know I should be concentrating on "Kumbaya, my Lord, Kumbaya," but all I can do is listen to my heart change beats as Marco walks down the center aisle, approaching closer, then closer, his pretty, puffy swimmer lips together so nicely he could almost be whistling to me.

Right when he nears my position, I turn my glance away, admiring the swirls of my eight-panel skirt that is almost as bright as Marco's hair. I wonder if he peeks at me sitting in pew number eighteen. I wonder if he notices my soft cheeks. This is love, I say to myself, when someone sneaks in a glance.

His shoulders linger on, but Marco Scarpelli does not look at me this time. Maybe he will when I see him in a few short days, at CCD. This is the Confraternity for Christian Doctrine—a religious education class held every two weeks for us publics. I would like to know what it feels like to look into his green eyes and watch him look into mine. I think it will be like standing on top of a mountain in Switzerland, surrounded by orange and red and yellow wildflowers, smelling the ham and cheese sandwiches from the picnic basket that rests on the gingham blanket spread out like a puddle of warm rain in spring.

•   •   •

At night when I go to sleep, I don't bother saying prayers anymore—well, I say them very fast like *please God protect our entire family*. Then I play my new album, *Angel Clare*. As I listen to Art Garfunkel, who's got the purest voice in the world, my mind flies off to dream of Marco, Marco, Marco. I jump up from bed, open my heavy curtains to let in light from the streetlamp, pretending it is gilded fireflies streaming from the moon. I light three candles situated on top of the old console in the corner. When Art Garfunkel is finished, I put on *Bread* and listen to David Gates sing so gently how he'd do anything to hold his sweetheart just one more time.

That song, "Everything I Own," just mesmerizes me until someone tells me it's really about the singer's wife or girlfriend who died. Sometimes I get tired of hearing about tragedy, but still, that is the last song I play each night when I lie in bed with the silver light flooding my corner bedroom on Margaret Rae Drive. I stare at the flicker of the orange flame, pull the pillowcase closer to my lips, and wonder if Marco Scarpelli will ever know I am alive.

The night of our religious education class, I do the dishes after our stew dinner. The dishes are easy because everyone has cleaned their plates—there was so much gravy, thank God, to wash down the carrots and potatoes and the beef, loaded with huge chunks of lard.

I get dressed for class, button up my red shirt with the two pointed darts, and wonder where I left my blue sweater. At 7 P.M., Dad, who is my ride for the evening, knocks on my bedroom door and asks if I am ready to go.

"Three more minutes," I call out, brushing my hair one more time so I get that little flip on the bottom.

I find my blue sweater draped over the sewing machine in the family room. It rests against the wall Mom has dedicated to Father Jack. I pull my arms through the sleeves as I stare at his photograph, remembering the day Mom repeated over and again, "I can't take Daddy's silence anymore!" She cleared the dining room table and spent two days assembling a dozen pictures and newspaper clippings about Father Jack's life. She wrote *No Man Is an Island* on felt, then hung the frame opposite the letters from J. Edgar Hoover. As far as I can tell, Dad's never sneaked a glance.

"Mom, see you later." I dash by as she gets Joey ready for his shower.

"Have fun!" She always says this. It doesn't matter where I am going, even if it's to religion class. I wonder if she knows that I'll have loads of fun because I am going to see Marco Scarpelli and not because I will be discussing Catholic dogma. I smell my perfume. I hope Marco Scarpelli will notice it as I walk so free and easy into McKinley Hall, which always smells like the previous night's sweaty basketball game.

As I leave the house and go into the dark night, I see Dad standing in the middle of the driveway. I wonder why he hasn't already rolled the car backward, like he usually does. His head is bent down to his chest and he is making some noise I've never heard before—stiff, sharp, like a horse who's galloped too fast uphill. I run out.

"Dad?"

He is coughing, in between gasps, almost choking, then he coughs, wheezes again, like he can't find air to tell me what is wrong. He throws his head up, looking to breathe, but he can't.

I reach out and hold his arm, which is always so full of muscles, but now his skin is wet, and I say, "Hold on, Dad. Relax. Breathe, breathe. *Breathe!*"

His choking goes hoarse and I repeat, "Dad, please—breathe!" and he keeps trying and I do not know what else to do. And so I run back into the house and yell for Mom. "Help! Help! Dad can't breathe—something's wrong—he's choking!"

"Oh, God!"

Mom tears out of the house in her apron and I don't know if

I should chase her outside and help her save Dad or stay behind to supervise Joey, who sings *la la la* in the shower.

I look out the front door and see the shape of Mom wrapping her arms behind my father's chest and Dad tossing his head up, then down again. I run back to Joey, who calls out, "Ready! Ready!" and I tell him "I'll help you out of the shower in just a minute," and then I race back and see Mom's arm on Dad's back and now Dad finding something, some spot of air, some ounce of breath, as Mom yells, "Come on, Joe. Come on, Joe," as if her words will save him. "Come on—come on!" Mom's voice echoes from the driveway into the street, calling like an owl to the moon.

And then there is silence, and something releases. A few seconds like broken glass and then the crickets start roaring again, like they decided to resume just at this precise minute.

I push the screen door and walk out to my parents because now I think it is safe—that Dad will not die on our driveway tonight.

He stands still, conserving his energy, and Mom backs away to let him find deeper ground in his chest. I stand behind her, not knowing what to say.

"Are you okay?" I ask, my heart still caught in turbulence. "Is he okay?" I ask Mom, who turns around to tell me with her eyes that he is okay and it's his cigarettes that caused this choking spell.

Dad does not say anything. I think he is sad because he just choked on his own cigarette smoke. Or maybe he is embarrassed, or maybe I am embarrassed because I see that look on his face, that look that might have something to do with love. I give him a small hug, keeping my face grave, like that is the best way to show my father I care.

"Dad, maybe I shouldn't go up for class tonight. I can just stay home."

"Come on. Let's go. We're late," he says, a loud whisper, as he looks at the ground under me and Mom, a soft film wiping his eyes.

It has been a long time since I've thought about breath, how it comes in and goes out, like the tide. I wonder if the ocean ever thinks about its ebb and flow, or whether it keeps its mind on other things, like how many people are sailing on its skin that night or how full the moon will be.

In the car, Dad rolls his window all the way down and cool air rushes in. I wish I could smile and tell him I am glad he is alive, that he did not have to choke to death, that he is my father, and how I appreciate him driving me up to CCD. I don't smile, however, because doing that right after someone loses their breath is forbidden, even if your smile is just to hide your fear.

I remember the time I was ten years old, still sharing a room with Julie. It was almost midnight and I was awake, standing in blue light. Even though the vaporizer for her asthma was humming along, Julie was not in bed. I looked down the hallway, saw the bright light coming from my parents' bedroom. I sneaked down and peeked around the door frame. Mom was holding Julie, and Dad was breathing into her lips. Julie's face looked nearly blue.

I gasped, ran back to my bedroom to stare at the vaporizer steam spraying up like empty fireworks. All I could think was that this is not good, this is scary, what is wrong, how is Julie, what will we do, will it go away, this thing that takes her breath? I stood in my flannel pajamas, shivering with these thoughts.

An ambulance with its light flashing pulled into our driveway, its high beams stabbing my gaze from the bedroom window. It was quiet in the house except for the push of breaths, and

I didn't know what else to do except to stand, to hold the earth under my feet to stabilize it, and not allow it to take my sister away.

Dad came into my bedroom, a pair of pants pulled over his pajamas. He looked at me. I looked at him and thought as his fellow FBI agent that we could solve this together, even though I shook like a dog caught in a house fire. He told me they were taking Julie in the ambulance because her asthma was so bad she couldn't breathe. I already knew this, so I didn't say anything. No, I just smiled at Dad because I was so scared I didn't know what to do, smiled because I wanted Dad to see I would handle things at home, take care of everyone as he and Mom rushed Julie to the hospital.

As I stood there smiling, Dad gave me a twisted stare, like I was some slimy, middle-of-the-night criminal. He said, "How dare you smile at a time like this!" Then he turned and dashed off while I stood at the window crying so hard, watching the paramedics open the ambulance doors, wanting to tell Dad I was just trying to be brave, like him, as he held Julie in his arms, with Mom climbing into the ambulance that rolled out of the driveway and silently sped down Margaret Rae Drive.

I watch Dad's chest move in and out as he drives me to religious education class this dark night. I am in love, I realize, with breath. With breath, with the longing and the quaking of the lungs, with the ebb and flow called breath.

I lean over, kiss Dad's cheek. "I am glad you are okay."

He nods his head with just a trace.

I walk into McKinley Hall and find my seat and there is Marco Scarpelli, with his hair and a red sweatshirt, sitting two rows away. But tonight, even though I am in love with Marco Scarpelli, I think I do not want to look at him. I don't want to feel my heart race. I don't want to feel the lumpiness of my breath as I dream of touching his lips. I don't want to feel clammy when he walks past me, with my head staring down at my lace-up shoes.

I want to feel this thing called love, but tonight, most of all, I want to keep my head up and breathe.

Mom and Dad's courting days in New York.

chapter 19

These days I write tons of poems. Sometimes I speak them into the tape recorder I bought up at Parker Five and Dime. I have filled up two sixty-minute tapes so far. I don't listen to what I record. My voice can sound so, I don't know, searching. I decide I will listen to my tapes when I am eighty years old. For now, I just talk.

Conversation is what it's all about. This is what Mom says. Conversation. Communication. That is what life is all about. You have to tell someone how you feel or what you think and then listen as they do the same. You say this, they say that, back and forth like a tennis ball sailing over a net. If someone says something you don't understand, you pursue them for an explanation.

Mom says this at the dinner table. She signed up for an Assertiveness Training class at Magnolia Community College. I baby-sit Joey when she goes up on Wednesday evenings. At dinner now we are not allowed to stare at our plates and listen to ourselves chomping food anymore. We have to come to the table prepared with something to say. Since I talk so much on my tape recorder, I'm not always sure what to share with my family while we eat. Still, Mom is persistent.

Dad doesn't like Mom's new approach. I know this when Mom asks me to tell everybody dinner is ready, and so off I go, telling Julie and John, who play ball on the grass outside, grabbing Joey to get his hands washed, then looking for my father.

"Dad? Dad?"

My footsteps take me traveling in and out of four bedrooms, the bathrooms, the backyard. Finally, in the garage I hear the AM radio tuned to its permanent California Angels channel. I still wonder how he can listen to so many games and never want to play ball himself. I listen to AM as well, but at least I dance when I hear music like Stevie Wonder's "Living for the City" or Helen Reddy's "I am woman hear me roar, hear me knocking down the door," or something like that. Half the time I make up my own words when I dance.

"What do you want?" Dad's FBI shoes are nestled tight in his hands and he polishes the tops and sides, meticulously, like they could be the ruby slippers in *The Wizard of Oz*.

"Dinner's ready."

"Yeah, okay . . ."

Dad never comes in right away. Now that Mom is in Assertiveness Training, he comes to the table only after I've told him three times and everybody is already seated and has started eating and then, of course, we must stop because as soon as Dad arrives, Joey extends his hands.

"Grace, grace . . ." Joey likes saying grace even though he can't say the prayer. He just introduces it by saying *grace, grace,* but then Mom has to say the actual prayer as we all hold hands. No one else ever volunteers.

Dad sits down and immediately lifts his fork, bending his head low to the food. The rest of us wrestle in our seats because Mom's determined eyes shoot like flares to Dad, who sits across the table from her.

"Hello, Joe." You can tell she is warming him up.

Dad looks up, with innocent eyes like he's a schoolboy busy with his doodles. "Oh, hello . . ." Then he smartens up, lays his fork down, and puts out his hands. "Well"—he looks to all of us—"here I am."

Mom's eyes then circulate to us as we race to start chomping down our food. Our eyes fall to our plates, knowing she will give Dad a little more time to warm up, meanwhile calling on one of us to talk. I hope she does not speak to me. Thankfully, she returns to Dad, who eats without breathing, hoping to leave the table before Mom forces him to say another word.

"Joe, how was your day today?"

Even if Dad were not an FBI agent, I bet he still wouldn't say a thing, but since he is an agent, he always has an excuse to keep his mouth shut. His ears turn red and he coughs that cigarette cough from deep in his chest.

"Fine." He pushes the word out of his mouth as if it is the shape of a quarter moon.

Mom's cheeks steam up. "Fine, fine? That's it? I rack my brains making dinner and *fine* is all you can say?"

Dad looks up and gives her an evil eye as if she should be grateful, since *fine* is the nicest thing he's said at the dinner table in ages.

"All right, Mary." He rests both arms on the table, instead of one as he usually does. "What would you like me to say? Would you like me to recite the Gettysburg Address?"

Julie yells, "Yeah, yeah!"

Mom touches her hand, shushing her.

I take my first bite into my pork chop, which is lined with fat. I scoop out the soft potato from its baked skin, mashing it down on top of the pork chop. I hear cars outside make their required stop at a stop sign in front of the house, then speed on. Another stops with squeaky brakes, then drives on. When I hear the next car hit its brakes, I know too much silence has passed.

"So nothing is new at work?" Mom picks up her knife and makes an incision into her pork chop, looking at Dad with eyes that say it is not a difficult question. Dad's face is caught as if the stage curtain has gone up prematurely.

"Work was fine."

Mom lays her palm flat on the table, loud like the sound of a basketball passed to your gut. "You know, Joe, this way that you simply do not converse with anyone at the dinner table—is this really the example you wish to set for your children?"

All our mouths full of food dart toward Dad. Mom has said the "children" word to him, the word that gets Dad every time. No one should dare say anything negative that pits him against the *children*.

All of us, but mostly me because I am fourteen and understand these adult tensions, stare at Dad, wondering what he will do. Mom meanwhile sits, her brown almond eyes barely patient behind her blinking eyelashes. The timer on the dynamite stick ticks, ticking, ten, nine, eight, seven, six . . .

I eat my spinach and gulp and then look at Dad and hope just this one time he might come through. I could help him think of something, since I have been practicing with my tape recorder. I could tell him to say something like this:

My day was a busy one. I was up in the Los Angeles office all day, working on a special assignment—sabotage. You meet with an informant. He thinks you're gonna buy him lunch, you know—ham and cheese on rye—then you tell him you're not going to buy him lunch and then he retracts his position and excuses himself from the clandestine appointment. These sabotage cases can drive you batty!

And then Dad would be all set and Mom would be happy. He could stop talking because we all know we can't ask follow-up questions about *sabotage!* All Dad has to say is *sabotage, sabotage, sabotage* as he eats his cabbage, and we could sit there and just imagine him being an FBI agent, like we usually do.

Mom says another sentence including the word "children," and this sets Dad's eyes in motion, going round like ripples in water. He spoons in another mound of potatoes, then looks to all our faces, his eyes stopping at mine.

"The children are just fine, right?"

Everyone nods their heads in slow motion except for me.

I figure this is my time to become juror number eleven again, to become an immigrant and proclaim at the dinner table we should be grateful for all the freedom we have in our wonderful country, freedom to have conversation whenever you please and without fear of persecution.

"Well, Dad, other families, you know, they actually talk at the dinner table. I ate at Jill Sutherland's house, and Mrs. and Mr. Sutherland talked all the way through dinner and I could not get in a word, not that I had anything to say."

Mrs. and Mr. Sutherland also sit on the living room couch holding hands, but I don't want to overwhelm Mom or Dad with this information.

Mom looks at Dad with her Assertiveness Training glance, which means that she knows better now and she isn't going to take it anymore. Dad dodges her glance, throwing his at Joey, his jaw softening.

"Well, what do you think about that, Joey? How would you like to eat at someone's house and not be able to get a word in?"

Joey's mouth is full of roll with butter and he opens it so we can see the food he grinds. He then closes and opens his mouth like a fish. Dad asks the unanswerable questions—always to Joey.

"Dry, dry—" Joey points to his throat, which means he needs something to drink. Mom stands up. She gets more milk out of the refrigerator, places the blue and white carton on the table, pours Joey's milk, and sits back down.

"What about the *other* children? What would you like to ask *them*?" She looks at me and Julie and John, the other children, the children *other* than Joey, as if we have a special category all our own.

Mom's Assertiveness Training questions give Dad indigestion. Maybe this is why he leaves the table even earlier than before, so we don't have to watch him subdue the acid bubbles flaming up his throat. His head buckles, lowers to the chest, compressing air back down. His cheeks redden like apples and his gulps become thick, like Joey's. I know that indigestion is the first sign of a heart attack. I wonder if it's Mom's new approach or the cigarettes or some ghost that is the culprit.

"Dad, you want some water?" I get up and pour him water even though he waves his hand, saying no, that it's just a matter of time and he'll be over his indigestion. Still, his breathing seems irregular. I stop chewing. I can't bear the thought of Dad having a heart attack and dying right there in the kitchen. I can't bear the thought of being in the same room where Dad dies. I can't bear the thought of ever losing Dad. He coughs, his chest like a barrel, sweat leaking out his red pores.

"Excuse me!" I leave the table and go lock myself in the bath-room and pray if Dad is supposed to have a heart attack, he will have it when I am not there to watch him because I don't know CPR and I wouldn't be able to save him. I stand in the bathroom with its loud fan going and hang on to a perfectly folded towel and look at my small waist in the mirror, and my strong arms and my monster pimple I wish would disappear, until I think it is safe to return to the kitchen.

Dad has left the table and everyone else has disappeared too, except for Joey, who's already digging into his ice cream. I walk over and lean against the back of a dining room chair, wonder-ing if other kids my age have to ponder all the mysteries about their parents. I stare down at my bare feet, not sure which di-rection to go—to run into my room and talk into the tape recorder, or ride off on my bike, or sit in Dad's vacant chair and watch Mom stare into her coffee cup, orange at its rim from her lipstick.

I take a seat, lay my hands flat on the kitchen table, and start drumming my fingers.

Mom looks up. "What are you thinking?"

"Why did you and Dad get married?"

She hesitates, like she's rounding the corner on a thought, then takes a napkin, places it on Joey's lap. She looks back and studies my face, my shoulders, and then notices my hands. "You keeping those nails filed? There's nothing wrong, Maura, with becoming a woman."

I hide my nails against my palm and pretend I am in As-sertiveness Training class too.

"Why did you and Dad get married?"

She pushes away her cold Sanka, helps Joey wipe ice cream off his fingers, then leans forward to sip her coffee, placing the mug square to her plate. Her eyes are slow as resting water.

"Daddy had this dreamy way of looking at me. It was as if he worshiped the ground I walked upon."

I study her still face, imagining Dad with dreamy eyes, then think of all the Hollywood movie stars and how the leading man always throws down his jacket to prevent the leading lady from having to wade through a puddle. I can see Dad doing this with his jacket, sort of, if he was in the right mood, though his happy moods would hardly last long enough for Mom to get across a puddle.

"Was Dad so—I don't know—the way he is now, before you guys got married?"

"Hmmm."

Joey stands up. "Aw, babee," he says, making the sign for "love." He points to me. "You?"

"Yes, Joey." I sigh. "I love you too."

He smiles. "Okay—buh bye." He waves like some entertainer holding a straw hat, and heads to watch the loud television with the others.

Mom scoops up the crumbs on Joey's seat, folds them tight into a napkin, and drops it on her plate. She moves the milk carton to the left so there is nothing on the table between us, then takes her time before speaking again.

"When Daddy and I were engaged to be married, his moods were getting a little hard to handle." She hesitates, then goes on. "Even Nana, who was never one to say anything, was concerned."

She loosens the tie strap on her red apron, her shoulders slightly rounded. "Well, you see, I mentioned this to Daddy— this problem. I said maybe we should wait, postpone our wedding date, so we could figure things out. Maybe get some help." Mom leans to the right, looking past me to make sure no one is around.

I start picking at the threads from my denim shorts, tugging them, pulling the strings tight until they break.

"So, what happened?"

"Daddy started to cry when I said all that." Mom clears her throat. "I thought about it for a while, thought how with my looks and charm and all that, I could change him. I was naive back then, you see. You don't marry someone thinking you're going to change them."

I look at the Jell-O molds hanging above the sink, the pink telephone surrounded by the ripped Betty Crocker cookbook and a few framed Mother's Day cards, then watch her massage the handle on her mug, which reads *You're Number One,* that I bought for her last birthday. I don't like the idea of my parents almost never getting married. When I look up, Mom has recovered her usual smile. I lean from my seat and look out the sliding glass door at the sky, which has turned so dark so fast.

"So, Maura, what do you think?"

It's as if Mom wants me to say something so I don't forget the lesson she is teaching me.

"I don't know." I am uncomfortable with what to say next. I look at her and yawn, even though I am not tired, and start counting the hairs on my arm.

She takes a deep breath, twists around in her seat, and looks out the window. "How about we go outside? Who knows, maybe we'll find the first evening star."

I rush right up as if Mom couldn't ask a second sooner, and nearly knock off the cushion as I wait for her to stand. We find the perfect spot in the backyard next to the edge of the pool, then look up into the sky. The night is wet with sprinkles and threads of creeping ocean mist. I feel my mother's arm wrap around my waist.

"Look! Do you see it?" She points beyond the backyard fence, past the tall palm trees, almost as if her finger touches some spot from the future. "See that glow, over there, not too far from the moon?"

I feel Mom's hand snug against my shirt and marvel at how we are about the same height. My head falls back and I let the sea air lick my cheeks, my hair hanging past my shoulder blades.

"Boy, that one's awfully bright . . . Maybe it's one of your planets," she says, her voice like wind up from the cliffs.

"Maybe." I close my eyes, breathe in the smell of my mother's skin for five long seconds. "Or maybe it's one of *our* planets?" I put my arm around her waist, wondering if the real reason she and Dad got married was so we kids could come along.

. . .

Julie finds me after my talk with Mom and reminds me it is my night to do dishes, as she helps Joey. We trade off every night. I prefer getting Joey ready. It's the same old routine. I pick out his pajamas, make sure he's got clean underwear, fill the bathroom sink with lukewarm water so he can wash up, put toothpaste onto his brush, help him with his teeth, button up his shirt, and comb his hair so that he looks handsome when he goes off to bed.

Mom's Assertiveness Training techniques must still be upsetting Dad, though, because he's returned to the kitchen to assume my spot at the sink, rinsing dishes and sticking them in the washer, smoking fast and furious.

"Dad, it's my turn to do them tonight." He does not budge, but I remain steadfast, holding my ground, my arm nearly touching his. I look out the kitchen window. The moon is bright now, its light hitting the swaying palm trees.

In the living room, Mom plays "Man of La Mancha" loud

enough so I can hear the lyrics. Joey dances the do-si-do that he's mastered in square dance class, and Mom claps with him after each beat.

Finally, Dad steps aside to give me my spot. He takes the dishrag and leans over the kitchen table, wiping back and forth. He starts talking to himself, under his breath. I want to ask him what he is muttering, but I don't because I know he will stop. So I keep at the dishes, stare out the window before me, where stars pop up like wandering sheep, their heads down and minding their own business. I wonder, as I rinse off the next plate, if stars had voices, what they would say. Maybe they converse in silence, sending messages by waves of light. Maybe they leave it to us to make up the conversation.

"Dad . . ." I shut off the faucet and tuck my shirt into my shorts. "I know you love us so much, even though you show it in strange ways." I am not used to being so direct with my words. Neither is Dad, because now he leans up from the table and puts his hand in his front pocket, which means he is about to say something important, his eyebrows worried.

"Things were so much better around here before your mother got involved with that Aggressiveness Training."

"It's *Assertiveness* Training."

"Yeah, right." He snaps the dish towel as if to scare a lunging lion, then folds it and walks back to his bedroom for a cigarette. The more direct you talk to Dad, the faster he leaves the room.

• • •

Mom's Assertiveness Training class ends the following month. Still, change keeps creeping in. Maybe the fact that President Nixon was caught lying and had to be excommunicated from the White House explains why all Mom can talk about is open and honest communication. She's got her eyes on something called Marriage Awareness. Mom never quits and all I can say is *good luck.*

Marriage Awareness is sweeping the St. Bede parish like a plague. This happens just as Father McKinley retires and a new young priest, with curly hair and a hearty laugh, takes over as pastor.

First off, Father Jerome officiates at something called the folk mass on Sunday evenings. Dozens of parishioners who play the guitar, flute, mandolin, and tambourine, and who wear long hair, file into the first two pews of church. Instead of reciting dry responses to old Father McKinley's cues, we sing every prayer, every response to every prayer, even sing between responses, so loud because the jamming musical instruments shake things up and it's hard to compete with them. Mr. Flanigan does not approve of the folk mass. "Damn hippies" is what he says, calling on the phone after dinner. "You can ask your dad—they're probably voting with the communists."

The guitars, mandolins, and tambourines must make people feel romantic, because now when I go to the folk mass, I see couples touch one another in church. They tap each other on the shoulder and smile, or they stroke each other's arms, or they take each other's hands, and sometimes they kiss one another on the cheek. Once I saw Mr. Adams tap his wife on the rear end, even though her eyes whacked him afterward. All this makes me feel uncomfortable. It takes my concentration away from everything, even from staring at Marco Scarpelli. Julie notices all the affection too. She starts pointing her finger during the service.

"Marriage Awareness people," I tell her. "Marriage Awareness is like Assertiveness Training, except you learn to talk and touch at the same time."

"Do you think Mom and Dad will go to Marriage Awareness so they can touch each other too?" Julie is only eleven years old, which makes her too young to know her question is a silly one.

"Fat chance. FBI agents don't do Marriage Awareness." I know that even if Dad weren't an FBI agent, he still would never sign up for one. Mom says he's got too much to hide.

•   •   •

It is Father Ed's turn to come out to California. He sometimes visits twice a year because he travels with his work. Father Ed still loves to talk about family and open communication, even while he eats. He gets so excited, sometimes he chews with his mouth open, and we have to do our best not to watch all that food go chomping around.

Dad gets tense when Father Ed is about to visit. He grumbles a lot, repeating that he's never seen a house like this in all his life. Something about Father Ed makes him stand on guard. Father Ed is an independent priest. He doesn't work in a parish like Father Jack did. He is on special assignment, flying around the world leading communication workshops for couples. When he arrives at our house, Dad does his best to stay in the garage, where he feels it's safe. At night, though, he knows Father Ed will have a Manhattan, so he makes a strong one for Father Ed, and an extra strong one for himself.

"So, Joe . . ." Father Ed has a smooth voice, like a coo.

Dad drops three ice cubes in the glass monogrammed with *C,* serious as a scientist in a top-secret experiment.

"You take a cherry, Ed?"

Father Ed smiles. I bet he is amazed because just when he is going to ask Dad about his relationship with Mom, Dad expertly switches the subject to maraschino cherries.

"Sure, Joe. I'll take a cherry." Father Ed plays along, scratching his nice drape of silvering hair, looking over at Mom, who cuts Joey's toenails in the dining room. Joey's toenails grow ten times faster than normal people's, sometimes making him walk on his tippietoes. I stay seated at the kitchen table, writing in my journal and pretending to mind my own business.

"So, Joe." Father Ed accepts the Manhattan with a cherry floating above the ice, thanking Dad as he sets it down. Dad remains standing, however, still in his white-collared shirt and black tie from work. Perhaps he wishes to look official while Father Ed is here so Father Ed will ask questions only about the FBI, even though Father Ed has learned like the rest of us not to expect an answer.

"Mary, are those toenail clippers working? I bought some new ones the other day." Dad would rather discuss toenail clippers and maraschino cherries than talk about Father Ed's favorite subject, which is relationships and open and honest communication. Mom knows Dad's tactics and does not answer his question, escorting Joey to the family room to watch television.

Father Ed has been encouraging Mom and Dad to enroll in a Marriage Awareness weekend for years. He writes it in his letter every time, including it in his P.S., like he had almost forgotten: *Joe, what about that weekend? I believe you and Mary would benefit from it immensely, and so would the children.*

That "children" word again.

This time Father Ed says it not in a letter but in real life, taking a loud sip of his Manhattan.

"Joe, you have any thoughts about the Awareness experience? Anything you might be wondering about?"

It's like a bullet fired, and Dad, who is already making his next Manhattan, a cigarette alight in his palm, is ready to catch it between his teeth.

"Wonder, my a—" He says this so low I think I may be the only one who hears. He does not quite say the word "ass" because FBI agents do not swear, and even if they did, they would not do so in the presence of children and a priest. Instead, he sits down, sipping on his new Manhattan, his voice the sound of a skipping rope spanking pavement.

"So you think Mary and I ought to join the other fools and go spilling our guts, do you?"

Father Ed grabs the opportunity to explain all the benefits of a Marriage Awareness weekend, almost as if it comes with a "results guaranteed or your money back" coupon. He gives examples of the McKnights and the Carters and the Caputos and the Garcias and all the other Awareness couples—and tells how their newly mastered, open communications have enriched the entire family.

Dad, engulfed in smoke, sips, sets the glass down, picks it up, sips just enough to wet his tongue. He bites into the maraschino cherry, munching it flat, swallowing it, then rolling an ice cube around in his mouth long enough for the ice cube to disappear.

"Okay . . . Ed. Tell me. Who takes care of Joey?" Dad always mentions Joey whenever someone tries to entice him to do something he doesn't want to do. I am just about to raise my hand and volunteer, but Dad sneers and I realize now is not the right time.

"And clean the pool, Ed, who will do that?"

I think about it. I could probably clean the pool, which involves testing the water for the chemical level, adding chlorine, and raking the bottom with the sweeper as tall as the roof on the house. Still, I don't raise my hand.

"In addition to my work for the Bureau, I've got leaves to rake, doors to fix, clothes to fold, lawns to mow. And, oh, by the way, did I mention Joey has a hole in his heart requiring an operation? Open-heart surgery, that is. Now, what is it you want from me?"

Dad must think he has stumped Father Ed with this one because who can argue about a Down's syndrome boy with a hole in his heart, even though Joey's had it since birth, just like some other Down's kids. Father Ed is calm. He never moves very quickly or raises his voice. He is like a sponge, soaking in Dad's words.

"I see . . ." Father Ed strokes his Manhattan, fingering circles, ice peeking through the glass. "Mary's told me about Joey and the surgery. I know that will be a difficult time, but it's not for a while there, Joe. Why not go on a weekend before then, hah?" Father Ed always says *hah* in that New York relations accent. "If you did an Awareness weekend before then, you and Mary might have more strength for later on."

"Strength, huh?" Dad says, cocking his head, the veins in his neck bulging. "You fly all the way out here and have the nerve to talk to *me* about strength?"

• • •

Father Ed must have cast a spell, or maybe Mom just put her foot down, because the following month my parents pack their valise and drive to Los Angeles for a Marriage Awareness weekend. Mike comes home from the University of California and stays with me, Julie, John, and Joey. Mrs. Flanigan comes by with Kentucky Fried Chicken. I worry what will happen when Mom and Dad come back Sunday night, how strange if we started talking through dinner like the Sutherlands when I could not get a word in, or how I would feel if Mom and Dad held hands while they sat on the couch or tapped each other's shoulder at church. I tell my tape recorder my concerns and say I will report back upon their return.

Sunday night at six o'clock, the front door opens on Mom and Dad and their old valise. Mom's face shines. Dad looks around, then with a clear voice asks if we remembered to take out the trash. This time, though, he believes us when we tell him we did, not venturing to check for himself.

•   •   •

In three months, Joey has his open-heart surgery. The hole in his heart is fixed, and after twelve days, he comes home safe and smiling, even though he is pale and eats very little. In my journal with the angelfish swimming freely on the cover, I draw a sketch of Joey's heart without a hole in it, draw a smiley face, and show it to him.

Dad takes time off from work, and Mom and Dad stay at Joey's bedside day and night. When Mom is in the room, she strokes Joey's right shoulder, and when Dad comes in to relieve Mom, he touches the left.

I enter the room and smile. Dad's eyes attempt to nudge me out, maybe because he thinks it's too much stimulation to have an extra person in the room.

"Dad, I have something to tell you . . ."

His finger goes to his lip, as if he says, *Shhhh, can't you see. Tell me later.*

I look down. Joey's eyes are heavy as they close for sleep. I back out of the room as Dad covers him with a second blanket, clearing the bangs from his eyes.

I can't wait to tell Dad later, so I tell my tape recorder now, pushing the record and play button and hearing that low static, kinder than that of Dad's FBI car radio. My stomach fills with adrenaline because I know this static is waiting for my voice:

This has been the year of the hearts. Father Jack was shot in his. Mom and Dad went to Marriage Awareness and softened theirs, at least for a little while, and Joey is healthy, he does not have a hole in his heart any longer. It's weird. How could someone who is so loving, like Joey, ever have a hole in his heart to begin with? Mom says that's called irony. As for mine, I don't know. All I can say is that my heart feels— so much.

A Conlon gathering.

chapter 20

bicycle near the house of Marco Scarpelli, who lives on a fancy cul-de-sac in Jacaranda Highlands, his home surrounded by a white picket fence with a red gate bordered by a lilac tree. I'm on my way to Parker Five and Dime to buy fabric for a new dress, but I take a detour on Susan Louise Way when I discover Marco out front, washing the fancy convertible and wearing a yellow tank top that shows off his bronzed skin.

"Hi there, Marco!"

Marco waves with one hand. Only after I stop on my bike does he turn the water lower, a slow leak still streaming over the suds.

"You on your way to church, huh?"

How could he even think this? "No, I am on my way to the

store, but I had a question for you—well, generally speaking—
and here you are, outside your house and everything, so I had to
stop." Marco Scarpelli stands with his hands gripping the hose,
his big eyes looking like those of a golden retriever ready to
prance toward his next goal.

"Well, what's your question? I'm kinda in a hurry—I got
water polo practice in fifteen minutes."

I try to imagine Marco in the water, balancing like a star athlete while grabbing the ball and whacking it across the pool for
a goal and the crowd jumping up and down and asking for his
autograph afterward, asking what year will he be going to the
Olympics, because Marco Scarpelli is so handsome and so strong
you just know he will end up in the Olympics.

Mrs. Scarpelli calls out from the gate as soon as I am ready to
ask my question. I look at her and stare, never having seen a
mother with hair as blond as hers.

"Five minutes, Marco!"

Mrs. Scarpelli's eyes get caught peering at my new red and
white sneakers that Dad and I bought at J. C. Penney. I bet Mrs.
Scarpelli would love to know where I got my shoes, but the
phone rings before she gets a chance to even say a word.

"Well, anyway, Marco. My dad is organizing a special dinner
dance with food and celebrities and music and everything—at a
fancy restaurant in Los Angeles—and I get to invite someone to
go and I was wondering—"

"What kinda dance is it?"

I am not expecting this question from Marco. I don't really
know what kind of dance we will be dancing or what kind of
music will be playing. I only know Dad has started some new
group called STADD, which stands for Society to Aid the Developmentally Disabled. He is still working to raise money for
group homes for when people like Joey get older and no longer

have parents. This is not an idea I want to even think about, let alone explain to Marco Scarpelli.

"I don't know—my dad's putting it on. It's at some fancy Italian place, three weeks from tonight. It's for a special cause."

"What cause?"

I scratch my forehead. Maybe Marco only goes to dinner dances for water polo causes or for getting athletes to the Olympics. If he asked me to one of those causes, I'd say yes in a heartbeat.

"Well, you know, it's for—you know, people like Joey."

"Joey your brother?"

"Yeah."

Marco looks to the front gate as if his mom is calling out again, but she is not. Then he looks to the living room window with its white shutters complete with engraved hearts to see if his mom is calling from there, but she is not. Then he finally looks at me, just above my mouth, trying to avoid the pimple on my chin, I can tell.

"I got a water polo event three weeks from tonight."

"Oh, you do . . ." My voice trails. This is sad news. Still, I wonder what a water polo event is like. I've never been to one. I wonder if they dance at water polo parties, even dance in the pool like Esther Williams, who is Mom's favorite movie star. I close my eyes, imagine floating with Marco, and me wearing a shimmering mermaid outfit. I can practically smell the chlorine on my skin.

"Besides, my parents do muscular dystrophy."

Marco starts up the hose, his Popeye arms leaning over the car, wiping off all the soap. "Thanks anyway."

I stand with my bike and pretend to adjust the gears, telling my eyes to stop blinking, telling myself to just get back on the bike and ride to the store and pretend I never saw Marco Scarpelli in the first place.

"Well, it's not your parents I was asking—it was you." I jump on my bike, ride away, not giving Marco Scarpelli a chance to speak, as if a water polo player could say anything intelligent anyway.

• • •

The next afternoon the phone rings. It is some fellow named Anthony Brodick. That's what Dad says as he knocks on my door while I speak into my tape recorder.

"Phone for you," he says, "and why do you have to lock your bedroom door all the time? I've never seen a house—" Dad always says this. He doesn't like to let on that I need privacy for my tape recorder, just like I did for my log.

I take the pink telephone, winding the cord around my right hand.

"Hello?"

It is Anthony Brodick, for sure. He was the stagehand for *Twelve Angry Women*. He had to play my part in rehearsal when I was feeling queasy one day. I ask Anthony if he'd like to come along to the STADD dinner dance with me. He does not even ask if it is a benefit or what group it is supposed to support. He just knocks out his loud voice, every word he says like you know he means it.

"I'll go for sure!"

"We'll ride with my family," I tell him. "We'll pick you up at six o'clock—and we're taking two cars, just so you know."

"Two cars?" he asks, so certain he wants to say those two words. I think someday Anthony Brodick should become a famous actor.

"Our New York relations will be visiting. They'll come too," I say, even though I wonder if Dad has told them about the fancy event.

"New Yorkers talk so funny, don't they?"

I wonder how Anthony Brodick knows this. I wonder if he and his family are all alone—exiles in California—like us, with all relatives living three thousand miles away.

"Yeah, but New Yorkers think we talk weird," I say, stretching the telephone cord around my waist. "Oh—and my Gramma Molly might be coming. She's got an Irish brogue. I'm hoping she'll finally fess up and tell me some Irish stories."

"Groovy. I love the brogues you hear in the movies."

Anthony tries to imitate a brogue, but it comes nowhere close to Gramma Molly's, which is the original. I wonder what movies Anthony is talking about. Maybe he will tell me the night we are all dressed up and I am wearing an orchid behind my ear and another one on my dress—a Butterick pattern, floral with a Tarzan strap.

• • •

Gramma Molly and Father Ed come out in two weeks. Even though Gramma loves my uncle, you can tell by the sad slits at the corners of her eyes that he's not the same as Father Jack. The worst thing that can ever happen is to lose your own child. That's what Mom has told me.

I sit in the kitchen, finishing the last part of my hem. Gramma walks in and asks if I would like a hearty breakfast. I put my dress down and say yes, knowing Gramma will cook a meal anyhow even if I tell her I'm not hungry. I watch her assume command position, whisking her hands this way and that, as grease slowly fills the air. She sets a full plate before me, sits across the table, ready to inspect how I chew.

"If that's not enough, I'll make you some more." Her brogue floats like a wavy magic carpet.

"This is plenty, thank you very much." I inspect what's on my plate, then let out a chuckle.

"What is it that's so funny now?" Gramma Molly crosses her arms.

"Oh, nothing." I try and hide my grin as I pick at the slightly undercooked eggs with the yolk spilling on top of shredded toast, and with hard butter secured on top.

"What in God's name do you think you're doing, laughing this way?"

I start giggling again, my breakfast nearly dropping out of my mouth as I try hard to swallow. "Gramma, you make eggs the exact same way Dad does," I gulp. "That's so cute!"

"Cute!" She scowls like who do I think I am saying such a word? "For God's sake, it's your father who makes his eggs like me! And what about the rashers?" She points at me sharp, then finally gets up to cook herself some breakfast.

"I've never heard of rashers. Is that Irish for 'hashed browns'?"

"Aw, God Almighty—doesn't your father tell you a thing!"

• • •

We dress in our finest clothes for the STADD dinner dance and gather outside by the juniper tree as Mom snaps photos. I smile wide as passing cars slow to examine our family. Once we're finished with the pictures, Father Ed, in his priestly white collar, takes the driver seat in the station wagon, adjusting the seat for his long legs. Julie in her paisley dress and John in his new brown suit climb into the rear with its seat facing backward. Michael, his hair now as long as Jesus Christ's, takes the backseat with his date, Sophia. Dad looks at Michael, then mutters he'll be buying him a set of women's hairbrushes for Christmas. I chuckle to myself while watching Mom climb in front with Father Ed, who no doubt will talk about all things related to marriage and family life as soon as he turns the key.

Anthony Brodick, Gramma Molly, Dad, Joey, and I hop in

the other car. Dad lets Joey sit in the front seat because this evening is a special occasion. The whole way to Los Angeles, Joey turns around, reaching out to touch Gramma Molly, but I grab his hand first, because Gramma maintains an unusual look around Joey. Anthony Brodick takes Joey's hand too, sings some merry song about the high seas, and I wonder if the song may be about sailing from Ireland.

Gramma Molly stares out the car window, her lips mouthing Hail Marys and Our Fathers as we drive along. She stops when Joey touches her knee. I can see a smile attempting to break through, but the smile is unrehearsed and so stays small.

• • •

La Buca Italian restaurant is set up for the big affair, with helium balloons streaming from the twenty-some tables, each with a centerpiece of white roses and yellow tulips. A man who looks like Lawrence Welk gestures in front of his fellow orchestra members, all of them wearing tuxedos, carrying instruments, lifting them carefully from black cases.

Dad, being president and all, is the emcee of the first annual STADD dinner dance in downtown Los Angeles. He talks to the Lawrence Welk guy for a while, then walks toward the kitchen to chat with the chef, who arrives just as Dad is about to push open the kitchen door. Dad motions around the room, which smells of carpets that have soaked up many a party throughout the years. The maître d', some guy named Sammy, comes up to me where I stand with Anthony Brodick, waiting to find our table and hoping we get a good one, since we're the first ones to arrive.

"Hey ya, you must be FBI Joe's daughter?"

"Who, me?"

Sammy slaps my arm. "You got the big eyes like your old man. Now, where in the hell did he go? We need to get the table chosen for the hotshots, ya know, the celebrities coming, ya know."

I point to the kitchen door, where the chef motions this way and Dad motions that way, trying to set something right.

Sammy runs over in his tuxedo and the chef disappears. Dad and Sammy go strolling, stop at a table, and Dad taps it, saying this will be the one.

"What celebrities are coming?" Anthony takes out his notepad to write down the answers, like he wants to be sure to get the names right.

"You're not going to introduce yourself, Anthony?"

"Sure, we've got to make them feel welcome, don't we?"

"Don't worry. Dad will do that. Just watch—he'll pull out this strange, kinda charming Irish humor, pull it out from nowhere. He always does this when he's around the retarded. It's like he becomes a different person."

Anthony Brodick folds up his notebook, inserts it in his pants pocket.

"Different, like how?"

I look into Anthony's actor eyes and wonder where I should begin. "Well, for one thing . . . he talks."

"Talks?" He scratches his head. "That's different?"

"If only you knew."

I listen to the musicians tune their instruments—tubas, violins, French horns, saxophones, and clarinets sending out all sorts of mismatched notes—and try to predict what songs they will be playing tonight.

"Well, speaking of different . . ." Anthony turns, notices my orchid, then looks me in the eyes, his mouth soft.

"Yes?"

"How'd you ever get a name like 'Maura'? I never heard of it until I met you."

I listen to the saxophone player do a C scale, the notes rippling upward, then back down like silver confetti. Anthony Brodick is the first person in my life to ever ask that question. I pull my hair back, so that my white orchid, all of it, shows, and try to sound like one of those famous actresses, like I've told the story a million times before.

"My dad—he heard the name a long time ago, before he even met my mom and got married."

"Wow."

"He loved it. He waited forever to have me, to have a daughter in the first place."

"So he could name her—"

"Maura. Which is Irish for 'Mary,' in case you didn't know." I look at him, grin, then turn back to the musicians, a couple of them still fine-tuning.

"Your dad didn't give you any old name. He must have known you were going to be unique." He holds my hand, quick, then releases it. I feel warm all over, then think of Marco Scarpelli, who'll never know what he's missing out on.

All around us the parties come strolling in through the archway, Dad welcoming everyone. Angela Larson, with her new hairstyle, Otto and his parents, and some other families with the developmentally disabled begin to arrive. I watch Dad lean over and shake Otto's hand and kiss Angela on the cheek, his face beaming as he starts spooning out stories, and all the families eating them up, clapping their hands and laughing, like my father is the most entertaining man in the world.

Other parts of the room fire up with conversation and merry toasts. Dad never mentioned who all were coming, but I see several tables already filled up with couples shaking hands and kissing cheeks. A few men glide through the door and look a lot like Dad: they wear dark suits, walk to the edges of the room and check out the place, just to be sure the Mafia's not running La Buca restaurant in downtown Los Angeles. I walk past them, through the shadows, and they don't even glance my way. I come back and report to Anthony that they are indeed agents.

Other tables are filled with people from St. Bede parish, including the Flanigans. Mr. Flanigan keeps his whole table rolling in laughter as he tells one joke after another. Mr. and Mrs. Sutherland are at another table, holding hands next to their glasses of champagne, talking with another couple who occasionally peck each other's cheeks. Mother Perennial and Father Jerome sit at another table with batches of couples from St. Bede wearing pearl necklaces or sport jackets. Father Jerome throws his curly head back each time he laughs, the rest of the people at the table smiling, some peering over to the band.

Sammy, the maître d', has seated our family at the table closest to Angela and Otto and all the others. He seats Gramma Molly next to me. The table on the other side of us is filled with the celebrities. A cartoonist from the *Los Angeles Times* smokes a cigar and talks to two professional baseball players wearing beige suits. Anthony dashes over and shakes their hands and they seem pleased to meet him and give their autograph.

The Lawrence Welk group, who are actually called the Gray Seals, since most of the thirty men have silver hair, play music nice and low during our steak dinner, and then afterward start turning up the volume, luring the crowd to the dance floor. Anthony and I walk to the edge of the floor, stand next to a stucco pillar, and watch all the spinning and swirling ahead. I fold my arms, start singing along to "Some Enchanted Evening."

"You must know the words to every song out there," Anthony whispers, then leans and listens to me.

"I've an excellent memory for lyrics," I say.

"Maybe someday you'll be singing onstage," Anthony says, applauding with the crowd when the song ends.

"Huh! I can barely carry a tune." I grab Anthony's coat sleeve and suggest we return to our table.

The next song begins and Mom leads Dad out to the dance floor. The blue spotlight melts on his face as he puts his arms around her, his eyes going big as his hips rotate this way and that. He watches his belt buckle almost like he's too shy to look at Mom. She looks him right in the face, her dance speaking louder than words, and then she glances around the room to make sure everyone's having a good time. Dad reaches for Mom's hand, twirls her around in a clumsy way, but her smile balances them after the spin.

I watch her moves, so smooth and graceful, and remember her story about the time she almost became a dance instructor in New York. The owner must have felt it was the eyes of Ingrid Bergman he was looking into when Mom walked in. He must have asked her for an interview on the spot, saying, "We'd like to see the tango, waltz, fox-trot—why don't we get started with those!"

I imagine Mom holding her white gloves, not expecting anything like this as she places her stole in the corner of the mirrored dance studio, adjusting her dress, trying to remember the last time she danced with anyone other than Joe Conlon. I can see the owner whisking her around, asking about her husband, Mom staying quiet, saying nothing about the FBI, just dancing, dipping this way and that, warm and dizzy, then blushing when the owner announces that she is hired so long as she removes her wedding ring. Mom must have been happy when Dad announced the news of the FBI transfer; maybe she figured that only in exotic Los Angeles would God give her the family she always desired.

Now Mom grins as her long legs twirl in a floor-length red satin dress. She glances over to Anthony and me, smiles, and lets Dad fold her back into his arms as the light catches a glint of blue gold in his eyes.

The Gray Seals go right into the next song. The spotlight hits a strobe in the middle of the ceiling, and flecks of silver travel the room, hitting painted faces, dreamy eyes, shiny lip-sticks, glasses of champagne raised in the air, diamond specks chasing each other in mad pursuit.

I look across the table to Gramma. She keeps a leaden stare on Joey, then shakes her head as he spins not too far away on the dance floor. I look at my brother so full of joy, and wish I could tell Gramma Molly what life with Joey is really like. I wish I knew the choice of words to make her understand. If I told her that in some strange way Joey's been our salvation, she might look at me as if I were a *haratick*—but it's true.

The lead singer takes the microphone, announces that it is time for a special request as specks of light keep sprinkling the air. A solo violin pierces the silence, then the Gray Seals begin to play "When Irish Eyes Are Smiling."

Dad strolls over to Gramma Molly and then taps her shoul-der. Gramma turns around and looks up, as if for a moment she's found land. She and my father dance, slow, stiff, as if they wear thick socks, maybe the way they dance in Ireland. I watch their feet and listen to the lyric: "there's a tear in your eye, and I'm wondering why." I look at Dad and Gramma Molly go around in their silent embrace, Gramma's eyes shut, Dad's eyes to the floor, then think of the tragedies, and for the first time in pub-lic, I learn how to cry.

When the song ends, Dad turns toward the Gray Seals, nods a thank-you, then escorts Gramma back to the table. Dad bows quietly, then walks away, weaving through the crowds, shaking some hands, dodging others, as if he's looking for someone in particular.

"You about ready to dance?" Anthony Brodick asks, straightening his tie.

"Sure."

Just as I take off my shawl, Dad slips through, returns to our table, and stands right before me, bobbing on his feet like an anxious schoolboy.

"I've been searching everywhere for you."

I look at my father, who must know I've been here almost the entire time.

"I've got a question for you," he says, offering a shy bow.

I look down to Dad's freshly polished, hard-soled shoes, then over to my new black pumps.

"May I have the honor of this dance?"

Anthony Brodick steps away as my father reaches for my hand.

Dad, in his fancy new suit, leads me past the crowd and to the dance floor. I can tell by his gait that he is happy. Maybe it's because hundreds of people—his fellow FBI agents and hordes of people from St. Bede and Father Jerome with his clarinet laugh and all the nuns and Angela and Otto and the others—are here at the STADD fund-raiser, which means someday the group home for the developmentally disabled will be built. For one night, maybe my father's heart has found its place.

Dad twirls me like a ballerina. I hear him whimper as I spin round and round in my black heels. His whimper sounds like the language of birds, like his heart is about to burst its cage, as if he can barely stand the fun.

"What song is this?" I ask, warm and a little out of breath.

" 'String of Pearls,' " he says, his hand at my waist, taking a few steps back, another forward.

"But this is one of Mom's favorites!" I look around the banquet room, searching for my mother, and see her sitting next to Father Ed, deep in conversation. I turn back to Dad. "You could be dancing with her."

He spins me around faster than before, his whimper melted caramel. "I've got my dancing partner."

Dad and his catch.

chapter 21

My New York relations have invited me to come back East, see a Broadway musical, and ride the waves at Jetty Point. Dad is either excited or nervous about me going to New York, I'm not sure which. Perhaps I should be nervous as well. I won't be too far away from where my uncle was murdered, staying with Gramma Molly for a few days.

Father Ed says I am a bit spoiled, living in sunny Southern California, twenty miles from Disneyland and forty miles from Hollywood. He plans to take me for a ride through Harlem and other places so I can see how the real people live. But I feel I already do that—live with the real people.

Dad says he has a surprise for me in the trunk. He doesn't

store mitts and bullet shells in there anymore, just uses it to stash our birthday gifts. We walk out to the garage, and he pops open the trunk. I look inside—and can't believe what I see.

"How about this?"

Dad takes out a brand-new valise, the color of a tangerine, larger than any suitcase I've seen in my life. On top is a long strap and underneath it are four black rollers.

"Watch—it's magic."

He grabs the strap and starts skipping down the driveway, the vibrating suitcase with its loud rollers chasing him as if he were the Pied Piper. I don't know what to think as I watch him skipping along, doing a few figure eights. I hardly notice the passing car and its driver staring at Dad as he cavorts with the suitcase that is soon to accompany his daughter to the dangerous place called New York. At the edge of the driveway, he turns around, more serious now, rolls the valise back to the car, the wheels rattling as if it's a plane ready to sail off the tarmac.

"We'll keep it in the trunk until it's time for you to pack."

"Okay, but, Dad . . ." I sigh, barely sure of what to say next. "I can't believe you got this just for me!"

"Yeah, well, you know. If you're old enough to go to New York, you may as well travel in style. At least, that is what your mother says."

I stroke the soft sides of the tangerine valise and admire its firm clasps of silver. I punch them in and out, loving the clicking noise they make. I imagine walking through the streets of New York being followed by a suitcase given to me by my very own father.

"Wouldn't it be great if you could come with me? We could visit your old stomping grounds." I brush the bangs off my face, then stick my hands in my pockets.

He coughs, stoops over when I say this, lifting the valise back to its storage place and gently shutting the trunk. He glances at Joey's new yellow go-kart sitting in the corner of the garage, as if to say it's time to move on to the next business of the day. Dad takes Joey to the school yard every Saturday, smokes his cigarettes, and watches as my brother maneuvers around the basketball poles, zooming with glee.

"Dad, do you think today you and I could go for a drive somewhere? Maybe you can tell me a story—so I'll have one on hand for the New York relations."

"Aw, enough already. I've got other things to do." He waves at the air, walks to the washing machine, and starts pulling out wet clothes.

"Come on, Dad. Let's go up to St. Bede field. We haven't been there in ages."

He looks at me, pulls gray threads off the lint screen. "Some other time."

"When?" I swivel around him, almost backing him into a corner. "Just this once, please, Dad?" I put my hands together like a prayer.

He looks into my eyes for longer than a precise second, then raises his freckled arm, inspecting his wrist even though he doesn't wear his watch today.

"I've got a half hour before I report in to Joey. I don't like to keep the busy executive waiting."

•   •   •

Dad and I drive past rows of houses in Jacaranda Highlands, each lawn manicured with the precision of a barber, lined with rosebushes, birds-of-paradise, and lilies of the Nile. Dad drives slow, his eyes looking straight ahead, ignoring the rearview mirror. We cross busy Jacaranda Boulevard and he pulls into the parking lot adjoining the St. Bede ball field.

We climb the wooden bleachers and find a seat. Dad takes the lower one, and I go a step higher. Spread out before us, the ball field looks slippery green in the sun.

"I bet you'd love if our grass looked like this," I say.

"Yeah, sure." He squints, pulls his California Angels cap up over his eyebrows, and looks out to the pitcher's mound, then to the center-field fence, and lights a cigarette. I sit quietly and wait. Dad is like a shepherd counting invisible sheep in some lush pasture, keeping silence company until he wears it out and it lets him speak. Meanwhile my mind goes as blank as one of those sheep, just taking in the green grass and the sky, waiting for the coming of words. When Dad is finished with his Lark, he throws it under his shoe, his nostrils sending forth chutes of smoke.

"So, it's a baseball story you wanted?"

"Uh, er, yeah."

I never asked my father for a *baseball* story, but I don't dare push my luck. I raise my arm under the baking sun and inspect the hairs, count my slow breaths, then start chipping the green paint off the bleacher, so Dad doesn't think his words are all I'm waiting for.

Finally, the silence cracks.

"One day I was going to a meeting at the downtown head-quarters. I was sitting at a red light, the corner of Pico and Blair."

I listen, knowing only my father can link a story about the FBI to one about baseball. "So, you were somewhere in Los Angeles?"

"Waiting for a green light. I look to my right and notice a different sort of fellow standing at the bus stop. A portly young fellow, with Down's syndrome, like Joey. Except this one doesn't wear socks or shoes."

"You mean, like Shoeless Joe, of the Chicago White Sox?"

"You want to hear the story or not?"

"Sorry."

He leans forward, his clasped hands hanging between his knees. "I pulled up to the curb. 'Hello there, young man.' That's what I said to the fellow standing all alone. 'Hel-lo,' the fellow says back. I say to him, 'Now, I realize you're not supposed to talk to strangers and I am a stranger, but will you tell me something?' "

Dad goes on almost as if he's speaking with himself, although just as I lean closer, he becomes quiet. He does that sometimes—just stops, or walks off in the middle of a conversation, as if some voice has beckoned him elsewhere.

He glances over to home plate, brown with scuff marks from the last hard slide, then turns to me. "Where were we?"

"You were about to ask Shoeless Joe, I mean the portly fellow, something." I sigh. I've waited forever for Dad to tell me one good story, and who knows where this one will go? I think he just likes to test my patience, to see if I will stick around, if I'll pursue the hidden meanings within his silent ways, or if I will just say forget it and walk away like he does.

"That's right. This fellow was high-functioning. He was reading the bus schedule." Dad looks at me, as if reporting a most amazing feat.

"He was reading a bus schedule?"

"No slow fellow, this one—smart enough to get around by bus." He goes back to staring at the field.

I nod, keep my stare on Dad, thinking how all of his stories—if ever he were to tell them—would be about the same thing.

"So I notice this poor fellow."

"Which is why you got out of the car?"

Dad frowns like who do I think I am, getting ahead of his story? "I ask him for his address. He looks through his little glasses; he must have been scared. That is, who would ever ask him for this information?"

"Probably just you, Dad."

I take a deep breath, smelling the field's fresh-cut grass, its moisture being sucked up by the sun.

"So, this fellow lived at 235 Quincy."

Dad speaks slow, the way the Down's syndrome man must have. The fellow's name was Harold. The next day Dad pulled up in front of Harold's residence with a new pair of shoes. "These are for you. They should fit you fine. And don't tell anybody where you got these, okay?" That's what he said, handing Harold the shoe box. I can see Dad whimpering as he heads back to the black car, the radio blaring through the open window.

"Did you ever see Harold again?" I take a step down on the bleacher, next to him.

"No. That was it," he says, staring ahead, "almost like it was a vision."

I look down at my black sneaker and tie the right shoelace, tight with a double loop, then turn to my father. "Dad, when did all this happen?"

"What does that matter?"

A military chopper lifts from the Jacaranda Navy Base, pummeling the air with a low bass. Dad gazes up as if he might recognize the pilot, looks across the fence to where the helicopter came from, then drops his glance to the baseball field in front of us, almost as if someone has spoken to him, the grass dancing like ghosts under the chopper's heavy whirl.

"Hold on for a second, will ya?"

He sets down his car keys, puts his hands in his pockets, and starts to walk, slowly, away from the bleachers, past the snack shack, then steps onto the ball field. He goes ambling along, slower now, like how he does when he locks the windows each night, looking as if he's remembered something, and determined to find it now. He taps home plate, then strolls toward first base, his shoes leaving footprints in the white, chalky paint. He starts a light skip, like a child's skip, his legs hitting the ground, then lifting up, one-two-three-four, in perfect rhythm. I cover my mouth, waiting.

Dad skips all the way to second base, then stops, his shoulders rounding. He takes out a cigarette, lights it with cupped hands, sucks in deep as he turns and scans the entire field. A breeze kicks up from the east, hot, like the Santa Anas, running ripples across his shirt. He throws down the cigarette, stomping it under his shoe, then looks up, hollering something in my direction.

I can't hear what he says, so I step all the way down and lean into the fence, watching his lips and wondering if he's finally ready to tell me the baseball story.

"Dad, what did you say?" I call out.

He leans his head back, squints. "Remember what I told you the day you were born?"

I stand frozen, my fingers now hanging on to the wire fence as my father raises his hand and points to something behind me.

My voice drops to a hard whisper. "What did you say?"

"How about you get the bat and ball?"

"The . . . what?"

"Go ahead and get them."

"But?"

"Shall I tell you or not?" He points.

"Dad, we didn't bring."

"Sure we did—in the trunk."

I shake my head. "But there's just the vali—"

He crosses his arms. "Look in the valise."

I take his set of keys on the bleachers and walk twenty paces to the car. My cheeks start to burn as I watch the silver key turn perfectly as ever, making a popping noise, like the loud snap of bubble gum. I reach into the trunk, lift out the valise, bend down over the warm pavement, click open the snaps, and find inside a yellowed baseball and wooden bat. They look like museum pieces, but then I realize they are for me to touch and take back to my father, who waits.

I run back, and by the time I return, Dad has repositioned himself in center field. He takes two fingers out of his green pants pocket, motions for me to go stand at home plate. I scratch my head, unsure what to do next because it's usually me in the outfield, and so I stand alone with the ball and bat, watching my father among the boatloads of dandelions, as if he's been waiting forever.

"How about a nice homer?" he yells, then starts to smack a naked fist into his palm, then scooting back, closer to the jacaranda trees with their birds turning circles in purple blossoms.

"What? *Me* hit a home run? You got to be kidding." I don't move, just watch my father rock side to side, then I try and steady my balance. I toss up the ball, swing, then miss. I toss it up again, twice, three times, and miss. I choke up on the bat, slow, my hands in a fat sweat, dust kicking up to my eyes, my legs shaking. I let go of the ball and swing one more time and my bat sends something sizzling all the way out toward my father. He stares up to the sun, scurrying back, reaching as the ball sails high, then higher, flying deep into center field.

"*Weee-hah!*" I drop my bat, go running for the bases, fast, like a wild mare. I run serious, not jumping up and down at all as I glide over first base, and gallop hard toward second. As I get closer, I can hear my father's voice coming from the outfield, his words rushing on a warm wind toward me, slowing me down to listen. I turn and see him standing, his hand placed over his heart, as he says over and again: *Bee-utiful, Maura.*

I close my eyes and remember.

• • •

It is the Feast Day of All Souls. My father sits with a cigar in his coat pocket, a fedora on his knee, and waits hours for news of my birth, falling asleep in the hospital sitting room, dreaming of waiting—waiting for what seems an eternity, like the time he was a kid playing in New York, snagging a ball in center field and hoping one day someone might notice.

"Joe, Joe—I've got some wonderful news."

My father's eyes open as fast as they had shut when he sees Dr. McGann, the obstetrician, hovering above.

"Doctor?"

"She's all eyes, this one—not going to miss a thing."

"She?"

"That's right, and quite the catch."

• • •

None of us, my father nor my mother nor myself, say anything at first. Introductions can be so awkward. Instead, we stare at one another in happy shock, looking for words; I suppose that's what humans do. My father cradles me closer, strokes my cheek, and whispers the name he's held in reserve for so many years, waiting for me to come along and claim it. He starts telling me a story, but I can't understand all the words yet. All I can do is rest at his belly after spinning for so long—ages soaring through dreams, hurtling faster, winds whooshing me farther afield—in my slumber sailing out to the man, or is it a boy, who runs like mad when he spots me flying out to him, his arms outstretched.

epilogue

Shortly before Joe Conlon was diagnosed with terminal lung cancer in 1992, he sent me his complete correspondence from J. Edgar Hoover, warning me to keep the letters in a safe place— to show them to no one. The letters were not concerned with top-secret issues, nor referred to specific Bureau cases: my father left his one coded directive, spurring me to write these records of the heart left untold.

The local parish erected a memorial honoring my father's work nearly forty years after he built the field of his dreams, where today hundreds of young boys in spring uniform still yell *play ball.*

The John P. Conlon LIHFE Towers, in Queens, New York, providing low-income housing for seniors, were named in honor of my uncle under the auspices of New York City Mayor John Lindsay in 1973. It stands to this day.

Mary Conlon bought me a new typewriter when I was a teenager still talking into my tape recorder. On her manual machine, my mother typed letters to presidents and popes, hoping on mine this story might be told. She cared for our brother Joe until he was thirty-three years old. She saw the book's early chapters before passing away on Solstice, 2000.

Joe, Jr., resides in a group home that honors the physical,

emotional, and spiritual needs of those who "hold the keys," and to this day loves the beach, music, dancing, and checkbooks. Mike, Julie, John, and myself spend time with him regularly, and always crave for more.

At the age of eighteen, I traveled to rural county Clare, Ireland, to see the original homestead of my Gramma Molly and the place where my people come from.

That's another story.

acknowledgments

This book started as a dream many years ago. At the age of thirteen, I confided to my older brother that I wished to write a book about love for the entire world to read. Thanks to Mike, Julie, John, and Joe, who share the love of family that Mom and Dad inspired.

To Barbara Sullivan, my West Coast editor, for her compassion and unparalleled brilliance, "thank you" barely suffices. Thanks to Sandy Farrell, who never allowed me to forget the dream; to my writing mentors, the members of the Wednesday Night Critique Group headed by Elizabeth Lyon; and to Karen Karbo, for all the sage wisdom. Thanks to dream agent Stephanie Kip Rostan of the Levine Greenberg Literary Agency for her absolute enthusiasm and love of story; to Beth de Guzman, mass market editorial director at Warner Books, for her infectious energy and for catching the book quick when it came her way; many thanks to Jamie Raab, publisher, and to Maureen Egen, president and COO; to Jennifer Romanello, Ivan Held, Melanie Murray, Candace Ayers, Becka Oliver; to Penina Sacks and Bill Betts; to Tom Whatley and his production crew, to the entire sales force and marketing department, and all others at Warner Books—a boatload of thanks.

To families who have "special needs" children, you do the

work of the heart within the realm of the invisible. This story is for you. And for all the other shy girls (and boys), you too have your story to tell.

Finally, to my husband, Andrew, thank you, the love *de mi vida.*

about the author

Maura Conlon-McIvor graduated from the University of Iowa
and has worked as a journalist, editor, and producer on both
coasts. She holds a doctorate in Depth Psychology and lives with
her husband in Portland, Oregon. For more information visit
www.fbigirl.com.